A Joyful Noise

BOOKS BY JANET GILLESPIE

A Joyful Noise
The Joy of a Small Garden
Peacock Manure and Marigolds
Bedlam in the Back Seat

JANET GILLESPIE

A Joyful Noise

1817

HARPER & ROW, PUBLISHERS

NEW YORK AND EVANSTON

103662

To Pop, my twin spirit,
in loving memory

CONTENTS

A Joyful Noise

Prologue

JUNE, THE MONTH of strawberries and roses, finds me up in our attic looking at old *Geographics*. I am really looking for the luggage, as it is almost time to start packing for the Point, the family summer place by the sea. I always try to pick a rainy day for my attic operations, partly because I love the pattering of rain on the roof but mostly because it's cool. On sunny days it's so hot up there and smells so powerfully of mothballs that it's hard to stay conscious. Ours is not an efficient attic with neatly labeled drawers and boxes like some I've seen and resented. It would be more efficient if it didn't contain nearly complete sets of the *National Geographic* and *The New Yorker*, but it does and probably will until the floor gives way. Traffic through the attic is further complicated by a kind of Berlin wall of gigantic trunks where the family woolens are stored, or are supposed to be stored. One of these is the green steamer trunk which helped to move our grandmother's menage from New York to the Point and later became part of our parents' equipment for moving us down there. Here, too, are the packing trunks in which my mother shipped the bedding and table linen.

My branch of the clan does not believe in trunks. We travel soft, with a collection of canvas Car-pacs, duffel bags, laundry bags stolen from several laundries, squashy suitcases bought with green stamps, and some zipper bags known as Toads. Of course these are supplemented at the last minute by cartons, and in the final convulsions of departure all sorts of items are stuffed in naked—snorkels, swim fins, underwater goggles and other necessities of life by the sea. In the old days there were also sterilizers, diaper pails, a pale blue thunder mug with a rabbit on it, and a potty seat embellished with a chicken. In one way I regret their passing but on the whole I prefer traveling with people who are housebroken and don't get carsick.

What is there about the Point that is so magic, so heart-rendingly beautiful that no other place will do? Nothing, I guess, but the fact that we were all little there in summer. Nothing except that it's home. On that part of the New England coast where the Westport River flows into the Atlantic Ocean, among the stone-walled fields and oak woods of the land and the mud flats and eelgrass jungles of the river, members of my mother's family have spent their summers since the dawn of creation, or at least since before Mum was born, which to us was the same thing.

My father only married into the Point and had spent all his summers on the Old Farm in upstate New York, swimming in the old swimming hole, riding on hay loads, and throwing green apples at beehives, just like a barefoot boy in a book. We were brought up on stories about the Old Farm but saw it only once, because in the dark ages before we were born Pop had gone to Union Theological Seminary, where my maternal grandfather, Charles Cuthbert Hall, was president. One day Dr. Hall walked into the gymnasium at the precise moment that Pop ran into an iron bar and knocked himself cold. When he woke he was in the presidential quarters, where he saw my mother, a golden-haired child of thirteen. After that one thing led to another and when the smoke cleared away they were married and he was committed to the Point for life. Sometimes we used to think about that iron bar and realize that it was, in a sense, the reason for our existence. Pop admitted it freely.

"If it hadn't been for that iron bar," he used to say, "I would never have met your mother."

He always delivered the last words in an emotional croak,

as any reference to mothers or the home affected him powerfully.

"Don't tell us you fell in love with a thirteen-year-old kid!" we cried, but he claimed he had, which was, of course, a bit of luck for us and Mum, too.

The grandfather who had so fortuitously opened the gymnasium door at the correct moment was at that time one of the most distinguished ministers of his day as well as a man of great charm and wit. I never knew him, for long before I was born he died of an illness contracted while on a lecture tour in India. In our eyes his greatest claim to fame was that he had discovered the Point and founded the family summer place.

As far as I can make out there was a time in the late nineteenth century when a vast army of bearded and mustached grandfathers advanced on the Eastern Seaboard and bought land. They were either on a fishing trip, a walking trip, or a cruise when they looked with wild surmise on their future summer place, said, "Here it is," and then founded it.

One group, who either didn't mind swimming in ice water or didn't like swimming, settled in Maine; another gang of eccentrics went inland to the mountains; and the rest took over the Cape and the South Shore. To this latter species my grandfather belonged. One summer he went to visit friends at Westport and was overcome by the beauty of the place—the wide estuary behind its barrier beach, the old fishing village on the Point and the checkerboard of fields and pastures on the hills above the tidal river.

Like all good Victorians he went for long walks and on one of these excursions he discovered our hill. It was the highest land in the area and commanded a breathtaking sweep of river and ocean. At that time it was treeless and reminded him of the moors in Scotland. For some time he had been looking for a site for a summer place and this seemed to be it.

Synton was named after the family mansion near Hawick,

Scotland, as in my mother's clan everything was named after things or places abroad, preferably in the British Empire. The house was built to my grandfather's own design and painted a rich cocoa brown, which became the official color for all family structures on the hill. It wasn't that anybody especially liked cocoa brown—Pop didn't for one—but it was the tradition.

My grandfather caused his new house to be built in a turnip field on top of the hill. He inadvertently built without reference to rights of way and so had to buy a lot more land to cancel the gridiron of invisible streets that had been laid out on the hill. These wretched streets, which existed only in a legal sense, have haunted the family ever since and given us all a very low opinion of the law and its insane methods.

Shortly after I was born Pop built our house halfway down the hill to the river. He built it on a right of way that he didn't own, and an invisible road called Riverside Drive ran through the living room, a situation that made lawyers stick straws in their hair and which wasn't cleared up until my brother Dave managed to buy Riverside Drive and give it to Pop, who had been living on it for fifty or so years. Our house was built to Pop's own design, painted cocoa brown, and named Snowdon after a mountain in Wales.

When we became aware of things the dominant figure at Synton was our grandmother—Baba, we called her, with the accent definitely on the first syllable. After my grandfather's death she moved to the Point for good, bringing with her Aunt K., her oldest daughter, a son, our uncle Tink and a staff of family retainers, most of whom were well stricken in years.

In our day Synton was buried in a cloud of trees, and the famous view was almost obliterated. The Scottish moors had become lawns and flower gardens, orchards, paddocks, chicken yards, and berry patches—a royal domain. There was still a horse in the stable, there were carriages in the carriage house, chickens in the chicken house, boats in the boathouse, and servants in the servants' quarters. It was a paradise for children because it was planned around a child, our dearest playmate and companion, Uncle Tink, Baba's youngest son. Tink was about twenty-five when I was born but he had never grown up and was two or three years old inside.

The boundaries of Tink's little world were the valley, halfway down the lane on the east; the river on the west; Synton's flagpole to the south; and the barn to the north. Within this area he roamed freely, following the sneaker-padded paths that wound through it. We traveled these paths with him, and as long as we were small the boundaries of Tink's world were ours, too.

We shared this small peaceable kingdom with rabbits, peacocks, hummingbirds, chipmunks, mice, butterflies, and all kinds of other creatures that buzzed, warbled, scratched, scampered, flew, and dug holes. Some of them lived in our house with us. We knew almost all of them well because we had been taught to feel that home was not just a building, it was the earth and all its wonders outside our doors. We knew the hill by heart, which is the only way to know anything. We belonged to it and it belonged to us down to the last chickadee, spider, and buttercup.

Throughout my childhood we spent the winters in Holyoke, Massachusetts, and drove to the Point in our old Dodge, the great Artful Dodger. In those years when we turned off the main road into our lane the doors of the twentieth century slammed shut behind us and we were back in the golden age of Queen Victoria. Snowdon, our own house, was barely finished and was just a half-empty box of unpainted wood—honey-colored and smooth as cheese. When we first went inside in June it smelled of pine boards and of months of stored-up sunlight, sweet and toasty. After our big city house with its dark woodwork and thick Oriental rugs it seemed wonderfully clean and resonant—like a shell from the beach. It was furnished with castoffs from family houses and odds and ends picked up at country auctions. The first things you saw when you walked in the front door were two spinning wheels, a parlor organ, and a Rochester Burner—one of those nickel-plated kerosene lamps with a milk-white china shade. There were a few golden oak monstrosities, some old straw chairs and assorted antiques. Rag and braided rugs were scattered about the floors, and on the walls were sepia photographs of India, some Japanese scrolls, and other souvenirs of the trips around the world.

As far as comforts went our establishment was easily a hundred years behind the times. Our plumbing, to use the word loosely, consisted of a black hand pump in the kitchen and a privy. The pump water was from the cistern and was unfit for drinking, so Pop had to lug all our drinking water from Synton's artesian well in two huge milk cans he'd brought back from France in World War I.

The privy was in the woodshed and was a two-holer with one large and one small orifice. Added attractions were a nail keg of chloride of lime and copies of *Punch* to read. It was quite pleasant by daylight but dreadful at night, when shadows lurked in the corners and unseen spiders lay in wait below. However, under the beds upstairs were thunder mugs covered with flowers of various species and edged with gilt. Each one matched a set of bedroom china consisting of a large washbowl and pitcher, a smaller tooth-water pitcher, a cup, a vase to stand toothbrushes in, a covered soap dish and a slop jar, also with cover. The best set had pink azaleas on it, there was another with blue morning glories and another with violets. These sets stood on washstands—wooden tables with holes in the top for the washbowl and pitcher, towel racks on the sides and a shelf underneath for the other equipment. The slop jar was on a square of linoleum to the right of the washstand, and after you washed you were supposed to dump the soapy water into it. You could hear the clank of slop-jar lids all over the house because we had paper ceilings upstairs and the walls were so thin that Pop said you could hear somebody change his mind in the next room.

We took our baths in a flat green tub that used to belong to our grandfather. The bath water had to be heated on the kerosene stove in the kitchen and carried upstairs in the French milk cans by Pop. He also emptied the slop jars and filled the water pitchers every morning.

The grownups took either sponge baths or "chatty baths," which involved standing in the green tub and pouring dippers of water over yourself. (They learned this in India.)

The simple life was just right for summer and opening up was easy. Put a cake of ice in the icebox, fill the kerosene lamps, prime the pump, carry a few nests of baby mice out into the woods, and you were ready to go.

Of course at that time we had a thing called the "servant problem," so opening up also included the installation of a female or females in the servants' quarters. In the city we had two red-headed Irish girls—sisters—that Mum had imported "green" as the expression went. They were young and gay, and on their nights off they liked something more exhilarating than watching the blue herons fly home to roost at sunset. When summer arrived they went off to work for a rich family where there were electric lights, running water, and other luxuries not provided at the Point. As a result we either hired some strange beldame or brought along an elderly spinster, a sort of part-time retainer, known as The Fiddle. The Fiddle was Scottish and bore an amazing resemblance to a haddock with false teeth. Her hobby was disease, and she was deaf so you could hear her lecturing on it all over the house. Conversations with her had to be conducted in screams, very tiring.

Conversations with Synton and the boathouse at the foot of the hill were also conducted in screams or bellows through megaphones. Baba naturally never screamed or bellowed but then on Synton's veranda she had a megaphone as tall as she was. This sacred object was constructed of some sort of glazed brick-red cardboard with a metal mouthpiece.

Baba at such times as she wished to speak with us at Snowdon would rest the megaphone on the porch railing and, applying her lips to the mouthpiece, call out a musical "Heigho!" Whoever heard it would rush out with one of our small, inferior megaphones and screech a reply. Sometimes quite long and complicated conversations ensued, punctuated by innumerable "What's?" "Who's?" and "Where's?" Pop was apt to come away from one of these sessions with his voice worn down to a whisper, but Baba's was as clear as ever.

A large number of the megaphone interviews had to do with the telephone, as the only one on the hill was a wall model in the butler's pantry at Synton. People were always calling Pop and asking him to do something and Baba would have to get out the megaphone again and again. We used to hear the repercussions from some of these calls, especially those from women. Mary E. Woolley, president of Mount Holyoke College, kept calling him long distance about Sacco and Vanzetti, and then there was the attractive but autocratic wife of one of his friends who used to call him and summon him to her house for dinner without Mum so that he could meet some distinguished guest. Pop was fearfully embarrassed by these invitations and Mum had no mercy on him.

"You encourage her," she said. "You enjoy it."

"I do not," Pop would cry. "Egad, I can't insult the woman!"

As for us, our parents summoned us with a tin fog-horn. I was one toot, Aldie was two, Dave three, and when they became mobile Bobs was four and Targ five. You couldn't answer back or argue; you just went home. It was an excellent system in parental terms.

Summers were endless when we were little and we looked from June down a vista of blue-and-white days that stretched to infinity. Then there came a time when we realized they would end on Labor Day and after that they seemed shorter. After the middle of August we could feel ourselves slipping downhill toward fall, when we would shoot out into the world again and be shut up in school. This knowledge made the last of summer unbearably poignant.

This book is an attempt to capture some of the magic of the little kingdom of the hill and of those happy summers when we were all under one roof. I'm writing it down for myself and for my family and for anyone else who likes to get up early on summer mornings or sail a boat on a blue day or watch birds and babies, pick flowers, dig clams, or maybe just laugh. I guess what I really am trying to do is celebrate life itself and the beauty of the earth as I have known it, and in gratitude to make a joyful noise unto the Lord.

CHAPTER ONE

Life in the Back Seat

WHEN WE LIVED in Holyoke, Massachusetts, we drove to the Point in the Artful Dodger, the family Dodge, but it might have been quicker to ride horseback or go in a covered wagon. After all, horses don't have flat tires nor do they boil over, and the Artful Dodger always did both. Covered wagons could go cross-country while we had to stay on what were laughingly called highways. In the twenties practically all the roads in the land were being torn up, widened, and resurfaced. To wait in line behind a dirty man with a red flag was, as far as we knew, a normal aspect of travel by car, and so were detours, which we believed to be part of the national highway system.

It was a hundred and twenty miles from the horse block in front of 231 Oak Street to our lane at the Point and it took us a whole day to get there. By the end of the afternoon we felt as though we'd been in the back seat since birth, but we didn't mind.

As a member of one of the pioneer generations to travel in the back seats of automobiles I would like to say that those were the days. What with punctures, picnics, engine trouble, diaper changing, road construction, and stops to go to the bathroom, we had opportunities to explore the countryside undreamed-of in these days of superhighways. The front seat was something else again. Why Mum and Pop didn't go stark staring mad I'll never know. By the time we actually started driving they were both already worn to a frazzle and Pop would say he was worth about two cents in the open market.

The whole process of moving the household began a week before departure, when Pop went up into the attic for the luggage. You could hear him wrestling with the trunks on the stairs and it sounded as though he were trying to take a horse down them. Finally everything was in place: the green steamer trunk in the upstairs hall, the blue canvas duffel bags draped over the banisters, the medicine bag in the big bathroom, the silver trunk in the dining room and the brown packing trunks in the guest room and Mum's room. A gigantic affair of rust-colored canvas called "the roll-up" was on the floor of the front hall.

They really closed up a house in the old days. Rugs were rolled up with camphor, curtains were taken down, furniture was draped in dust sheets. We used to sit on the steps of the front veranda and watch the life of Oak Street going on as usual and feel as removed from it as though we were already at the Point. Mr. Allen mowing his lawn, the ice-man driving his yellow wagon from horse block to horse block, our friends climbing the Allisons' horse chestnut—all these seemed like part of a bygone time in a city under the sea. We felt the lush, melancholy atmosphere of cities in summer. The mornings smelled of cut grass, the afternoons of hot tar and the evenings of wisteria from our big vine. Soft, sweet and narcotic, the night came down and it was too hot in our beds even under one sheet.

The year I was twelve and the Artful Dodger was eleven Pop said at breakfast that it was time we faced facts and realized that we didn't own a moving van.

"There is no need," he said, "to take along every dad-gasted thing you own. We're only going away for the summer, not for life."

He himself, he said, had packed all his things and was taking only the bare essentials. These were, we knew, his doctor's gown, which he stuffed into his Gladstone bag with a black leather collar box, two hairbrushes, and his razor. He had also a brown suitcase full of yellow "sermon paper," books and other religious equipment, as well as a huge carton of tools and his ship model, the *Charles W. Morgan,* then under construction. He naturally packed no clothes, considering this woman's work, which it certainly was. Mum and the maids had already packed the green steamer trunk, the brown packing trunks, the roll-up, and several duffel bags with clothes and bedding, and the trunks had been shipped off. Pop could never see why Mum wanted to pack anything more. He said she seemed to be under the impression that we were going to the North Pole for three years.

Nobody paid the slightest attention to these directives and we all went upstairs to pack everything we owned—everything that is except clothes. I don't remember once packing so much as a sock. I had enough trouble packing my binoculars, my books, and my collection, which included essential equipment like an ostrich egg, a snuff box and some miniature figures for a Japanese dish garden. That year I had the added burden of a baby robin which had been found on the lawn after a thunderstorm. He was revolting in appearance, being a mere bag of skin covered with bluish pin feathers, but you know how it is about orphans—you can't leave them on the lawn.

Aldie considered himself packed when he had attended to his paints and canvases. Even at eleven he was an artist and had already copied a painting called "The Concert" by Ter Borch and another of some woman in green reading a letter called "Study in Black and Green," and had done an original still life of a blue tea set with irises on it.

Dave, who was eight and torn between the career of a farmer and that of a sea captain, took along his peaked cap, his jackknife with a marlin spike and Bailey's *Manual of Gardening.* Bobs and Targ were of course too small to count and their nursemaid packed for them. At this point in their lives we called them the Hideons—short for Hideous Ones—most unjust as they were both extremely attractive to look at. While all three of us had blue eyes, they had brown.

Bobs was a slender, quiet little boy, and Targ, whose real name was Margaret, was a replica of Mum as a child. We heard a lot about that. Pop would compare their baby pictures and become completely speechless with emotion.

On the morning of departure everyone was occupied with his or her own affairs and I had to deal with packing the robin alone. I finally put him in a basket with a lot of dry grass, but he wouldn't keep quiet. Every time I passed the basket his head shot up and he yelled for food. It was very irritating and I was already bored with parenthood.

Nobody showed any sympathy for me and my robin and even Pop, who had started me down the primrose path of bird watching, had no time for my problem. When he went away for the summer he left his congregation at the mercy of the Holy Ghost, as we called his assistant of the moment. That year's Ghost was terrible and kept talking about the efficacy of prayer so Pop was naturally concerned about the fate in store for his flock.

Besides training the Holy Ghost for his duties Pop had to pack the car, an operation of which he was theoretically in charge. His attitude toward car packing might have struck an outsider as bizarre, as his one aim was to prevent people from putting things into it.

At breakfast on the last morning Pop made his usual announcement. He said this time we were going to make an early start, a statement so absurd that nobody even bothered to challenge it.

"I want everybody booted and spurred by eight-thirty," he said, and left to bring the car around for loading. When we went out with the first round of duffel bags the Artful Dodger was parked by the horse block and Pop was lying under it with his feet sticking out into the street. He was putting on the luggage racks.

Putting on the luggage racks is a lost art like chipping flint, and a good thing, too. They went on the runningboards, where we carried the smaller suitcases and duffel bags. To hold this luggage on some fiend in hell had invented a kind of folding fence of metal strips so designed that whoever tried to unfold it pinched some or all of his fingers and became mad with fury even before he began fiddling with the nuts and bolts that held the fence in place.

We could hear Pop under there swearing and talking to himself and sometimes to God. Being a minister, he couldn't use profane language and take the name of the Lord in vain. To solve this problem he had cleverly made up his own swear words.

"Eye Guy," he was saying, "whoever invented these dadgasted things ought to be boiled in oil. Oh, shoot! I've dropped the nut again."

The Artful Dodger was our first car and a noble vehicle, possibly the best ever built. He was technically a convertible, but as no one had invented the term he was called a "touring car." He had a canvas roof that could be folded back like an accordion, or could if you happened to be a gorilla or Charles Atlas. The Artful also had big round headlights, a horn that said "Ah-oo-gah!," a crank to start the engine, and a thermometer on the radiator cap. The expression on his face was one of benevolence, for cars had faces then as well as personality. The Artful's personality was rather like Pop's—merry and wise and kind. Like Pop he had low moments when he thought he would never amount to anything. Like Pop he kept having trouble with his insides although his diseases were usually real and Pop's a figment of his imagination. Pop was really a very healthy man but never knew when to stop and wrote sermons in his head all night. Then he was so tired that if he heard of a disease he thought he had it. The Artful didn't do this, but then he wasn't a minister. He had plenty of diseases—blocked feeds, oil on the points, ruptured fan belts, broken fuel pumps, just like everybody else, but he also had diseases nobody had ever heard of. There was the whistling disease, the tapping disease, the hiccuping disease, and the disease that made him warble like a cageful of canaries. Pop had learned to drive in the horse-and-buggy era, and although he could harness up and take stones out of horses' hoofs as well as the hero in a cowboy movie, he was helpless in front of an engine. We spent many dreary hours in garages while a series of greasy men peered into the Artful's bowels.

There were days when, like Pop, the Artful looked depressed. These moments usually coincided with our trips to the Point. Then he had a hang-dog expression and seemed to cower beneath his load as though ashamed to be seen by other cars. This was understandable, as when we finally pulled away from the curb we looked like a traveling slum.

Pop always started packing the Artful in a scientific way, explaining that if you really planned properly everything could fit in like pieces of a Chinese puzzle. He said that same thing this time and climbed around inside building a complex structure rather like a dam in the space between the front seat and the back, our foot room.

"What are we supposed to do, cut off our legs?" we asked, but Pop said he washed his hands of the whole business. It turned out that the visible pile of luggage strapped and ready in the front hall was merely a rough sketch or first draft of what Mum intended to take. Cartons of leftover food, the last collection of laundry, her sewing basket tied up in a pillow case, a lot of rubbers, plants, special roasters, and indispensable frying pans kept arriving on the sidewalk. Mum had a firm belief that you could always get one more thing into a car either by forcing it into some crevice in the back seat, putting it under somebody's feet, or tying it to the outside. (You can.)

Pop stood rubbing the end of his nose with his forefinger and tried to figure out a place to put each new offering, then suddenly he had had enough. Abandoning the humble role of laborer he became once more the captain of the ship. He stood up straight; his voice hardened.

"NO MORE JUNK!" he bawled, and everybody snapped to attention.

"Go and pee, every one of you."

We went. Mum was inside rushing about, grabbing last-minute items.

"We're leaving," we yelled. "Hurry up!"

There was a moment of horror when the dog, Kelt, was thought to have vanished, but he was discovered in the back seat sitting with a piglike expression on top of a duffel bag. I tied my robin's basket to a brace overhead but the boys complained that he was in their territory so I had to move him right in front of my left eye.

"I can't see anything but the robin's rump," I said angrily, but Pop said I didn't know when I was well off. He said I should have been with Mum's family on one of the trips abroad.

"Do you realize," he said, "that they went all the way around the *world* with a sunfish called Dear Baby in a lard pail?"

Mum said on the contrary Dear Baby had perished in the Indian Ocean and been buried at sea with full military honors. Then she began to reminisce about the golden summers of her childhood, when the trip to the Point was a gracious and beautiful thing. My grandmother and her household had traveled from New York on the Fall River boat, then made a royal progress down to Synton in horse-drawn vehicles of various kinds. The servants went in the carryall, the luggage in Tripp's wagon, and the family with Lizzie, their English nurse, in the three-seater, a covered carriage. It was clear that Baba had never been exposed to the more abrasive realities of going to the Point but then it is only since the invention of the internal-combustion engine that parents have plumbed the real depths of traveling with their young.

It took a little time to sink into the old rut of back-seat life, but at last most of the complaints were ironed out and by then we had crossed the Connecticut, left the mills behind, and were out in the country. The morning was fresh and sweet, the fields of daisies and buttercups gay in the sun. The wind splashed through the uncut grass with big silver footsteps, and bunches of trees swung past, tossing us snatches of bird song. Swallows dipped on sleek wings in front of the car, and the truck gardens were still dewy-looking, with crisp rows of lettuce and celery lining the black earth. Men weeding stood up and waved to us and we waved back. Then Pop threw back his head and yodeled.

"This is the day the Lord hath made!" he yelled.

In this lyric vein we went on our way until Aldie punched Dave because he kept poking his elbow into his (Aldie's) side, and there was a short struggle.

"Hey, cut that out," I said, and then Mum, harking back to the old Fall River boat days, said that as children they never fought, never even exchanged a cross word. This information was not well received by us. We were faced with ten or twelve hours wedged into a back seat with two siblings, a drooling dog, and an incontinent robin, and we didn't want to hear about people who never exchanged cross words. The whole idea was sickening.

"I'll bet God would fight if he had to sit back here for a whole day," Aldie said, but, of course, we never were in the back seat the whole day and we knew it. About half the time we were thrashing around in the underbrush looking for a good place. Pop said he couldn't understand it.

"Why in Sam Hill does everybody have to pee every five minutes as soon as we get in the car?"

"It's not something you can help," I said indignantly.

On this particular trip he had decided to handle the problem in a businesslike manner.

"I want to say right now," he announced, "that when I stop for cover, everybody gets out and I mean everybody, including that dad-gasted dog."

"What about the robin?" somebody asked impudently, but Pop ignored this.

"Stopping for cover" was the family expression for going to the john in the woods. In those primitive days the expression "rest room" hadn't been invented and neither had rest rooms. In any case we weren't allowed to use public johns because we might catch some sort of disease, the exact nature of which no one would explain. As a result we took to the woods and the whole route to the Point was studded with places where we had stopped for cover. We always greeted these oases with glad cries.

"There's the place I saw that man going on the other side

of my bush," I would say and somebody else would call our attention to the exact segment of sidewalk in a small town where Aldie had been caught short and gone.

The test of Pop's new system came very soon when Dave said he had to go.

"All right," said Pop, "but remember what I said, everybody out."

"I don't have to," said Aldie.

"You can't go if you don't have to," I said, but Pop claimed you could if you tried.

Finding a good place was very hard, as opinions differed. Pop would have settled for a large tree, a billboard or even a bush. I wanted a place with a brook because I always used these stops to look for birds' nests, flowers, rare birds—anything. At no other time did I have such a wonderful chance to explore new territory. Every flat tire, every stop for cover was a little adventure, a miniature expedition. As a result my trips into cover were apt to be extended.

Now Pop was beginning to get impatient, as one place after another was rejected as too transparent, too low, too small, too this, too that. Finally he got tired of arguments and braked to a stop beside a plantation of firs with trees in parallel rows like columns in a cathedral. Inside the plantation it not only looked like a cathedral, it felt like one—dim, religious light, long aisles receding into the distance—everything.

"This is no good," I said to Pop. "It's like trying to go in church."

It was just like one of those dreams when you're hunting for the john and think you've found it and then the lights go on and there you are up in the chancel in front of a huge congregation. The males in the group, however, said it was perfectly O.K. and only laughed when we said they had an unfair advantage.

We christened this place Cathedral Cover.

The next cover was a beauty, rating four stars on the list since Pop, stumbling through a thicket, found an ovenbird's nest— a real treasure. These nests are hard to locate because they are roofed like old-fashioned ovens and camouflaged with dead leaves. The mother bird, which looked like a tiny thrush, now put on the famous broken-wing act to decoy us away from the nest. Pop was delighted and we got down to peer in at the freckled white eggs neatly arranged in a cup of grass. You don't see ovenbirds' nests in Howard Johnson's rest rooms—just one of many reasons why the pioneer days of car travel were so much fun.

While I was on my own quest I was attended by a nervous red-eyed vireo and knew that a nest must be in the vicinity.

"All ashore that's going ashore," Pop bellowed after a while.

The vireo had a green grub in its bill and was clearly en route to its babies, so I couldn't yell back to Pop. However, I had to leave when he began tooting the horn.

"Holy Caesarea Philippi!" he said when I appeared. "There's no need to go on a cross-country hike."

He didn't seem to be in the mood to hear about nervous vireos; he was worried about the Artful Dodger, who was beginning to show symptoms of the canary disease. After a few miles he chirped and warbled so loudly that people a block away stopped dead in their tracks. Eventually we drove to a garage and Pop tried to explain our problem to the oily man in charge.

"It sounds as though there were canaries in the engine," he said.

The oily man looked at him sharply.

"Birds," said Pop, "chirping and warbling."

"You think you got birds in the engine?" asked the oily man evenly.

"It sounds like canaries, I mean," said Pop.

It was clear that the oily man believed Pop to be some sort of eccentric, if not actually insane, but he decided to humor him.

"Canaries, eh?" he said. "Start her up."

The Artful ran as smoothly as a sewing machine.

"I don't hear no canaries," said the oily man reproachfully, so we left.

The canaries began warbling again as soon as we were back on the road but Pop said we couldn't stop for every little noise.

Presently there was a loud report like gunfire, and at first we thought the canaries had blown up, but it was only a flat tire. We all poured out of the car to explore, and Pop removed the front seat where the tools were and untied the baby's bathtub from the rear tire. Spares were carried on the back of the car then, a system so convenient that the designers naturally abandoned it. We then took the old tire to a garage and waited for it to be fixed, which was lucky because we had another blowout soon afterward.

I am a little confused about the exact sequence of events during the latter part of the day, but I remember that we had to stop at a diner to heat Targ's bottle, and then the dog, Kelt, threw up on the steamer rug, so we stopped and rinsed it out in a pond. This episode made me feel carsick and then somebody was—I forget who. We had a picnic in a field and Kelt got into some cow manure and also ate some sardines when no one was looking. He threw up after we were back in the car, and then we got lost on a detour and found ourselves on a rutted dirt road down which we rumbled and crashed for so long that a lot of the luggage worked loose and an iron frying pan fell on my foot, causing me considerable anguish. Finally Pop got out and asked a man in a field where we were.

"We're in East Hardwick," he said, getting back in the car.

"Where's that?" said Mum.

"God knows," said Pop.

Bobs said he had to go pee-pee so Pop simply slammed on the brakes and stopped. There was nothing around but some clumps of grass and several people objected, but Pop said it didn't matter whether anyone saw us or not as they didn't know who we were.

"Just stand beside the car," he said. "We'll all look the other way."

On this road we got stuck in a herd of cows, lunging along with swinging udders.

"A cow's rear end has nothing to recommend it," said Pop, as we crawled along behind the row of manure-caked pelvises.

In order to escape this vision he turned down a side road,

which by a stroke of luck took us back to our route. Shortly afterward Pop was arrested for speeding and lugged off by the police.

To be perfectly fair about this, it was all the fault of us backseaters. We had persuaded him to play Bag, a terrific car game of our own invention. It was a great game from a parent's point of view, I see now, because we were all on the same side. Our opponents were the rest of the human race, or that portion of it unlucky enough to be behind us in cars. The road behind us was the Bag and to capture more victims we forced Pop to pass the cars ahead. As the driver he played the key role on the home team and was most cooperative, even exceeding his usual speed of twenty-five m.p.h. to collect a new prisoner. Our role, of which he was happily unaware, was to kneel on the back seat and make faces at the victims through the rear window. We had a large repertoire, ranging from basic faces like thumbing the nose to complicated ones involving every feature plus the hands. I remember one in which you pulled out the corners of your mouth with your little fingers, slanted your eyes with the forefingers, and turned up your nose with the middle ones. At the same time you stuck your tongue out to its full length and waggled it. After a few miles of this treatment the occupants of the car behind became so inflamed with rage that they would risk death in order to pass and escape. Pop maneuvered to foil them and there was never a dull moment. Sometimes truckdrivers, a hard-bitten lot, would turn down side streets and try to cut in ahead of us on the next block.

This trip Aldie added an extra touch that had very satisfactory results. He wrote things on a piece of paper and held them up to the window for our captives to read.

"Go boil your head," he wrote once, and the man behind us—the father of a family—reacted so violently that he nearly wrecked his car trying to escape.

He almost passed us, and when he drew abreast he shook his fist at Pop and bellowed something in a very uncontrolled way. Pop stepped on the gas though and pulled ahead again.

"That chap seemed upset about something," he said.

"He looked insane to me," said Aldie.

"Probably drunk," I said virtuously.

It was at this point that we were arrested and our victim got away. As he passed, shouting invective, his children made horrible faces at us out their rear window. Altogether it was an unfortunate incident.

In these innocent ways we passed the time until we came to the outskirts of Fall River and saw the green towers of the Catholic church high against the sky. Few landmarks in my life have filled me with such unadulterated joy. Every stone wall, tree, and building from there down to the Point was part of the enchantment.

The countryside is flat here, with walls of squared granite and trees blown crooked by the prevailing winds, and the old houses are silver-shingled with white trim. There are hollies in the woods, and sassafras and wild roses grow right up to the road's edge. There is a curve after Central Village where you first see the ocean, and then there is the harbor ahead and our river on the right and the big white farmhouses riding the crests of the little hills all the way down to the Point.

In those days we could see Synton's chimneys and Baba's twin spruces on the top of the last hill.

When we turned off the main road into the lane Pop said it looked as though they'd put gravel on. We were back in the Synton world, where "the road" was a major subject of conversation.

Baby rabbits ran ahead of us down the ruts and in the green center strip were Gyp's hoofprints. Wild roses and honeysuckle sent out a gay light perfume and the catbirds were singing from the tangles of grapevine.

Pop blew his horn at the corner where the big laurel was a cloud of pink blossom. Then we passed the twin spruces and came out on the top of the hill where Synton stood among her trees, her wide-skirted verandas spread around her like the brown wings of a broody hen. The blossoming lindens roared with honeybees and the whole hilltop smelled like hot lemons. Baba in her violet dress stood on the steps by the smoke bush, one hand out in welcome. Aunt K. was with her, carrying a trowel. Tink, his face all crinkled up with joy, was there in his new summer clothes, put on in our honor. Also present were Synton's dogs—Lad, reputed to be a "black-and-tan," and Thistle, a Scotch collie. They kept up a fanfare of hysterical barking while in the back seat Kelt lunged against his collar, making hoarse, wheezing noises. Nobody could hear himself speak and it was just like every other summer.

We tumbled out of the car and hugged Tink hard while he gave us big, smacking kisses.

"I love you, dear Jan," he said when it was my turn. It was his usual greeting. We kissed Aunt K., who was tall and sunburned with merry eyes and hair like pulled molasses candy. There was a fragrance of wood smoke, spices, and hay about her, left over from her various activities in kitchen and barn.

Last of all we went and received Baba's kiss, for she waited with dignity for us to come to her. This year she seemed smaller but she was just as erect and straight-backed as ever, the nearest thing to royalty I ever hope to see. Her face was highly colored, aquiline, with hooded brown eyes like a falcon's. There was only a little gray in her bright brown hair, which she twisted into memorable coils and fastened with historic hairpins and combs of tortoise shell. I suppose when we first knew her she was only in her fifties but we thought she was very old. She dressed always in shades of violet and looked exactly like a grandmother.

"Dear Jan," she said to me, as usual. She retained the Victorian habit of address, putting "dear" before the names of those she loved. Tink did the same but he also dropped his h's in imitation of Lizzie, his nurse, who had a cockney accent, and this gave Tink language a peculiar charm.

During the initial exchanges the grownups shouted at the tops of their voices to make themselves heard above the dogs and each other. Even Baba was forced to speak louder than she felt a lady should, and we knew she did not approve of such yelling sessions. Neither did Pop, for different reasons. He was, he said, ready for the chip basket and called out several times, "All ashore that's going ashore!" but nobody paid any attention.

We three oldest took Tink and galloped down the path to Snowdon.

As we ran out at the other end of the path, the world opened up—all was sky, water, and treetops. There were the sea, the harbor, the river—the design of land and water that we knew by heart. We stood there drinking it in, breathing the sweet special air scented with bayberry and red cedar and salt. We listened for the loon laughter of the gulls, dreamy and nostalgic with distance—the signature of the Point. Then we ran down to the house.

CHAPTER TWO

Tink's World

THE FIRST DAY AT THE POINT we spent settling in and Tink came down to preside, rather like the little fat Chinese god of happiness, round bellied and wreathed in smiles. It was his first day of summer too; our arrival marked the beginning of his vacation, the peak of his year, for which he lived all winter.

Like birds and animals all his movements were determined by the seasons of the year, the days of the week, and the hours of the day. He did the same thing at exactly the same time every day and nothing and no one could make him omit the tiniest ceremony. The iron-bound ritual with which he began every day of his life was unaffected by the seasons. Winter or summer it was the same with certain extra rites to celebrate Sunday.

Tink's day began at seven but no alarm clock was needed, for he possessed an internal clock that told him the time. He simply woke at seven in his bed, a huge antique four-poster, with a kind of rope hammock instead of springs. This had sagged so that Tink could only lie in the deep hollow in the middle of the mattress. When asleep in this valley he was all but invisible.

Upon arising Tink repaired to the bathroom, where he brushed his teeth and washed his face and hands. Back in his room he dressed carefully in clean clothes and brushed his hair with his two military brushes. He then polished his " 'peckies" (spectacles) on all the towels in the bathroom, on his bedspread, and finally on his clean handkerchief. Then he made his bed, pinching a little pleat all around to make it smooth and shipshape. After this he came downstairs in a special way—leaning his arms on the banisters and thudding his heels down stair by stair, hitting the exact center of the hollows he had made over the years.

Next he went into the drawing room and straightened Aunt K.'s rocking chair. From there he made a beeline through the dining room, pantry, and kitchen to the sink and had a drink of water out of his special blue enamel cup. Only when these rites had been observed could he turn his attention to the day's business.

Once Dave, using all his blandishments, tried to make Tink omit the rocking-chair sequence and come directly to the blue cup.

"You don't have to do that," he said. "It's all straight—see?" He pointed to the chair.

Tink was very upset and stood still, rubbing his eye.

Dave argued and reasoned with him but was, I'm happy to report, unable to move Tink a single inch. The chair was adjusted.

After the blue cup Tink always turned and beamed upon the assembled company. Then he went around and greeted each one of us with a kiss. This included any dogs or cats present. Tink always kissed his pets full on the mouth. If the pet happened to be a baby chicken he kissed the end of its bill. Good mornings over, he sat down in his office, the sunken counter by the north window. The kitchen was his headquarters, from which he surveyed the world and to which he returned to rest between engagements. It was also the headquarters of all the hill's children.

When at Synton we left the front of the house and passed through the butler's pantry into the kitchen, we knew that practically anything we did would be accepted. This included forbidden activities like belching, risqué dances, and backhouse humor of a particularly primitive variety. Aunt K. always cried, "Oh, sto-op!" but it was more a shriek of laughter than an order, so, of course, we just showed off some more.

We would shut the pantry door so Baba wouldn't hear us and settle down into the lovely sweltering bedlam of the kitchen like kittens into a basket. I suppose it couldn't always have been as hot, light, and noisy as I remember it, but it seems from here a perfect heaven of red tablecloths, geraniums, dogs, and people stewing in the brilliant heat from the stove.

When Bessie, the last cook, died, Aunt K. took over the cooking, having somehow figured out how it was done. Under her rule the kitchen blossomed with flowering plants, and more and more animals and birds kept creeping in. Once there were twin kids leaping like mountain goats from chair to table. Sometimes there were new puppies, blithely unhousebroken. In spring flats of seedlings stood in the sunny windows, and in early summer there were sometimes baby chicks cheeping in a carton behind the stove. The place was part kitchen, part zoo, part greenhouse, part animal hospital. Whenever anyone found a fallen nestling or a wounded animal he brought it to Aunt K. and she would give the patient to some roughly comparable species to bring up. If it had fur she chose somebody with fur; if it had or was supposed to have feathers, she gave it to somebody with feathers, and so forth. Some pretty amazing combinations resulted.

I remember a parakeet feeding a one-legged robin that had come to Aunt K. at a very early and revolting age. After it grew up it lived in a cage with the parakeet, a canary, two cutthroat finches, and some English sparrows that had been frozen in the goat's water pail. Another time one of the dogs brought in a baby rabbit, which was put in with an elderly guinea pig named Brown-eyes. On reaching adulthood the rabbit made a pass at its foster parent and had to be given away. Nobody seemed certain as to the sex of either party or even whether they were of the same or opposite sexes. However, this was irrelevant. Brown-eyes was cast in the role of victim in this affair and was put in the cage with the birds to help her (or him) adjust. However, she got so covered with bird droppings that she had to be moved out again.

The rest of Tink's private zoo was out at the barn and the next item on his daily agenda was chores. For this enterprise he put on his rubbers and work hat—a curious flat affair of stitched khaki very like those worn on K.P. duty by members of the armed forces. He then set out for the barn. Aunt K. came along carrying the garbage pail for the hens, and one or more of us trailed behind with Thistle, the collie. We always halted by the chicken yard while Aunt K. dumped the garbage over the fence. Then we trudged in single file across to the carriage house, which contained a buckboard and a buggy (Baba called these the dos-à-dos and phaeton), a privy called the "men's outhouse," and the apartment of Rajah, the peacock. Next door lived Gyp, the bay mare, and a barn swallow which had a mud nest up on a beam. Upstairs in the hayloft was Moni, a bachelor goat of the lowest moral fiber, who slept there with a setting hen and a cat.

The presence of Moni in the hayloft used to upset Pop, whose standards of barn etiquette had been learned on the Old Farm. You didn't put goats in haylofts.

"I'll bet that dad-gasted goat pees all over the hay that benighted horse has to eat," he said often, but Mum said he had no proof.

Tink's job was to hoe out Gyp's stall, put in fresh bedding and sweep the barn floor. We helped with the stall but the floor was Tink's sole responsibility, and he was a purist of the first water on the subject of clean floors. He swept and swept, bending double to examine the floor between bouts. He always ended up brushing it with his handkerchief and picking up the last hayseeds with his fingers. While he did this he never spoke, being completely absorbed.

After chores Tink returned to his office in the kitchen and waited until the clock with the yellow morning glories on it struck eight. Formal breakfast in the dining room followed. Here the inexorable part of his schedule ended and there was now room for variety.

During the spring, winter, and fall he worked, cutting the grass, chopping wood, and doing simple jobs around the barn. His axe was easily as sharp as a spoon, but with it he was able to bang down trees and fracture billets of wood. It was in the off seasons that he carried out projects suggested by Baba to surprise us. He loved surprising people; it was one of his greatest pleasures. To see someone else happy made him absolutely radiant with joy.

The day we came he laid aside his axe, put off his winter work clothes, and assumed the summer dress of a gentleman of leisure. In his case this entailed a khaki shirt or short-sleeved jersey, khaki pants, and high brown sneakers. Baba seemed to be under the impression that Tink was of enormous size—a giant— so she always ordered pants so large that the legs had to be cut off at the knees to fit his rather unusual figure.

Tink kept himself as clean as a whistle, and when we hugged him he smelled of freshly laundered shirts, wood smoke, and hay. He always carried two handkerchiefs, one to blow on, one for polishing his " 'peckies." Once a week—on Sunday—he shaved; then, his chores done, he put on a gray suit, white shirt, and tie and observed the Sabbath as a day of rest. There was something serene and orderly about Tink's arrangement of his life, and he was meticulous about decorum. He knew what correct drawing-room manners were, and if we indulged in any Rabelaisian kitchen behavior at the wrong time he reproved us.

Baba was magnificent when she introduced Tink to a roomful of garden-party guests—ladies in flower hats, one or two gentlemen in white flannels, and Baba like a small queen standing in the doorway with Tink at her side. I can see her now—her falcon eyes fixed on the company with a kind of defiance.

"My son Theodore," she always said, and Tink would come forward and shake hands with everyone.

"Theodore will entertain you while I see to the tea," Baba would say later on.

And he did, too, in all kinds of ways. Sometimes he regaled them with tidbits of gossip no one was supposed to know. Sometimes he told them about his pets. Sometimes he proposed marriage. This was one of his ways of expressing love. He proposed to all of us regularly and we always accepted. Tink had an uncanny sixth sense about people and only proposed when he felt they appreciated him. In Tink's company there was happiness of a particularly peaceful kind, for he loved us just as we were. The grownups seemed to make life unnecessarily complicated and you were often accused of being naughty, disobedient, impudent, or impolite. Tink had the same problem and worried terribly about being good.

"I am good boy?" he would ask humbly over and over until he was reassured.

I'm sorry to say that we led Tink astray all the time. I was the first grandchild to play with him and my earliest memory of the hill is of such an occasion. Tink and I were both three when we crawled in under the raspberry bushes and gorged ourselves until I was sick. Tink wasn't but he had the edge on me, having been three for a much longer time. Aunt K. rescued me and carried me down to Snowdon while Tink followed, giving aid and comfort. Everyone said how naughty we'd been but neither Tink nor I knew what we'd done. We had been encouraged, even compelled, to eat raspberries at the table, and nobody had ever told us not to eat them off the bushes.

When Aldie was three like Tink, and I was four, Dave was born. We had been left at Synton for September as there was a flu epidemic in the city, and Buffy, our nurse, stayed on with us.

One night we were having our supper at the kitchen table, warm and sleepy from the heat of the coal range. Tink was by the window on the sunken counter picking twills off his sweater. Twills were fuzz, loose threads, bits of hayseed, lint—anything that stuck up from an orderly smooth surface. Tink hated twills and waged perpetual war against them.

In the middle of this domestic moment the telephone rang and Aunt K. answered it. Presently she uttered a loud shriek and turned to us: "You've got a baby BROTHER!" she cried.

Then she and Buffy took turns at the telephone and there was a lot of meaningless grownup gabble. I think Pop eventually spoke to us, in a quavering voice, but I can't remember. We had not felt the need of any baby brother as we had each other and were quite self-sufficient. I had a dim idea it might be fun to hold a real baby, but I saw no need for Pop and Mum to get one when they had us.

There the mists close in, and the summers until that baby, Dave, was three blur together. Nothing earthshaking seems to have occurred. Oh, Pop went to the war—something that was going on in France—but I don't remember his leaving. We stayed at the Point with Mum, Buffy, and a cook called Fishy-Fishy, who drank vanilla. Of the horrors of war and its bloodshed I recall two episodes. Mum cut a black snake in half with an axe, and she and Buffy killed a large fish with a baseball bat on the porch after a long battle. We were appalled at this carnage, but then war is a brutal business.

Tink spent the war chiefly in our hammock reviling the Kaiser, for whom he had conceived a passionate loathing. All three of us realized that this monster was the one everybody was fighting, and we used to roar out the lines:

> Slip a pill to Kaiser Bill
> And make him shed a tear.

The Kaiser's picture was on a large recruiting poster on the front of Manchester's store in Adamsville, so we used to see him every time we drove there with Aunt K. in the buckboard. He had a spiked helmet and a fierce mustache and was pointing directly at us. His hand was dripping with blood so it was easy to see why Tink disliked him.

After a while Tink composed a chant about the Kaiser, set to the rhythm of the hammock's swing. It was called "Missa Willema" and went like this:

> Míssa Míssa Wíllema Wíllema Wíllema Káiser, *yái*-yow!
> Míssa Míssa Wíllema Wíllema Wíllema Káiser, *yái*-yow!

and so on indefinitely, with a lingering howl on the "yai."

After Pop came back from the war, hollow cheeked and thin, he used to object strongly to "Missa Willema." Mum said the war had made him very nervous, and as Tink sang "Missa Willema" for most of the day Pop got tired of it. He got sick of the hammock, too.

When Tink was on his summer schedule the hammock was the next step after the completion of his regular routine. He put on his hat and headed downhill to our house, and no human agency could stop him. He went around onto the veranda and climbed into the hammock, his summer office, from which he had a clear view through the window of much that went on in the house. We always left that window open about a foot, and in this space Tink's face was usually visible, sliding back and forth to the rhythmic squeaks of the hammock's moorings. He had two hammock chants, the other being exactly like "Missa Willema," with our iceman's name substituted for that of the Kaiser as a concession to peacetime.

Between bouts of chanting he conducted conversations with himself or anybody who happened to be in his range of vision. At intervals he played a tune on his mouth organ. This tune consisted of two chords, one played as he inhaled, the other as he exhaled. It was pretty monotonous and Pop, who was upstairs trying to study, would eventually yell down in despair. We could see the war had made him very nervous.

"Hey, Tink," he'd shout, "call it quits, will you?"

"O.K., dear Brother Bob," Tink would call back. "You love me?"

"Yes!"

"You want to marry me?"

"Yes, if you shut up!"

"O.K., dear Brother Bob!" called Tink happily, pocketing his mouth organ.

As long as he was alone on the hammock he kept the speed down to a rhythm suitable for singing "Missa Willema," but when Aldie and I came aboard we led him astray as usual, pumping harder and harder until the hammock crashed into the side of the house. Then Pop would stamp on the floor upstairs.

"Hey!" he'd scream. "Cut that out!"

Hammock time ended when everyone except Baba went down to the river to swim. This was about eleven o'clock.

Tink, in a curious bathing suit with cap sleeves and tubular

legs, would stand on the beach and throw himself full length
into the water even if it was only ankle deep. Then he forged
out from shore, churning the water to foam and leaving a wake
like a motorboat. After a short pause to breathe he turned to
plow back.

Following the swim we all went up the hill to lunch, Tink
resuming his place in the hammock. Presently we would hear
Baba's voice through her big megaphone calling, "Theo-do-hore!"
in musical, ladylike tones. Every day the same thing happened.

Tink's blissful smile would fade and "Missa Willema" stop
in mid-verse.

We would tell him he had to go. He would refuse curtly.
We would lay hands on him and pull. It was like trying to move a
tree. We would try bribery and an appeal to his better nature.

"Want fun tomorrow?" I would say.

"Yes, I do, dear Jan."

"Well, then go on up the hill."

"No," said Tink, "I will not."

In the end we had to get Pop, who could make Tink do anything, and presently they'd go off up the hill, Pop's arm around
Tink's khaki shoulders, Tink's arm around Pop's khaki waist.

After his lunch Tink's schedule required that he go down to
the river and play "Hanky Wind Take," a game of his own invention with which he whiled away the summer afternoons when
we were out sailing. He walked to the river by the path from
Synton that came out at the old boathouse. Down on the shore
was a huge square of teak deck that had lodged there one winter,
and here he sat down with his legs straight out in front of him.
He then took out two handkerchiefs and picked all the twills off
them. When they were in proper shape he held them delicately by
the corners, one in each hand, using only the tips of his fingers.
They streamed out in the breeze like flags, fluttering, snapping,
furling, and unfurling in the most delightful way. Tink watched
them in a happy trance. He did this every pleasant afternoon until
we came back, when he folded his hankies and went swimming
with us.

At five o'clock he was summoned through the megaphone to do the evening chores, and while we were small that was the last we saw of him. However, after Dave grew old enough he used to go up with Tink, because he had decided to be a farmer. He wore during this phase a real farmer's straw hat, and he and Tink spent hours together out at the barn doing the chores and fraternizing with Moni, the goat, whose obscene antics appealed to their low humor.

Tink never stopped singing "Missa Willema" nor did he himself ever change, and this made all the summers merge into one, a summer without end, blue and serene forever. Babies were born, grew to be three and then older, but Tink stayed the same age until summer seemed like a separate country where time had stopped.

When we went to the Point we went back to our childhood and the country of summer, Tink's enchanted land. However, the summer after Targ was born I realized for the first time that I couldn't play with Tink in the old way. Also, I had grown as tall as he was. Bobs had finally arrived in Tink's age bracket and it was he who now rolled on the grass with him in fits of laughter. Dave was still Tink's closest friend and the world authority on Tink language, but even he had moved a step farther away from that magic, timeless country where Tink lived. We all ran down the hill howling and screeching in the traditional manner, but I felt just a little foolish doing it.

CHAPTER THREE

Beulah and Granny Gooseberry

THE EUPHORIC MOMENT OF ARRIVAL on the hill was immediately followed by a hectic interlude called Getting Settled. This operation was entirely directed by women, Pop playing the role of serf, or so he claimed. He said that a man couldn't call his soul his own around the place as long as there was a woman unoccupied.

"Haven't sat down for four hours," he would report, trudging by with some article that was too heavy for female hands.

First, of course, he had to unpack the car because the women had to have something out of it right away in order to feed the Hideons, and just as he got started on this they said he had to get some water. All the pitchers upstairs had to be filled and a good supply of drinking and cooking water carried from Synton. Pop struggled up and down hill, up and down stairs, with his two French milk cans until he said his shoulders were pulled down right to his waist.

"I look just like a gorilla," he said. "My hands are dragging on the ground."

He began to get miserly about the water from Baba's well and guarded it as though it were vintage wine.

"Hey, don't use that water for washing," he'd yell. "Use the cistern. Holy Caesarea Philippi!"

Even when we went in for a drink he'd try to persuade us we didn't want it.

"But we're thirsty," we protested. "It's hot."

35

"You're hot! What about me?" he asked, mopping his face and neck. "I'm melted down to a grease spot."

Mum and her cohorts would go into shrieks of laughter at him. When both his hands were occupied she always seized that moment to tickle him or dangle a wet diaper in front of his face.

"Stop that!" he'd yell, and after a while he'd laugh so hard he'd have to sit down.

During his menial labors among the washstands everybody called him Beulah.

"Beulaa-ah," Mum would cry. "The pitcher in our room's empty!"

"What in Sam Hill do you do with the stuff?" Pop would ask, toiling upstairs with his French milk cans.

"We wash with it," said Mum. "The whole place has to be scrubbed."

"Well, use the cistern water, dad-gast it. I think I've already ruptured myself."

Mum said the cistern water smelled. "I think something must have drowned in it," she told him. "There's fur coming out of the pump. Why don't you go down and see?"

"I haven't time to loll around in cisterns," said Pop, "and stop those women from using water as though they were millionaires. Nobody needs to be that clean. Look at me. Filthy."

He was, too, as he had been crawling around under the house, climbing onto the roof to remove the cover from the chimney, evicting mice from bureau drawers, and burying the corpses of whatever members of the wild kingdom had been trapped in the house during the winter. Among these that June were a partridge—a soft drift of leaf-colored feathers in a corner —and two squirrels which had spent their final hours eating the window frames. Practically every frame upstairs was gnawed to the quick, and there were wood chips all over the place.

While Pop gave the squirrels decent burial out by the garbage pit we buried a dead mouse that we christened Tuttle at the last minute in order to use as a gravestone a brick with "Tuttle" printed on it. Before we were done one of the women inside gave a piercing scream and Pop rushed inside. Shortly afterward he came back carrying a ball of shredded toweling that squeaked.

"Baby mice," he said, and showed us a pile of pink lima beans with blue lumps for eyes. To our horror he said he was going to expose them, so as soon as he left we made them a nice home in a strawberry basket, which we concealed in the woodshed.

After that Mum said her room was full of bees and it turned out there was a swarm in the gable.

"Get them out!" she cried. "Do something!"

"How am I supposed to get them out?" asked Pop. "What do you think I am, a queen bee?"

He said he'd have to call the bee man, and then he got the ladder and climbed down into the cistern. We peered in and saw a circle of blue sky, our faces, and Pop's bald spot.

"By George," he said, "there is some dad-gasted animal down here. I think it's rabbit—abbit—abbit."

His voice echoed around the walls like the voice of a man with his head in a pail.

At some point he had to put up the hammock for Tink, as it didn't seem like summer without his face sliding back and forth in the window. "Missa Willema" soon began and served as a kind of ground bass to the chorus of slop-jar lids, the braying and gagging of the pump, and the shouts of grownups calling back and forth.

Getting settled that particular summer was even more hectic than usual as something was missing in the home—a cook. The Fiddle was unavailable as her sister had been killed by a train—"neatly sevaired at the waist," The Fiddle had said with ill-concealed relish. The grownups were in a panic. Conferences were held. I think they had ordered a cook by mail and were betrayed by the employment agency. In any case, there we were, seven of us, marooned on the hill with starvation staring us in the face. There was even talk of looking up Fishy-Fishy, the temporary cook who had drunk vanilla, but Mum said nothing was worth that.

We had been dimly aware that there was a crisis in the kitchen department, but with the callousness of the young we thought it a lot of fuss about nothing. As long as we were fed and there were plenty of women around, we felt quite secure. There were plenty of women: Mum, Buffy (the so-called mother's helper), and Aunt K., who had come down with a basket of new peas, some fresh eggs, and a bunch of flowers from Baba, who stayed aloof from the shambles of her child's menage.

There was a strange picnic atmosphere about. In the city we were used to having the house's machinery running the way you get used to the throb of engines on a steamer. It was a comfortable sound—the vacuum humming, pots and pans clattering, stove lids clanging, and the murmur of voices out back. We woke up to smell breakfast cooking—bacon and coffee and bran muffins warm from the oven. We came in at noon for dinner and the whole house was rich with savory odors of meat and vegetables, and at intervals the hall smelled sweetly of new-baked bread or apple pie. There is a lot to be said for this way of life but it had its drawbacks. Without the maids a house was like a ship without an engine, at least ours was. The maids' night out was rock bottom, gastronomically speaking. We always ate shredded wheat or crackers and milk at the kitchen table, these being the only dishes Mum knew how to prepare. Pop could cook steak, chops, or brook trout over an open fire outdoors, but the only thing he could do indoors was pop corn over the bed of coals in the furnace.

"If you had ever let me learn to cook," Mum said unfairly, "things would be different. It's all your fault. Don't blame me."

We knew she was talking about her first years of housekeeping when Pop hired a holy terror named Margaret and told her never to bother Mum with domestic details. Mum had come to him from a household with a full staff and had hardly ever seen a kitchen. Pop and Baba felt that she was too young and too fragile to take on the job of housekeeping, so Margaret had been given absolute power. She seems to have been a sort of Scotch version of Adolf Hitler and soon reduced Mum and Pop to a pitiful state of slavery. Rather than offend her by saying they disliked some dish they would secrete food in envelopes, which Pop took with him on his way to work and concealed in a hedge along

the route. Their worst trouble was doughnuts, which Pop had pretended to like and which Margaret produced by the hundred. He
buried them in the garden at night, fed them to the dog, hid
them in the hedge, and even ate a few in despair. Both he and Mum
still bore the scars of this ordeal. Although Margaret had long been
gone there were all sorts of loathsome things that we children
had to choke down so as not to upset the cook. Faced with really
repellent dishes like apple tapioca or Brown Betty, which we rightly
refused to eat, we were put at the library table with the stuff in
front of us and there we stayed (theoretically) until we ate it.
If we stayed there long enough we were released, because if the
maids didn't get our dishes to wash they would be upset and might
leave. In those days the kitchen, far from being the heart of the
house, was more like the lair of a grizzly bear or some other
savage beast. People would put up with anything rather than
offend the inmate, because if she left they might have to get a
temporary.

The type of female who went out as a temporary was usually
so frightening that nobody could stand her for more than a short
time. Most of them didn't even know how to cook, but this was
considered irrelevant, especially by people reared in the British
tradition. You just had to have somebody in there banging pots
and pans together. Now, because of the train which had bisected
The Fiddle's sister, we were going to have to get one of these
gorgons. The home was drifting helplessly, headed for the shoals.

That night we had a grim supper of shredded wheat and
some burnt scrambled eggs that Pop had made. However, he said
it was good for us to see how some people had to live. Think
of the starving Armenians. We were always being told to think
of the starving Armenians when we gagged over lumpy oatmeal
or bread pudding.

The next morning I escaped breakfast because it was my
turn to go up to Synton, a ritual which Baba had initiated.

Breakfast at Synton was no mere meal but a festival to celebrate
the birth of a new day. It also had about it the glamour of a royal
levee, and in summer we took turns attending. As the eldest I had

the first day. Breakfast took place at exactly 8 o'clock and not one moment sooner, for Baba's routine was that of a lady of leisure in a Scottish country house during the reign of the late Queen Victoria.

I don't know how she did it, but Baba had the gift of turning the most commonplace event into a drama. A good example of this art was the morning flower ritual, when she selected (or was given) a perfect blossom to wear in her amethyst pin. In June I was supposed to procure a special symbolic flower—the purple milkwort —the herald of summer's beginning, as goldenrod was a symbol of its ending.

This milkwort—or polygala, as I was trained to call it—was an unassuming little plant barely visible in deep grass, but in Baba's hands it had acquired an almost heraldic status. For one thing it was *purple,* Baba's color, and one that she had taken over so completely that everything purple—amethysts, violets, lilacs, lavender, heliotrope—seemed to us her personal property. In Baba's family everybody had his own flower and color, her special flower being the violet. Mine was the Scotch harebell and my color blue like my eyes. A clump of Scotch harebells had been planted at Synton in my honor and they were supposed to blossom on my birthday in July.

On that first morning Rajah, the peacock, woke me at sunrise. It was his custom every morning to fly up on the carriage-house roof and shriek like a madwoman. The sun was just coming over Synton at the top of the hill. Outside the front door the morning fizzed and glittered like a shaken ginger-ale bottle, bird song bubbled up through wet leaves, and the whole hill was scented with honeysuckle and freshly opened wild roses.

I went up the path between bushes of wet sweet fern searching for the polygala. Across the path the wheels of the night's spider webs broke stickily against my face; I crawled under the best ones, and after a while I found one opened sprig of the sacred flower and ran the rest of the way out of sheer joy.

The kitchen was full of sun and steam; Aunt K. was stirring up some gingerbread in the yellow bowl, and there was a lovely smell of spices and sweet geraniums. Aunt K. rose at five and did most of the cooking and housework before dawn, thus creating for Baba's sake the illusion that a full staff of servants still operated beyond the door to the butler's pantry.

"Oh, what a day!" she said. "Oh, what air!" She said this every morning, whatever the weather, because she loved the world.

I gave her a hug and put my polygala in a glass of water.

"How are things going down there?" asked Aunt K.

"Oh, all right, I guess," I said. The whole business seemed senseless and boring. When you are lucky enough to be free of cooks, why go get one?

"Well, have something to eat," said Aunt K.

She cut me a thick slice of her bread, lathered it with butter and put it face down in the old yellow sugar crock. I went over to the sink and had a drink of water out of the blue enamel cup. Then I sat in the Boston rocker and went at the sugar bread. Presently Tink came in, and after he had drunk out of the blue cup we went out and did the chores.

Back at the house I shed my barn rubbers and went in. Baba was down and called "Heigho!" from the dining room, where I found her adding the last touches to the pretty table.

Unlike most Victorian houses Synton was full of light—the whole atmosphere was one of gaiety and color, and this was because Baba refused to have curtains. She liked to look out and see her gardens and the famous views of river and ocean, and she liked the sun to come in. Sun in one's morning rooms was, she said, very important. Now the dining room was flooded with sunshine, strained through showers of maidenhair fern, glowing in the red fleshy leaves and blossoms of enormous begonias and the green plush of mint geraniums. Everywhere were plants in damp, mossy pots. The air smelled of growing things and earth. The doors of the conservatory off the dining room were open, and the fragrance filled the whole front of the house. The canary—Pretty-Pretty—who lived in there was singing so loudly that it made my ears buzz.

Baba stood with her head cocked slightly like a small hawk while I presented my flower.

"Ah, my polygala, the first of the summer," she said, threading it behind her amethyst.

"Dear Jan, you never forget. Now, I have a little treat for you!" She flung out her hand toward my place, where the first sweet peas stood in a bud vase. One was pale pink, the other violet. The centerpiece was an arrangement of old-fashioned roses, and Baba called off their names: moss rose, cabbage, damask, old French. "All very old," she said, "and with the true rose scent. Modern tea roses are nearly scentless," she added sternly. Baba took as much trouble arranging flowers for me as she would have for the King of England; she entertained her family as though they were honored guests. The table was set with the best silver and glass, and today we had the blue Canton china and an array of Japanese and Chinese jars containing Baba's preserves and jams and various imported honeys and marmalades. We had damask napkins in silver napkin rings, Tink drank his milk from a silver cup, and I had Whitman's Instantaneous Chocolate mixed in a rose-medallion demitasse with a spoon that had a swastika on the handle.

"Always use the best of everything every day," Baba said often. "Who is more important than one's own family and oneself?"

When the French clock on the mantel struck eight in its clear silver voice, the kitchen clock whirred out the hour, and instantly Tink came through from the pantry, followed by Aunt K., carrying the oatmeal smoking in yellow bowls.

We all sat down. I sat opposite Tink, facing the conservatory, where the sun was shining through a jungle of green leaves.

Tink and I said grace.

"Thank you, God, for daily bread."

Then Baba looked up smiling and began the oatmeal rites, which started with cream. This was placed in front of her in a squatty white pitcher with mayflowers on it. She poured off the thick yellow top cream onto her own cereal and said as she did so, "The cream of the jest." Then she passed me the pitcher, now containing bluish skim milk. This little foible made Baba human even as we ourselves. After all, people have to have *some* weakness. However, sugar was out of the question. Baba didn't intend to turn breakfast into a Babylonian orgy.

There was apparently a law that people with Scottish blood had to have oatmeal for breakfast whether they liked it or not, and they had to eat it *without sugar*. No one in Baba's family *ever* put sugar on oatmeal, in tea, or in coffee, and they seemed to take pride in this fact. Going without sugar was a real virtue and built character. Pop put masses of sugar on everything, took tea and coffee with two lumps, and refused to be intimidated, but in some subtle way Baba and even Mum made us feel this was questionable behavior.

"Dear Robert has a sweet tooth," Baba said when Pop was visiting, and it was clear to us that a sweet tooth was a bad thing to have.

Tink ate his oatmeal with a large silver spoon that had a rabbit on the handle. He was so pleased that summer had come and we were back that he kept grinning at me between enormous mouthfuls.

"You, me, old chums," he said happily.

In front of Tink there was a plate of hot biscuits that Aunt K. had whipped up sometime before sunrise, and he could hardly take his eyes off them. As soon as Aunt K. had removed his empty bowl he reached out and took a biscuit. Then, tearing it open, he placed a huge slab of butter in its steaming heart. After closing it carefully he opened his mouth and engulfed the whole thing in one glorious bite. Baba deplored this.

"Theodore. Theodore," she said reproachfully.

After the oatmeal there was the rite of the boiled eggs, which came to the table in the small end of blue willow egg cups wearing tiny cozies that Baba had made from the crimson silk of an Indian sari. You had a choice of three ways to eat them: "dumped," or broken into the large end of the cup; "hat," eaten out of the shell with a special silver spoon; or "Yokohama," broken on a piece of buttered toast. The family had eaten eggs this way in Yokohama, Japan, hence the name. All of us at one time or another asked for Eggs Yokohama in restaurants and learned the hard way that they were a purely family thing. I really believed that Yokohama was spelled Yolk-a-hama.

During the meal Baba discoursed on the subject of servants and how to handle them. She used as a model the case of the late parlormaid—a girl called Miriam—who had kept her waiting on the front step of her New York house for five whole minutes after she had rung the bell.

"I simply walked right by her and gave her notice," said Baba.

"What's that?" I asked.

"I dismissed her," said Baba. "They have to know who's mistress in the house."

As breakfast drew to a close and Tink and I were each attempting to cram in one more hot biscuit with honey, the sound of steps on the porch heralded the daily procession of family. Hard shoes meant Mum; heavy, sneakered thuds, Pop; and light scampering sneakers the smaller members of the herd. After each one the screen door whirred shut and they came in out of the sun and the linden perfume to perch on a chair near the table.

On an ordinary day this was the time when reports were made, plans broached for discussion. Baba, sitting back with the air of a queen granting an audience, would reveal the program for the day as she had imagined it while lying awake in the dawn hours. She might decide that "probably dear Robert would want to go off in his boat if the weather was fine" or "probably you would choose today for a Newport picnic." The process was known in the family as "probablying" and served a valuable purpose, as it gave us something definite to accept or reject. Down at our house we often wasted an hour trying to decide on a project, with Mum saying, "Well, I don't know what anybody's going to do," every few minutes.

Today there was no leisurely discussion. The family was facing a crisis and quick action was indicated. Pop, who was in his poor-old-geezer role, went straight to the point.

"I think I'll try the Y.W.C.A. in New Bedford," he said, and went in to the butler's pantry with the hobbling gait suitable to an aging man bowed down with care.

"This is a Mr. Wicks," we heard him say in a conversational tone. "I live down here at Westport Point in the summers—have for years—down Scotch Pine Lane where Mrs. Hall lives. Katherine Hall runs the Westport Library, probably know her—my wife's sister."

"Don't tell them the story of your life," shouted Mum.

"What, dearie? No, no, that was my wife. She's right here. I'm up at Synton—that's the name of Mrs. Hall's house—her mother, you know, and Miss Hall's too. I haven't a telephone myself."

"Get to the point!" called Mum. "Just say we want a cook. They don't want to know the whole family history!"

This went on for some time and finally Pop came out, older than ever. He said they had promised him a dear old lady to begin work today. He would pick her up at the Y.W.

"She sounds exactly what we want," he said.

"How do you know?" asked Mum.

"Well, they said she was old," said Pop, who seemed to think this a real recommendation, "and she used to be cook in a boardinghouse on Martha's Vineyard."

"Oh, dear," said Mum, looking scared.

Baba tossed her head but said nothing. She wasn't afraid of servants, even cooks.

Pop now stumbled off and we followed.

"Stop seniling," Mum said. "Just because you have to go to New Bedford is no reason to act as though you were ninety-five."

Pop smiled in a patient, saintly way and went to the car. Changing gear with a horrible screech of metal, he drove off to get the dear old lady.

Some time later we heard the Artful Dodger's horn in the lane and rushed out to see what Fate had sent us. The car rolled to a stop by the flagpole, and we saw Pop looking glassy-eyed, with a tremendous woman sitting beside him. He gave us a ghastly smile and went around to open the door for her.

"Dearie," he said in a high, unnatural voice, "this is Mrs. Bagstock."

Out from behind the Artful's nose came a terrible figure with a stiff straw hat skewered onto its white hair, cold gray eyes glaring behind steel-rimmed spectacles, and a mouth like a bear trap.

"Hey, you," she said aside to Pop. "Get my suitcase." Her false teeth clashed like cymbals.

"Yes, sir!" said Pop, laughing wildly. "This is my wife, Mrs. Bagstock." When he introduced Mum as "my wife" we knew he couldn't remember her name. This happened when he was in a nervous condition.

Mum was nervous, too. We could tell by the way she was unable to stop talking and shouted as though the dear old lady were deaf.

Mrs. Bagstock may or may not have been deaf but she ignored Mum's babblings as though she were. We followed her down hill and Pop shambled after us with her luggage—a cardboard suitcase and some paper bags. When he knew he had made a horrible mistake he walked in a special way that Mum called "flumping." At these times his clothes seemed to be too big and looked as though he had slept in them. We recognized the symptoms but we were far more interested in the dear old lady's teeth, which seemed to have a life of their own. Sometimes when she opened her mouth to speak they snapped shut. Sometimes she clamped down on them to hold them in place; sometimes she just talked and let them clap and clatter all over her mouth. This made it difficult to understand all she said but it was diverting in an awful way.

"This your—snap—shtove?" she asked in the kitchen. "I don't like kerosene stoves."

"Well, it's all we have," shouted Mum.

"A pump, eh?" said Mrs. Bagstock. "I'm not used to places with pumps—snap."

Mum and Pop showed her her room off the kitchen and she glared around it in disapproval. Then Mum led her out into the woodshed and showed her the privy.

"No bathroom, eh?" said Mrs. Bagstock sourly, crunching her teeth together.

After we left her to change her clothes we all rushed into the living room, with Pop flumping ahead of us waving his hands in the air.

"I know, I know," he said. "I'm sorry, dearie, but what could I do? She was the only one they had."

"But she's a holy terror!" cried Mum.

"Well, we'll just have to do the best we can," said Pop. "She's probably just a lonely old soul who's had a hard life."

The idea of getting rid of Mrs. Bagstock never entered their heads. We were stuck with her and everybody knew it.

"Maybe she can cook," said Pop with pitiful optimism.

We came to the dinner table at noon with a feeling of apprehension. Pop said he was sure she could cook; she looked like a cook. Then we all sat and waited.

"Maybe she's had a stroke," said somebody after a while.

"No, I can hear her moving around," said Mum.

It was just like being at a bull fight, waiting for the bull to be loosed into the arena. We all giggled nervously and Pop began to eat bread and scoop the crumbs up with his spoon.

"What in Sam Hill is she doing out there?" he said.

"Ring the bell," I suggested.

Mum paid no attention to this silly idea.

Finally Mrs. Bagstock kicked open the pantry door and came in with the swordfish, which she slammed down in front of Pop. Then she went back and returned with the vegetables, which she plunked in front of Mum. After this she stood with her hands on her hips and watched.

"Thank you, Mrs. Bagstock," said Mum, but she just stood there.

"This looks good," croaked Pop, picking up the carving knife.

We were served and under Mrs. Bagstock's stony gaze began eating. The swordfish was cooked dry as blotting paper, the cabbage boiled until it was brown and the potatoes were a watery slush.

"Well, how is it?" asked Mrs. Bagstock.

"Great!" said Pop, heartily.

"Very good," said Mum.

We were doomed.

The dessert, which Mrs. B. obviously considered her masterpiece, was a steamed pudding, heavy as a wet mattress. She stayed to watch the effect.

"Pretty good, eh?" she said, regarding us narrowly.

"Wonderful!" cried our parents.

"It's good," we said sycophantically.

The minute she shut the pantry door Pop was out of his chair.

"Quick," he said. "Into the woods."

We rushed out on the porch and Pop, taking the body of the pudding, hurled it like a man doing the shot put far out into the trees. We flung our pieces and scrambled back into our chairs.

"That'll fix Granny Gooseberry," said Pop.

After that we never called her anything else—behind her back.

When Granny Gooseberry saw the empty dessert plates she was clearly gratified.

"Thought you'd like it," she said with a terrifying cackle. "I'll make you another."

"Good!" said Pop.

"What did you say that for?" I asked him when G. Gooseberry had gone.

"What else could I say?"

"Just tell her not to."

"No Sirree!" said Pop.

"Well, tell her you don't like it," I said. "What's the matter? Are you afraid of an old lady?"

"Yes," said Pop with simple dignity, "I am and so is your mother. It's her job to control the help, not mine." He took a bottle of Bell-Ans out of his pocket and tossed a handful into his mouth.

The next morning Pop began his usual chores of filling pitchers, dumping slop jars, and sluicing out thunder mugs. In the middle of this Mum decided to bathe the baby so she called, "Hot water, please, Beulah," and Pop said, "Yes, ma'am, right away," and went down to the kitchen. Granny Gooseberry was at the sink.

"Oh, it's you, Moses," she said. "Dump this swill."

Afterward we told Pop he should have protested.

"Did you dump the garbage?" asked Mum.

"Of course I did," he said.

"You shouldn't have," we said, "and you shouldn't let her call you Moses, either."

"Why Moses, I wonder?" said Mum.

"Because I'm a minister, I guess. Holy Caesarea Philippi, it's Beulah one minute, Moses the next," said Pop bitterly. "A man is just a figure of fun in the home."

From then on Granny Gooseberry addressed Pop as Moses and ordered him around all the time. We had steamed pudding again and again and finally Pop didn't even bother to serve it. He just heaved it straight into the woods after we had smeared some onto our plates.

All this was duly reported to Baba, who, in an unguarded moment, told me my mother didn't have a proper staff. One servant wasn't enough but even one should be handled properly.

"They have to know who is mistress," she said again.

Mum knew perfectly well who was mistress in our house: Granny Gooseberry.

This state of affairs continued until the end of the summer. Granny Gooseberry ruled the house with a rod of iron, called Pop Moses and had him dumping garbage, carrying water, and digging pits for rubbish from morning till night. In the last week on her day off she ordered him to drive her to Lincoln Park, where she took the trolley to New Bedford. At the end of the day he picked her up, and when they arrived home he flumped after her with his arms full of parcels. When G. Gooseberry had changed into her work clothes she summoned Mum to the kitchen. After a short interval Mum tottered out and sank into a chair.

"What happened?" we asked, alarmed.

"Do you know what she has out there?" said Mum. "*Presents* for all of us. She likes us. She's never had such a good time anywhere."

We were absolutely appalled. Pop lost his voice completely as he always did when deeply moved.

"Now don't start to cry," said Mum sternly. She's coming in here with them."

I don't remember any of the presents except my own, which was a length of blue serge for a new pair of bloomers. Pop acknowledged his gift in a warbling croak that caused Mum to give him a fierce, strengthening glance.

After the ceremony was over and Granny Gooseberry had retired there was a short reverent silence. Then Pop spoke.

"I told you she was just a lonely old soul," he quavered.

CHAPTER FOUR

The Time of the Singing of Birds

SUMMER WAS STILL NEW when my birthday occurred. Dave and I were the only ones lucky enough to have birthdays celebrated at the Point—one at each end of summer. Mine came at the time I loved best in all the year—the time of new-mown hay, of singing birds and hidden nests, the time when the woods smelled of wild grape blossoms and the leaves on the oaks were still thin and silky.

Whoever had a birthday in our house enjoyed twelve hours of absolute power and complete immunity from work. Not that we ever did much work, but on our birthdays if somebody asked us to feed the dogs or go down to the boathouse and get Pop's reading glasses, which he thought he might have left there, we said virtuously that it was our birthday and somebody else had to do it. The other members of the group, especially the Hideons, complained that we made them do all the work even when it wasn't one of our birthdays. The Hideons, being the smallest, were constantly exploited, but we claimed that they were so spoiled that it was our duty to train them. Our system of training was the one we used for dogs: we made them fetch and carry and even retrieve. What else were Hideons for? They had a terrible time on our birthdays, as the two senior siblings who weren't having a birthday passed all jobs on to a Hideon. Bobs always whined and said, "What do I have to for?" so many times that we composed a song or chant set to the tune of "Listen to the Mockingbird," as sung by Alma

Gluck on one of our records. We could reduce Bobs to a screaming wreck in no time flat.

Birthdays never seemed to change anything or make us grow any older—they were just days of festival like the Fourth of July until that momentous summer when I moved over the line into the teens. At thirteen you were still regarded as a child, which technically I really was, and except for dancing school life was wonderful and uncomplicated. However, thirteen was one step closer to the hideous fate of being a grownup lady who had to wear hairnets and *corsets* and do horrible boring things like sewing or knitting. Apparently there was a great gulf dividing twelve from thirteen and I was given to understand that no efforts would be spared in making this a day to remember.

At that time I slept on a cot that, instead of springs, had a kind of trampoline of knitted wire that twangled like a harp every time I moved. The mattress was thin and old, full of lumps and hollows, and smelled of mildew. The blankets smelled of mothballs at first and the sheets felt slightly damp, but all these things were part of summer and the Point and so extremely magic. We didn't want changes, even for the better. We wanted everything to stay the same, including ourselves, and we thought we were the same because we felt no different. We had, however, entered that brief but enchanted interlude between nursemaid rule and the sweet tyranny of love when you are really free, when for the first time solitude is a delight.

On the morning of my thirteenth birthday Rajah woke me as usual. I didn't mind; I liked to lie and listen to the stillness that Rajah's cries hardly disturbed. The long chord that was the voice of the city was missing. No brakes squealed on Oak Street, the trolley's far-off whine was gone, and so were the trains wailing down the valley and the clop of the milkman's horse. Now I could hear the hushed murmur of surf on all the beaches, the clamor of gulls from the river, fishing boats stitching their way down the channel to the sea, and a thousand birds warbling, chattering, and bubbling all over the hill.

My room was on the west side of the house, just where the

land dropped off sharply to the river, so it was always full of the rustle of leaves and bird song from the woods below.

After a while I hopped out of bed to see what kind of day I had drawn, as I was superstitious about the weather. I wanted it to be blue, my color—and this time it was, not a hard, dark blue but a tender blue, like larkspurs. Over the peaceful sea the sky was the color of Scotch harebells—my flower. Pleased that the omens were favorable, I went over and looked in the mirror at the thirteen-year-old person I had become. She looked the same—blue eyes, round pink baby face like Aldie's, and curtains of blond hair, which I loathed. Everybody else had bobbed hair but I couldn't because Baba had decreed that bobbed hair was "horrid." Then, too, Pop had the usual male obsession with long golden tresses. Mum wasn't brave enough to defy both of them, and Baba's opinion still carried a great deal of weight with her. Baba had seen to it that I wore my hair exactly as Mum had at my age, held back with a black velvet ribbon or a tortoiseshell thing called a fillet. I even wore Mum's best Liberty-silk dress for parties, a pale blue creation with a high ruffled neck and smocking at the wrists and across the bosom. When I was in this dress so many people said I looked like Alice in Wonderland that I could hardly bear it. I didn't want to be Alice in Wonderland; I wanted to be Robin Hood. The life of an outlaw seemed to me absolutely perfect.

Although I would have preferred to don a fair suit of Lincoln green I was now forced to don a fair outfit of blue cotton from Best & Co. This was a two-piece number with a sailor blouse on top and pleated bloomers below. I also had to put on long brown stockings because Baba had decreed that ladies couldn't wear socks—they showed one's bare legs—horrid. Viewing the results with distaste, I took my quarterstaff of holly wood and went out into the day. The hill was as wet as though it had risen from the sea. Drops of water flashed like prisms and the jeweled spider webs were unusually fine. I could see a spot of blue in every bead of curved crystal—myself at thirteen.

In the crevice of the granite steps my Scotch harebells were beginning to open—fragile sky-blue bells on wire stems that stirred in the faintest breeze. Here too the omens were favorable.

I checked in at Synton for a bite to eat as Aunt K. was bound to be up and had usually baked muffins or biscuits by this time. My birthday breakfast was always at home, with my favorite bacon-and-eggs menu and all the presents piled on my chair under a damask napkin. Still, it was a long way off and I had to make the rounds of the gardens. When you have a whole day of your own you want to visit all the special places the way queens used to make the rounds of the castles and manor houses in their domain.

I also wanted to find a peacock feather—one of the big round-eyed tail plumes—because in our clan we thought they brought good luck, not bad, as superstitious persons believed. Synton's gardens were the best hunting ground, for Rajah liked to poke around there looking for bugs.

The main garden covered about an acre and was like an English cottage garden—a mixture of flowers and vegetables all scrambled in together. The vegetables grew in neat little clearings of different sizes and shapes, but the rest was a lovely tangle, as undisciplined as a meadow, a sea of grasses and flowers from which rose a drowsy humming and the scent of honey. To an outsider it must have appeared a pathless jungle but I knew every inch of it. From the time I was peony high and could bury my face up to the ears in their great shell-pink blossoms I had played there, catching bees in foxgloves, making hoop-skirted dolls out of hollyhocks, collecting the pepper-box seed pods of poppies or simply standing and watching the busy insect life among the flowers.

The garden was also the laboratory in which Baba instructed me in the feminine arts of horticulture and flower arrangement. She had made up her mind that I, as the first grandchild and a girl, was to be a lady botanist like herself. Baba took her job of grand-mothering very seriously and had decided early in our lives what each of us would be. Aldie was to be a painter, so he was given one room in Synton's playhouse for a studio and an enormous book full of Meissonier engravings. In no time at all he had executed a relief of Savonarola's head in Ivory soap and copied in oils a gigantic painting of a fisher girl named "Graziella." Dave was to be an agricultural missionary to India, like a man called Sam Higginbottom, and he was encouraged to help with the chores and learn firsthand the facts of animal husbandry, except, of course, those of reproduction.

Baba was compiling a list of the wildflowers of the Westport area and kept her records in loose-leaf notebooks. I was provided with a notebook just like hers, and Mum helped me to paste a picture of a flower at the top of each page and write underneath its location and date of discovery.

I had no objection to being a botanist, as like all proper children I loved picking flowers; hunting for wildflowers in secret places was to me a real adventure and a field full of daisies, wealth. My year was measured out in flowers, and the arrival of real spring was the day I buried my nose in the warm yellow fur of a bunch of dandelions. That polleny smell, the golden dust on my nose went with the lilting song of the first robins so poignantly sweet after winter's brittle silence. Flowers seemed to me marvelously beautiful and valuable, and Synton's garden on a summer day made me feel almost dizzy. I stood and looked at it, my beloved kingdom, with its drifts of confetti-colored blossoms, its ballet of butterflies. Then I took a deep breath of its perfume and waded in. I went down the path, treading on lemon thyme and brushing the sweetness out of the lavender with one eye out for peacock feathers and the other for hummingbirds, whose nests I coveted above all others.

Among the heavy-headed old roses and the clumps of clove pinks and candytuft were the hummingbird flowers—scarlet salvia, buddleia and larkspur, salpiglossis and thick, sweet nicotiana— all trumpet-shaped and full of nectar. There were always hummingbirds there, probing the horns of salvia, throbbing on blurred wings up and down the delphinium spikes and around the cascades of honeysuckle that festooned the trees. They would appear out of nothing with a throb and a squeak—tiny, sequined creatures, whose supple bodies were scaled like tropical fish. Rajah's feathers had the same metallic sheen, and he and the hummingbirds seemed like exiles from an Arabian Nights tale.

Now as I stopped to gather a handful of Shirley poppy petals—coral colored and crinkled like silk—I saw one of Rajah's feathers—a gold fan, frilled with green—dropped on a carpet of thyme and as out of place as a Christmas-tree ornament. Near it was a neck feather, no bigger than a sapphire lost from a ring, caught in a bush of heather. Finally I saw my plume lying across a row of lettuces, and I carried it with me like a scepter, as I went down past the hollyhock and foxglove steeples to the lower garden. This secret enclosure with its clipped box and fringed white pinks was bound and fettered with honeysuckle, the rustic gate long since tied shut and the rotted fence toppling under its burden. Climbing roses had run up the trees and spilled their blossoms out of the tops of the junipers. The rugosa rose hedge was an impenetrable thicket and the trapped air inside the garden was almost suffocating, it was so heavily perfumed.

I went in under the Japanese torii at the garden's entrance and walked between the box hedges, under the Silver Moon rose and the pale pink Dr. van Fleet back past the old gate and up again to the big garden. Rajah was in among the lettuces, trailing his jeweled tail down the rows, his brilliant blue neck curving here and there, his bill stabbing at tidbits. When I saw him I stopped, and in the hot, sweet stillness he raised his crested head and gave me a brief contemptuous glance. Then he continued on his way. Presently the figure of Aunt K. carrying the garbage pail appeared on the path and Rajah, like Sir Galahad sighting the Holy Grail, uttered a loud squawk and took off. Tink came along in a minute and, giving me a bear hug, said, "Happy birthday." Baba, he said, had a surprise for me. I went inside and there she was with her hands full of sweet peas.

"Happy birthday, dear Jan," she said. "Come. I have something for you."

It was a small mahogany box with a little brass hook to close it, and inside was a microscope.

"It's not new," said Baba, "but it will help you in your botany. Look."

She adjusted various little wheels and focused down on a

glass slide that she had evidently prepared. When I squinted into the tube I was amazed to see what looked like oval amethyst beads covered with sugar or some other crystalline substance.

"The anthers of timothy grass," said Baba. "The white crumbs are grains of pollen."

I was thunderstruck and saw a whole new world opening up ahead of me. Baba and I examined part of a sweet pea petal, some salt crystals, and the wing of a small silver moth. Then I had to go down the hill for the family ceremonies.

At breakfast on my birthday Mum always reviewed the historic hours of my arrival on earth. I had taken three days to come and Pop barely survived the experience and was prostrated for some time afterward. Mum said that he had spent most of the time scorching to and from the doctor's on his bicycle. He was not a man who could wait. If things didn't happen on time he forced them to. However, I didn't cooperate and he suffered agonies.

When I came down from Synton and everyone was gathered around the table Mum began.

"Well, thirteen years ago tonight I wasn't feeling very comfortable. It was ninety degrees in the shade and my room was like a Turkish bath."

"Poor little girl," croaked Pop with a watery smile. "You gave her a hard time, Jannie."

"You were the one that gave me a hard time," said Mum. "You should have seen him. Never slept a wink. The doctor nearly went out of his mind."

"Probably I didn't have such a great time either," I said.

I had, at Targ's birth, been filled in on where babies were kept and how they got out (although not how they got in) and the whole business seemed to me highly improbable. Still, of the three of us—or four, if you count the doctor—I couldn't help but feel I had had the worst deal. I mean to say, *upside down* in there, no way to breathe, for *three days*. However, the saga had its own pattern, and we passed on to the room downstairs where Pop paced the floor, a shattered remnant of his former self. Then the door opened and the doctor stood there.

"It's a girl," he said.

"I ran upstairs," croaked Pop, "and there was your little mother" (Mum was always little in this story; actually she was twenty-three) "sitting up in bed with the biggest smile on her face you ever saw. And there was this little head."

Here he lost his voice completely.

Mum then took over and said Pop was so excited to have a baby of his own that he could hardly wait to get back from his parish calls to play with me.

"He'd run upstairs two at a time and pick you up. Then he'd sit with you in the crook of his knee and twirl his gold watch on its chain. He made his barnyard noises, too. You loved it."

We had heard Pop's barnyard repertoire all our lives. It included a cow mooing for its calf, the calf blatting, sheep, chickens, roosters crowing, a wonderful grunting pig, and a cat-and-dog fight that was a perfect masterpiece.

"Do the cat fight," I said as Queen for the Day, so he did. It sounded as though the whole room were full of snarling dogs and yowling cats.

"Now do the bottle," I said, and he pulled a cork by popping his cheek out with his finger, then poured out the water, making glugging sounds with his tongue.

"Now make the Eeyorkups face," I ordered.

Pop's "Eeyorkups face" was an amazing tour-de-force in which he stuck out the midpoint of his lower lip in a short cup, like an egg spoon, then he said in a kind of donkeyish bray,

"Eee   Eee   Eee   kups."
yore   yore   yore

It was a special treat and he refused to do it most of the time, as he said he didn't want us to become faded roués, glutted with pleasure. Also, he had to be in just the right mood.

"Well, now," he said, "I'm not sure I feel like the Eeyorkups face. It's a very difficult thing to do."

"Oh, come on," I said. "It's my birthday."

"Well, all right," he said, and went into his act.

We all shrieked with laughter and demanded an encore. "Certainly not," he said. "Once is enough. I don't want you getting blasé."

"Open your presents," said Mum, who could never wait long to observe the effects of her surprises on us. She had been hinting about them for days.

We loved surprises in our family, and during the period of preparation we built up tension about the surprise in various ways. As the moment of truth drew near we worked the victim into a frenzy of anticipation, and when the surprise finally broke we expected a violent reaction. It wouldn't be too much to say that we would have been gratified if the person had fallen to the ground insensible or had had some sort of mild seizure from surprise. Of course, Baba wouldn't have approved of such displays of emotion but we were of coarser fiber.

I removed my napkin from the pile on my chair and began the ceremonies, while everybody stood around to watch my reactions and tell me all the circumstances leading up to the purchase of the present.

"Mine cost fifty cents," said Bobs proudly.

Pop never had the faintest idea what was in the packages Mum had bought and given in their names, but he always said he had spent much time and thought selecting them.

"I hope you realize the trouble I went to to get just that color," he said.

"Oh, I do," I said. "How did you ever guess? It's just what I wanted."

After breakfast Pop and I went out to look at the day and decide what kind of expedition would be suitable with the wind and tide provided by God. Pop, who never let a milestone go by without a bit of homely philosophy, now said I had reached a new stage in my life. Pretty soon, he said, I would be a woman and he knew I would be a joy in the home. Here he broke down momentarily, but got a fresh grip on himself and went on.

"I know you want what every nice girl wants."

"What's that?" I asked, while he struggled for control.

"A happy home like ours, a good chap for a husband—better than your old man," he put in humbly.

"I do not," I said. "You're the best father in the world."

"Far from it," said Pop, "as your mother will tell you. However, now that you're growing older you'll realize that you have a pretty face and the fellows will be around. You may think they want a fast, hard girl, but, no, they want a friend, a sister."

He then croaked out the first line of a ghastly song called "I want a girl just like the girl that married dear old Dad."

"For Pete's sake, Pop," I said.

"Well, it's true," he quavered.

I saw it was time to put a stop to this revolting drivel.

"Now that I'm grown up," I said, "how about letting me cut my hair like everybody else? It's bad enough," I said bitterly, "that Baba makes me wear long stockings when everybody in my class wears socks."

"What's all this about hair and socks?" asked Pop, abruptly abandoning his dear-old-Dad role.

"Well, how would you like to have everybody say you looked like Alice in Wonderland?" I asked.

"The chances of that are very slight," said Pop, running his hand over his bald spot.

However, he was now bored with the whole subject and said it looked like a good breeze and what about a sailing picnic? I said that would be perfect and could we have chops?

"Not only could we have chops," said Pop, now completely restored to his normal merry self. "You see before you a tinted photograph of the man who will cook them for you."

CHAPTER FIVE

Messing About in Boats

A SAILING PICNIC was an experience that separated the men from the boys. It took a whole day and was rife with incident. The boat was so loaded with baskets, babies, grills, and bathing suits that coming about was like a stampede in a junk shop. The wind usually shifted at noon and the tide turned during the picnic so that there was always the chance of drifting out to sea backward, being stuck on a lee shore, going aground, or simply being becalmed. Then Pop would have to row with the boom banging against his temples and horseflies biting him, or guests would be forced overboard to push. Nothing out of the ordinary, but not everybody found it pleasurable. Some carping characters objected openly to the mud, but they were seldom invited again.

By the time my birthday rolled around the boats were painted, rigged, and in the water. As soon as Pop had recovered from the ordeal of getting settled he cleared the path to the river, scything the grass and cutting back the loops of honeysuckle and wild grape. After this there was usually a short delay while he recovered from a case of poison ivy. Pop was the worst patient known to man, and when he had poison ivy he talked of nothing else and behaved as though he were down with smallpox. However, he eventually got bored with the act and summoned his cohorts for action.

Painting boats in those days was a very relaxed affair, almost a recreation. We only sanded enough to remove the grosser incrustations from the previous summer. We painted over blisters, dead spiders, and bits of seaweed, and when some bug got stuck in the paint we just smeared it off with our gloves. There were no purists among us to suggest removing some of the layers of old paint, no one to insist that we sand between coats, and anyway we put on only one coat. There was no frenetic business about straight water lines. Pop did them free hand. Once the boats were dry all the adult males on the hill set to with ropes, blocks, and rollers, and launched them. They all sank at once and had to be bailed out, sank again during the night, and eventually settled down to their normal leakage, about four inches a day. The dock was put out and from it the men stepped the masts and rigged them. Nobody minded the gray, frizzy halyards, nobody ever thought of sanding and varnishing the spars, which had turned black over the years, and nobody dreamed of anything as effete as drying sails, which were dark gray with mildew and hung on the masts like sacks. If a sail rotted out or someone put a boathook through it, Mum took down her sewing basket and patched it with a piece of old sheet.

At this time the family fleet consisted of two elderly sail-boats and two rowboats of immense age and weight. They were painted pea green like the boat in *The Owl and the Pussy-Cat* and named after things or places abroad, as was the custom in the clan. All of them were sharpies—flat-bottomed skiffs designed for maneuvering in shallow water, something we had a lot of. The Westport River is an estuary—where an arm of the sea meets a fresh-water stream—and by then about three-quarters of it was salt marsh and mud flats. The whole center of the West Branch, where we operated, was filled with marsh islands that acted as a barrier between our bay and deep water. Behind the grass flats—as we called the marshes—the river had silted up until only one channel remained for deep-draft fishing boats. As a final touch there was eelgrass—we were born at a peak period and the river had a bumper crop—paradise if you were an eel or a black duck, not so good if you were a human being trying to get around in a boat. At low tide all the mud flats, sand bars, and mussel beds were exposed and the remaining space was filled with eelgrass, which lay over on the surface of the water in a thick, golden-brown mattress. In fact, the bald truth was that at dead low tide in the river you could hardly see any water at all, and our bay was indistinguishable from a wheatfield.

Our boats, at the time of this chronicle, were actually stored in our boathouse—a relatively new building. In the early years "the boathouse" meant Synton's boathouse—a narrow, cocoa-brown structure almost entirely filled by an East Indian catamaran, a gigantic and very primitive craft that my grandfather had bought in Ceylon. On one of his lecture tours to India, some potentate—the Gaekwar of Baroda, the Nizam of Hyderabad, or more likely the British Resident in Ceylon—had taken him to a beach, where he observed natives putting out to sea in catamarans. He was much struck by the picturesque character of these vessels and decided he must have one to sail in the Westport River. A catamaran was therefore shipped to the Point, where it became a permanent fixture in Synton's boathouse and was used as a clotheshorse by the ladies when they undressed for swimming. We were accustomed to see it draped in skirts, blouses, corsets, and bloomers, and we often played in it while the grownups were trying to dress inside their petticoats—a process that took time.

Technically the catamaran was a Singhalese outrigger canoe. Its hull had been hollowed out of a single gargantuan log, and there was an outrigger made of another log nearly as large. The topsides were fastened to the hull with coconut fiber. There were also a bamboo mast, a lateen sail of enormous size, and various unidentifiable pieces of equipment that we kept falling over in the dark.

Mum said that when it had first arrived they had launched the catamaran, sailed at terrific speed across the bay onto a flat, climbed out, hauled it around, and sailed like a bat out of hell back onto the shore, everybody aboard hysterical with laughter. This was a fairly accurate description of any family sailing expedition in our era, but we could never quite figure out how they or the natives had managed to fit into the catamaran, as the width at the top was a mere six inches—too narrow even for our small behinds. Maybe natives had behinds only six inches wide? At Synton we had seen glass slides of them taking their catamarans out through the surf, and pretty picturesque it all was. The natives were up to their armpits in water, pushing, but that's what we did out sailing, and we thought that's how people sailed—partly on foot. Still, even we stayed in the boat some of the time.

Pop finally straightened us out. He said that the crew of a catamaran have to stand with one foot in front of the other, the width being too narrow to allow them to stand with legs together. The helmsman, though, stands on one leg with the other over the side to control the huge paddle that serves as a rudder. You can readily see what an ideal boat this was for a tidal river full of eelgrass and mudflats.

At some point the catamaran was dismantled for good and Synton's boathouse was converted into a summer cottage for Mum's older brother, Basil—standard procedure in family summer places.

Pop, who still clung to the belief that boats should be stored in boathouses, had built one for us down the shore at the head of a small cove. By some fluke he managed to locate it on land we owned, even avoiding Riverside Drive. Outside, the new boathouse looked much like the original, as it was painted the traditional cocoa brown, but inside it was a great improvement. Of course, all a boathouse needed to be a success was not to have an Indian catamaran in it, but ours had all sorts of extra luxuries. For one thing, it had a row of bathhouses at the back, a revolutionary move. Being an upright, innocent man, Pop had not bothered to put ceilings over them, and one had a peephole where we had pushed out a knot. I'm sorry to say we used to climb up and look over the walls at people undressing and used the knothole to continue our research into human anatomy, a difficult thing in those days.

Our branch of the clan had two boats: a rowboat called *Mandarin* and a sailboat called *Dehra Doon*.

Mandarin, named presumably for a Chinese mandarin, was

reputed to be of solid mahogany, and this was easy to believe as she wasn't much heavier to row than a grand piano.

Dehra Doon had, in a previous incarnation, been the town ferry that for untold decades had carried people from the town landing across to the sand dunes and the beach. When the bridge was built she was retired and my grandfather snapped her up as she was perfectly suited to the kind of sailing practiced by the clan. This was to transport as many people as possible to some favorite spot for a picnic or a project like beach plumming. The ferry boat had been painted yellow and called *Gold Bug* when they bought her, but this was corrected and she was painted pea green and named *Dehra Doon* after some town in India.

Pop had once tried to break with tradition and bought a catboat which he painted white, but although he wasn't actually struck by a thunderbolt the boat seemed to be jinxed and spent most of its time under water. This was normal when our boats were first launched but they recovered in a few days. This one—whose name was *Hawick* after a town in Scotland—sank every night, so finally Pop got rid of her. I was very small at the time, but I remember sailing in *Hawick* wearing a yellow sunbonnet with my feet in a washtub full of water, which they took along to keep me quiet. Coming about with a washtub sloshing around amidships was not easy but no ex-member of the catamaran's crew expected sailing to be easy.

The only boat on the hill that embodied the poetry and beauty of sail was Pop's model of the whaler *Charles W. Morgan*. She was a miracle of precise workmanship, exquisitely scaled to the last marlin spike and the final thread of rigging. Pop had sanded her down until her topsides were smooth as glass, painted her with a camel's hair brush, resanded, repainted. In Pop's eyes the platonic ideal of a sailboat was a square-rigger, and when he spoke of the *Flying Cloud,* the most beautiful of the Yankee Clippers, he would croak with emotion. It was difficult for him to get all steamed up about the shipshape appearance of *Dehra Doon,* whose pitted and blistered pea-green sides were dyed a curious purplish bronze from contact with rotting eelgrass and red sea muck. *Dehra* always had a fringe of green seaweed around her waterline and often goose barnacles had made their home there. After reading about the great tea clippers racing back from China under a cloud of canvas, Pop clearly felt that an expedition in *Debra* was just transportation. She was a ferry boat and that's how we used her. When we went for a sail in those days every seat was filled and the boat so grossly overloaded that we made very little headway. There were babies and dogs and assorted relatives and guests. They used to sit around the cockpit chattering and gossiping like people at a teaparty.

Coming about with such a gaggle aboard was a frightful shambles. Pop would yell, "Ready about," and all the ladies would begin gathering up skirts, babies, and toys, and then at "Hard-a-lee" all hell broke loose. Ladies screamed, clutched each other, fell into the bilge, and laughed hysterically. Somebody always got a stunning blow from the boom or became entangled in the sheet. Any child trying to get across the cockpit was half trampled to death.

We went aground all the time, and people kept climbing over the side to push and climbing in again covered with mud and eel-grass.

We sailed to Adamsville to buy the famous Adamsville cheese and pick blackberries; we sailed to the beach to gather shells and pick beach plums; we sailed to a special island for marsh rosemary; and we sailed to the mail. On a certain kind of day, called a "blue day," we went on a sailing picnic.

Blue days were those crystal-clear ones when every leaf seemed edged with light and the horizon was cut with a knife— the kind New Englanders call weather breeders.

A blue day was, in our family, a day to be lived to the utmost. Mum and Pop believed in "using a day" and it wasn't properly used unless you dropped everything and did something special. You had to be outdoors and in or on the water the whole time. You had to *eat* outdoors. Obviously a sailing picnic was the solution.

The sailing picnic in honor of my thirteenth birthday has disappeared from my mind, probably because it was without incident. It's even possible we never had to get out and push, although that seems unlikely. Still, it may have been a day when the tide was high all morning—something that rarely coincided with the family urge to go on a sailing picnic.

We have talked a lot about low tide but high tide comes just as often, and then all the mud flats, eelgrass, and sometimes even grass flats are covered up—gone, vanished—and the river looks like a great inland lake brimming its banks and stretching full and sparkling into the heat haze up by Adamsville. Romantic little islands blue as gas flames float on its surface; sails like white petals blow across it. Compared to our river at high tide the Riviera looks like a dump (actually, it is a dump). It was on such a morning that Mum asked Aunt Danny and the Wheelers to go on a sailing picnic.

Aunt Danny was Baba's elegant younger sister, and the Wheelers were the two ladies with whom she lived. The Wheelers —Miss Hattie and Miss Emma—were sisters and as different as night and day. Miss Hattie had a rather racy sense of humor and according to family legend smoked cigars like a man. Miss Emma was very proper and carried a parasol, just like somebody in a Jane Austen novel. Aunt Danny had been a beauty as a girl and was still extremely attractive in a regal way. She had great charm and wit and was one of my favorite relations. The ménage was a happy one, and the three ladies had evolved a system that enabled them to converse on two levels at the same time. On one level they carried on a conversation with the public but all during it they communicated with each other in low but perfectly audible asides, known in the family as "sub rosas." These asides were couched in a kind of verbal shorthand which the ladies apparently thought was incomprehensible to others as well as inaudible.

We adored Aunt Danny but it was impossible to imagine her or the Wheelers on a boat, unless it was a yacht or an ocean liner.

"It's such a lovely day I asked them for a sailing picnic to the Harbor Rocks," said Mum defiantly.

"You didn't!" we cried.

"Holy Caesarea Philippi!" said Pop. "Look at the river! There's no wind and the tide will be going out all afternoon."

"Well, they're coming," said Mum, and "I've bought chops.

There's some wind. I just saw a leaf move. You go bring the boat in to the dock and I'll go pick them up in the car."

This was disaster, all right. A plain sailing picnic was bad enough, but a Harbor Rocks picnic could be an ordeal that made strong men wake up screaming in the night.

The Harbor Rocks are across from Horseneck Beach on the opposite side of the harbor entrance, a narrow gut through which the tide boils in a seething maelstrom of eddies and whirlpools. To sail across this rip on an outgoing tide in *Dehra* was almost impossible when she was loaded for a picnic, and sometimes people didn't arrive at the Harbor Rocks until mid-afternoon. Sometimes they never got there at all and just went home starving.

However, the chances of our getting as far as the harbor entrance were slight because we first had to sail through the barrier of grass flats that stood between us and the harbor.

"We'll have the tide against us on the way out, and by the time the dad-gasted picnic's over it will have turned and we'll have to fight it all the way back," said Pop, "that is, if we don't get swept out to sea first." Mum, however, was on her way.

"You know, don't you," Pop said to us, "that we can't expect Aunt Danny and the Wheelers to get out if we go aground? Have you ever thought what they must weigh as a group?"

"Don't blame us," I said.

"Not a breath of wind," said Pop later, loading the picnic baskets into *Mandarin.*

"You'll have to row all the way," Aldie said and Pop gave a mirthless laugh.

"Your Mother must be out of her mind," he said as we rowed out to *Dehra Doon.* "Dad-gasted boat leaks like a sieve. Look at it now." The water in her was ankle deep.

We bailed for a while and then Pop hauled up the sail and cast off.

"There they are," I said.

"Gosh almighty," said Pop, looking.

The three ladies on the dock were dressed apparently for a garden party at Buckingham Palace. They wore their tall Queen

Mary hats, which they called "jots," and were swathed in yards of veiling. They also wore gloves and hard black shoes with gun-metal stockings just visible below their trailing skirts. Standing above us they looked perfectly enormous, like three clipper ships under full sail. Actually the Wheelers, especially Miss Emma, were quite small, but with all those streaming veils and skirts they filled a lot of space. Beside them we all looked like peasants and *Debra Doon* appeared even more degraded than usual. She was already awash again with bilge, and the patched mildewed sail was like something salvaged from the dump. It hung limp. Pop had been absolutely right: there was no wind.

Aunt Danny extended her hand and Pop helped her onto the bow, where for a moment they tottered in a wild embrace, and the boat reeled under their combined weights. I could hardly look, but at last Aunt Danny was eased into the stern. Miss Hattie and Miss Emma followed somehow, and as Mum grappled with Pop on the cuddy he said he hoped the blasted dog was locked up.

One thing you could always count on during a sailing picnic was a dog crisis. Even the most iron-nerved member of the family could not contemplate the presence of dogs in a boat full of babies, meat, and picnic baskets. Consequently, the dog would be shut up at home with whatever maid or cook was then in residence. Every single time—just as we got off the mooring and were half-way to the grass flats—someone would spot the arrow-shaped ripple with a dog's head at the apex, and after that it was every man for himself.

Mum said of course Kelt was locked up and she had told the cook not to let him out.

"She will," said Pop, hopelessly.

He then pushed us off and struggled through the gear to the middle thwart, where he settled down with the oars. The boom slatted back and forth against his head, but he bent manfully to his task and we lurched off toward the grass flats.

It was by now what we call a "white day," the blue burned out of the sky and the water colorless as a sheet of glass. Down below, the eelgrass streamed toward us with the incoming tide.

The sub rosas had already begun in the stern, where the ladies and their skirts filled the entire cockpit.

While Pop labored at the oars they kept up a running fire of asides.

"Dear Robert," Aunt Danny said in her public voice, "what a bore for you to have such a load." (Sub rosa to Miss Hattie: "Handsome, David's nose.")

"Well, dear Jan," she said, turning to me, "did you enjoy your school this year?" (Sub rosa to Miss Emma: "Robert's eyes. Head on shoulders.")

"Head on shoulders" was a favorite aside and meant, in Aunt Danny language, the way one's head was set on one's shoulders. When you listened to Aunt Danny and the Wheelers you felt as though all your features belonged to somebody else, as most of the sub rosas were about family resemblances. Health came next and you were apt to hear, "Looks like death," or "Too pale; anemic." "Boyd eyes" was another favorite sub rosa. Aunt Danny was Miss Boyd and Boyd eyes were a good thing to have. Dave had them.

They were just getting to Dave's eyes when Mum uttered a cry of horror.

"There's Kelt," she wailed.

"Oh, shoot!" said Pop. "Well, we're not turning back."

He pulled on the oars and all of us watched Kelt strike out from shore and head for us. There was a brief period while Pop tried to outrow him. Then Aunt Danny said he was going under and might drown.

"Oh, shoot!" said Pop again but he rested on his oars and waited. Kelt, breathing stertorously, approached the boat and we hauled him over the side. Everybody fell back to avoid the drenching shower as he shook himself. When we were all soaked he mounted the rail and with an expression of heartrending anxiety began whining to go ashore. When wet he smelled powerfully and also drooled copiously.

It was broiling hot out in the grass flats, and pretty soon the midges began biting as they always did when the wind dropped. In the boat channel on the far side the tide was running, as Pop said, like a millrace, and his rowing merely kept us in one place. Then he got tired and we started to go backward up the river. It was, by now, way past noon and everybody was starved.

"Maybe we'd better eat in the boat," said Pop at last.

"You can't cook chops in the boat," said Mum. "The flag at the harbor almost moved a minute ago."

It was after two when we reached the Harbor Rocks, but the picnic was, Pop said, a howling success. The ladies sat about upon the rocks in their long dresses and all in all it was just like a picture of a Victorian picnic by the late Winslow Homer. From the rocks we overlooked the harbor entrance, where the tide had turned and the red buoy was pointing out to sea. Across the narrow gut Horseneck Beach stretched in a long curve of pale gold, and beyond the sand hills was the village and our hill with Baba's twin spruces on top. To the south was the sea, blue and scintillating to the horizon. The waves broke on the cliffs below us and withdrew with a long clattering of pebbles. There was a fresh breeze coming up.

"See," said Mum, "I told you we'd get a nice breeze to come home on."

Pop said it was from the northeast, which meant we had to beat against it every inch of the way. He was lying on his back on the warm rock with his hat over his eyes resting up for the return trip.

"We'd better get started," he said. "The tide's running out fast."

"Oh, not yet," we said, as we wanted to go out on the Point of Rocks to watch the fishermen.

Pop summoned us at last with his two-finger whistle and we joined the procession back to *Debra* which was high and dry on the beach. The tide was running out a mile a minute and the red buoy was under water. Pop took off his shoes and socks and told us to do the same and we finally got *Debra* into the water and headed out. We held her while Pop put up the sail, which snapped in the wind with a noise like pistol shots.

"Blowing up a gale," he shouted above the racket. The water had turned dark green and was covered with whitecaps.

Somehow Pop got the ladies aboard and the gear stowed up in the bow. Kelt leaped in, covered with wet sand, and then Pop climbed in and arranged himself at the helm. At the last minute we crawled over the side and fell into the bilge as *Debra* heeled over and roared out into the channel, shipping a good deal of water in the process. Aunt Danny and the Wheelers clung together in terror, all sub rosas forgotten, and we bailed for dear life, using tin cups as well as the bailer. When we hit the tide rip *Debra* staggered at the impact and a wave broke over the side into Miss Hattie's lap. She gave a kind of yelp and Pop apologized, but he didn't have much leisure to be polite as we were on a collision course with a red buoy.

"I've got to come about," he called. "Be all set to move! Ready about!"

The ladies leaned forward.

"Hard-a-lee!" shouted Pop and vanished behind a moving wall of skirts. Miss Hattie seemed to be lying in his lap.

"Hey!" we heard him screaming. "I can't move the tiller!" and then a lot of water came over the side and we went up into the wind with a hideous rattling of blocks and thunder of canvas. The boom met Pop's head with a smart crack like a baseball bat hitting a home run.

"Balance the boat!" he bellowed and Kelt launched himself into space, disappearing completely beneath the waves. Mum began to shake with laughter.

This sort of thing was par for the course on sailing picnics and ordinarily no one gave it a second thought. It was only the presence of Aunt Danny and the Wheelers in their gloves, "jots," and veils that gave this operation a certain classic splendor. It was almost a work of art. Somehow it was fitting that we went aground shortly after the incident I have just described. Gulls were walking dry-shod on the flats when we reached the other side of the channel, so Pop took the sail down and we helped him pull *Debra* across the mud.

"We have a perfectly good home," he said, "a cook, and a nice dining room, and what do we do? Row for miles, being devoured by insects, eat on a dad-gasted rock, nearly capsize in a gale and pull a boat full of women over mud flats in our bare feet in order to get back where we came from. What for? Why?" He broke off and pointed to the shore, where Kelt was shaking himself after swimming in, but this spectacle seemed to be the last straw and he doubled up, giving his celebrated wheeze laugh, the signal for the whole group to become hysterical. Pop's wheeze was the opposite of his croak as he was equally vulnerable to the sentimental and the ridiculous. The family curse—a tendency toward uncontrolled laughing fits—shared by Mum and inherited by all of us, has given us a lot of trouble but has also saved us from losing our minds in situations like the above.

The Aunt Danny affair was typical of the pea-green era of sailing on the hill. The pattern continued to be the same: collect every human being within reach, put them in a boat, and let the chips fall where they might. If guests didn't enjoy it it was their fault. It was *fun*. Then suddenly mutiny reared its ugly head right in the heart of the home. First Aldie, who as an artist had a very low threshold of tolerance for family gaggles, announced that he was not going on any more of these mass movements by water. This occurred after Mum had invited an old lady in white kid gloves to sail to Adamsville for cheese. The old lady, who clearly hated and feared boats in any form, refused to let go of the lee rail when a black gust hit us, and we *sank*.

"That was a great sail we had," Aldie said to Pop. "You fill the boat up with all these old bags and now look—we go to the bottom. What are you trying to do, drown us all?"

"Eye Guy, boy," said Pop, "we were only in one foot of water."

"Well, what of it? We could have been in the deep channel. If you want to take along everybody for miles around I'm not going sailing," said Aldie and from then on he didn't. His defection gave me courage to do the same thing.

For some time I had had a vague feeling that sailing must be something more than what we did. In books, sailing was compared to flight, boats to birds with white wings skimming lightly over the waves. *Dehra's* wallowing progress had no relation to flight and her appearance was far from birdlike. In fact, from a distance she looked almost exactly like one of those rafts that survivors from a shipwreck whip up out of a door and an old bedspread. Between the bow and the stern was a solid wall of human bodies and only about an inch of freeboard was visible. In order to avoid the scrum in the cockpit I used to sit on the bow in front of the mast and pretend I was riding a horse. I used to rig stirrups and reins out of the painter and take my steed over the waves as though they were jumps in a steeple chase. The day had come, though, when I felt I had grown beyond playing horse on a boat.

Dave, however, was not going to give up that easily. He wanted to sail, and as we only had one sailboat he had to reform the family, force them to comply with proper nautical rules. He was learning to sail—or trying to—and complained bitterly about the overcrowded conditions under which he had to operate. With so many people in the cockpit he couldn't come about properly but had to hang up in the wind while guests, elderly relatives, and small children stumbled over to the windward side. He criticized the appearance of the sail, the lines, the spars, the paint work and the quality of Pop's seamanship.

"What you do isn't even sailing," he said. "Half the time we're out pushing. The rest of the time we have to row."

"Just a moment," said Pop. "Did I hear you say 'we'? Who is the poor old geezer who always ends up at the oars on these occasions? You see before you an oil painting of that man. R. W. in person."

"It's your own fault," said Dave. "You take along so many people that *Dehra's* practically resting on the bottom. You can't sail a boat that way."

"That's your mother," said Pop.

Mum indignantly denied the charge and the point of the discussion was hopelessly lost, but when the gang next assembled for a family trek even Dave stayed behind and went crabbing with me in *Mandarin*.

For a while Pop tried on the role of a pathetic old gaffer, rejected by his children, too broken down to operate a boat alone, but it didn't work. He then built up Mum into the role of abandoned mother, mourning for her little ones who had left the nest. Once he quoted something by, I think, Abraham Lincoln. " 'All that I am or hope to be,' " he croaked, " 'I owe to my angel mother.' "

"Oh, Pop," I said, "cut it out," and he finally did. Shortly thereafter he ordered the shipyard to build a new sailboat for *us*. She was a small, *light* sharpie with a leg-of-mutton sail—an equilateral triangle and the safest rig for beginners. The boat was, naturally, painted pea green and called *Hawick* after old *Hawick* and the town near old Synton, the ancestral mansion in Scotland. He then designed and built with the boys' help a very small flat-bottom skiff to serve as our dinghy. This creation of his was an improvement on *Mandarin* insofar as it was light and easy to row. The only trouble was that if you stepped on the bow she dived straight to the bottom, and if somebody looked over the side she was apt to capsize. We didn't mind these little idiosyncrasies as they kept the grownups and Hideons out of her and she became our private rowboat. We named her the *Splinter*.

The addition of *Hawick* and the *Splinter* to the fleet marked a new phase in the maritime history of the clan. The old order was about to change. Dave persuaded the family to buy him an authentic naval officer's cap at the army and navy store in New Bedford and when we next painted boats he said we ought to put on two coats and sand between them.

"We ought to take some of that old paint off with a blow torch," he said, looking critically at *Mandarin* and *Dehra*.

"A what?" I asked.

"A blow torch," he said.

Still, even Dave never considered painting *Hawick* or the *Splinter* any color but pea green. We may have been mutineers but we weren't as yet revolutionaries. It was enough that we were able to sail alone in our own boat. It was miraculous how fast a boat could move with only two people in it and how easy it was to maneuver even in the snakelike creeks of the salt marshes. We were given complete freedom to explore not only our West River but the virtually unknown East River. We cooked bacon and eggs on strange shores, swam in new deep holes and, like the early navigators, named the capes and islands of our new world. The only thing we were not allowed to do was go out to sea. Pop made us promise on our honor not to, a low trick we thought, but we promised.

CHAPTER SIX

Through the Eelgrass Jungle

FAMILY SAILING PICNICS were only one form of tribal excursion to which innocent guests were invited. The ultimate in guest torture was a double-header—an expedition by rowboat to the middle of the river to swim and dig clams. This was a low-tide project, sanctified by time, and a special treat in our eyes, as ordinarily we just swam off the dock. Guests were considered pretty lucky to be present.

Going out to the middle of the river to swim was a tradition so old that we accepted it without question as the last word in swimming. Out in the grass flats—that maze of marsh islands— was a winding creek called the Bathing Channel, and in its course was the Deep Hole, a kind of glorified bathtub, where the water was over our heads and a wonderful blue-green color. We could run and jump from a mud flat right out into the deepest part. The tide was very swift there and swept us downstream like corks, wrapping us in strong silky currents, green and thick as mint jelly. It combed the eelgrass straight or swirled it like the hair of drowned girls, and we used to dive and swim down the dim blue corridors between the clumps.

All you had to do to get to this paradise was to row through the eelgrass jungle for half a mile until you got stuck. It was then a simple matter to climb overboard and push the boat a short distance—a mere fifty yards—through more eelgrass, walk across the mud flats, wade a shallow channel and you were there. It only took about half an hour if you didn't try to stay in the boat, but we didn't have a chance to enjoy it very often as it had to be dead low tide and Pop had to be in the mood to row us out there. Rowing through eelgrass is roughly comparable to rowing in a hayfield after a heavy rain and Pop didn't like it. Still, for years he was the only person strong enough to tackle it.

"I've rowed more dad-gasted women around this river than any man alive," he would say. "Enough's enough," but if he wanted a real swim badly enough he would finally give in. At dead low tide the water off our dock was about three inches deep, warm as soup and topped by a repellent brown scum. You could struggle out through the mud to deeper water but even there the eelgrass was so thick that it was like swimming through spaghetti and only the smaller members of the clan were willing to do this.

Swimming on the hill was a communal affair—people didn't just rush down to the river for a dip any time they felt like it and of course all children were forbidden to swim alone. The morning hour for swimming was eleven o'clock, after Mum had reported in at Synton and done the errands, Pop had completed his housemaid's duties and finished studying, and Aunt K. had done the chores, cooked the day's food, and weeded the garden.

Baba never joined us for a swim, having renounced this pleasure when our grandfather died. We would have been appalled if she had, as the thought of Baba in a bathing suit was impossible to contemplate. It would have been easier to visualize Queen Victoria doing the hula-hula in a grass skirt. Baba didn't even use the word "swim"—she said "bathe" and would ask us if we had enjoyed our "bath." We understood from Mum that Baba had in some prehistoric era done a certain amount of jouncing up and down in the water. For this exercise she had worn a bathing dress, long black stockings, shoes, gloves, and, I think, corsets.

The morning swim was one of the high points of a summer day, and once the summer was in full swing it occurred as regularly as sunrise or sunset.

Our regular swimming place was in the cove just below our boathouse, where a spindly dock reached out from the shore. At high tide this dock was up to its armpits in clear, dark blue water, and all members of the family went in off the end, men and children diving, women climbing down the ladder since it wasn't ladylike to dive. The act of diving meant an unnecessary display of the limbs and also involved the risk of showing unmentionable parts of the body below the skirt of one's suit.

All female guests and a large number of males insisted on wading in, claiming that they disliked the idea of going headfirst into eelgrass and meeting eels and crabs face to face. They would pick their way gingerly across the tumbled stones and matted eelgrass at the top of the beach, screaming whenever they stepped on a periwinkle or a broken clam shell. Then they staggered and slipped over the wet rockweed at the water's edge and took a few steps out into the shallows. There they stopped, hugging themselves, shivering convulsively and looking fearfully for crabs. Crabs were there, all right; usually one of the big blue crabs—known locally as "greeners"—would be barring their way with outstretched claws. Guests sometimes leaped several feet in the air at this sight and everybody howled with laughter. No sane person walked through "greener" territory; you swam over it. Crabs seldom attacked a swimming person although one—no doubt crazed with hunger— had bitten Pop in the chest once while he was floating on his back.

The art of swimming off our dock was to stay off the bottom. We spent most of our time soaring like birds over the eelgrass forest, over amber glades dappled with sunlight, and through narrow alleys between clumps. It was a landscape in sepia and gold, full of fascinating surprises. Schools of shiners flashed ahead of our shadows and baby flounders, the size of quarters, scaled along the bottom and disappeared in the mud in a puff of brown smoke.

At low tide it wasn't as easy to stay off the bottom, although we had learned how to swim in six inches of water. Ordinarily we had a reasonable amount of liquid to operate in but at intervals during the summer we would get a series of peculiar days when it seemed to be low tide all the time. The tide would be going out all morning so by noon the river was just mud and eelgrass. Then it would turn and come in all afternoon, although there wouldn't be much water until it was too late to go for a sail or a swim.

By some curious coincidence guests always arrived during these low-tide periods, and it was difficult to know what to do with them. The number of persons who liked swimming in eelgrass was severely limited, and you could count on the fingers of one hand those who enjoyed pushing sailboats through it, hip-deep in mud. Of course, normal summer residents would have taken guests to Horseneck Beach just across the bridge from the village. Horseneck at dead low tide was at its best, curving like an ivory tusk between Gooseberry Neck and the harbor mouth—four miles of golden sand as wide and flat as a super highway. It faced south and was sheltered from the north by its bastion of dunes and forests of tall pitch pines. The swimming was practically perfect, the breakers curling over in mile-long arcs of green glass and rushing shoreward in snowy levels of foam. There was a private beach club near the road's end and here the summer people rented bathhouses and congregated every morning to swim. We rented no bathhouse. We never went there.

Since Horseneck was a famous beach and people came from all over to see it, guests, who possibly had expected to enjoy the swimming there, seemed bewildered when we led them across our stony river shore into the crab-infested eelgrass jungle, and some of the braver souls actually refused to cooperate.

"Why don't you go to the beach?" they bleated.

We tried to explain to them that we *did* go to the beach but not to the private beach club where the summer people were, certainly not to the public beach where "the Cities," as we called them, swarmed on weekends, using *public* bathhouses and even *rented* bathing suits.

As we understood it, hordes of bobbed-haired, cigar-smoking barbarians spent the week penned up in the cities, shaking the gates of their prison, snarling through iron bars and gnashing their teeth at those outside. On Saturdays the gates were opened and the inmates rushed screaming out, leaped into their rattletrap cars and roared off toward Horseneck Beach in a cloud of dust and exhaust fumes. We knew because we saw them, crawling bumper to bumper past the end of our lane or stalled in a jiggling, smelly line the whole length of the village street. The Sunday crowds were a favorite topic of discussion at Synton, and the bigger the crowd and the more awful the traffic jam the more horrified pleasure observers seemed to derive from the spectacle.

Every now and then we'd hear the ladies at Synton discussing in low voices the latest scandal in the bathing-suit department. Baba had seen a man wearing a pair of *trunks* without a skirt or top. Imagine—a big hairy chest—bare! Horrid!

Another time I was alone lying on the grass below Synton's veranda where Baba was holding court and heard a report that Mrs. X had been seen on the beach wearing only the jersey underpart of her bathing dress—nothing else. Practically naked! This was worse than horrid; it was vile.

"You hear that, dear Jan?" called Tink, who was sitting on the floor behind a chair. "I call thile! Siskusty!"

"Theodore, Theodore," said Baba, shocked. Unmarried persons and children were not supposed to know about the vile side of life, but Tink was a terrific eavesdropper and instantly relayed his findings to all and sundry. We gathered from him and our own eavesdropping sessions that the private beach club was a dangerously corrupt place and summer people a group of Bohemians to whom nothing was sacred. They went sailing and swimming on *Sundays*, wore socks, bobbed their hair, and even avoided church by having a short early service of their own!

When we went to the beach we sailed to Sandy Beach—the western tip of Horseneck's ivory tusk—as far as you could get from the bathhouses without falling into the harbor. It was in those days a wild and lonely place, where the plaintive whistle of plovers sounded all day long over the hot, white desert of the upper beach. Swallows drew arabesques in the blue air hunting for bugs, and flocks of gulls and terns gathered on the point to feast off stranded clams and crabs or fish in the channel. They sat facing into the wind and, as you approached, rose in a white flurry of wings, filling the day with their harsh, grating cries.

Sandy Beach was a favorite spot for sailing picnics although the wind and tide had to be just right, the weather dependable, and Pop in good physical condition, as he bore the brunt of the work. If we got becalmed he rowed; if we went aground he pulled the boat; if we ever arrived he built the fire and cooked the meal. A Sandy Beach sailing picnic was an all-day operation and didn't happen very often. The swimming was good, yes, but you couldn't go through all that every morning, we told the guests. The summer people, we said, were forced to go to the bathhouse area because they didn't have a place to swim in the river the way we did. If it was dead low tide we offered guests the great luxury of a swim in the Deep Hole but even this left these queer characters cold.

I see now that to the uninitiated it might have seemed bizarre to row or wallow through seaweed for half a mile in order to swim in a mud hole when Horseneck was a few minutes' journey by car. At the time, though, we couldn't understand their attitude. They seemed to us peculiar—freaks—not quite right in the head. As an added attraction we used to treat them to a quahogging orgy, which, followed by a swim in the Deep Hole, made a combination of sensual delights a king might have envied.

Quahog is the Indian word for the hard-shell clam called cherrystone or little neck in restaurants. They aren't much to look at outside; inside, though, they are china white with a spot of deep purple—fresh as a violet. The Indians used them for wampum and the violet-colored beads were naturally worth more than the white. Our river was a perfect gold mine in Indian terms and the shores were rich in clam shell heaps.

The sport of quahogging was very popular with the clan. It combined life in a buffalo wallow with the joys of a treasure hunt and seemed to us an ideal form of diversion.

Quahogging as practiced by us was simple and pleasurable. You just churned through the sticky black mud until you stepped on something. This might be a crab or a piece of razor-sharp shell; then again it might be a quahog. You bent down and clawed it out of the mud with your bare hands, and if it was a crab it bit you, if it was a quahog you put it in the pail. A child of three could have done it but grownup guests made a great fuss about crabs, and when they cut themselves a little you'd have thought their legs were being amputated. Their peevish comments and screams of pain were irritating to us and for this reason you had to think twice before you asked someone to go quahogging. Did Mum and Pop think twice? No, they did not. They invited elderly librarians, spavined missionaries, church workers with a secret passion for Pop, fashionable summer people, embryo ministers who adored Mum—anybody in fact who happened to be hanging around the house. The trouble was that during the winter some holy man would come to Sunday dinner or a choir leader would call and stay so long that Mum couldn't think of anything more to say. Then she'd ask them to visit us at the Point, summer being so far off that it hardly seemed real. After that she'd forget all about it and the next thing we knew they'd write or telegraph that they were coming. Sometimes they called up from the post office to ask where our house was and on certain awful occasions they appeared on the hill with no warning at all.

I remember particularly a man of God who worked, I think, in the Y.M.C.A. and was a sort of holy boy scout. If there was one thing we couldn't tolerate in a minister it was muscular Christian behavior, and we watched Pop like a hawk to be sure he never descended to this level. The holy boy scout never behaved in any other way and his face was perpetually wreathed in Christian smiles. Let's call him Elroy.

Elroy, who like most muscular Christians had no consideration for anyone, telegraphed that he was arriving in the city at noon on a broiling day.

"Eye Guy," said Pop. "I never asked him, did you?"

"I can't remember," said Mum. "I may have. I thought he'd never go home."

"Tell him he can't come," I suggested. Elroy was one of Mum's worshipers and when in her presence goggled at her like a stuffed frog.

"He's already left," said Mum.

"Well, the poor fella's probably sweltering in New York," said Pop in his kind way.

At eleven, when everybody else was in swimming, Pop went up to New Bedford and came back with Elroy. When he climbed wearily out of the car he said it was a scorcher in the city. Elroy, a tall hearty creature, bore down upon Mum and gripped her hand.

"Your good wife is as lovely as ever," he said in a low, buzzing voice.

"Yes, she is," croaked Pop emotionally.

Mum rolled her eyes at us and gave Pop a scathing glance. Then she jerked her hand away from Elroy. We could see that she might start shaking with laughter at any moment.

Elroy then requested to be introduced to these little people and said he was sure we would all have some jolly times together.

Whether or not Mum and Pop took Elroy quahogging to give him pleasure is a moot point. Possibly they wanted him to suffer; we certainly did. In fact, we could hardly wait. At lunch Elroy had told Pop in merciless detail about his new job.

"A real challenge," he said. "Great opportunities for Christian fellaship. I wish you could see my boys' bible group—as fine a bunch of manly lads as I've ever worked with." (He really talked like that.)

We exchanged glances of revulsion and Mum opened her eyes very wide to signal to us that she appreciated the full horror of the occasion.

"We thought it would be nice to go quahogging this afternoon," she said, smiling falsely. "The tide's right."

"Quahogging?" asked Elroy.

"It's really just digging clams," said Mum. "We row out to the middle of the river and afterward we swim in one of the deep channels."

"A capital idea," said Elroy, heartily.

"Just a simple family tradition," said Pop, with a slight croak. The poignance of "family" always did him in.

After the grownups had had a nap we all went down to the boathouse and put on bathing suits.

Elroy went in with Pop; the boys got the knothole bathhouse and came out with a scholarly report on Elroy.

This unfortunate now emerged dressed in a one-piece black suit with a short skirt and tubular legs to the knees. He looked very strange. Beside our sunburned limbs his were so white that they had a violet cast. Nobody wore shorts then so the sun never touched the lower limbs from one year's end to the next and a ghastly sight they were. Mum always referred to men's legs, especially Pop's, as "lavender stalks."

Pop wore an almost unbelievable one-piece bathing suit of gray jersey with white stripes. It had tubular legs with a modest skirt to mid-thigh. He also wore a limp white duck hat against sunstroke.

Mum's bathing suit was two piece—a black wool knit underpart (never visible) with a dark blue cotton dress over it. This had a full skirt with white rick-rack around the hem. We wore miniature versions of the same designs, although I can hardly believe it now. Bathing suits were not supposed to enhance bodily charms but conceal them. We used to think it a miracle that people of the older generation ever got married.

"All aboard," cried Pop and steadied *Mandarin* while everybody climbed in. Elroy sat in the stern with Mum and the Hideons. Pop took the oars. Dave and Aldie shared the front seat. I sat on the cuddy, my favorite place.

Pop bent his back to the oars and Elroy playfully pretended to be a cox calling out "Stroke!" and laughing with an eye to the galleries.

"Better put that towel around you," said Pop to him. "You don't want to get a burn your first day."

Elroy said he wanted a burn. This was his only chance to get a good tan.

Pop lasted halfway through the eelgrass; then his oars got so tangled in the stuff that he stood up to work them loose. Everybody leaned over the side to see how deep it was and Pop yelled,

"Balance the boat, dad-gast it!" and then Bobs let go of the string of his toy boat and began to howl. Pop poled us back to retrieve it, and we saw him measure the depth of the water with the oar. He was testing to see when he could make Elroy get out and push. The eelgrass covered the water with thick green snarls and loaded the oars so that we were barely moving.

Pop struggled on for a short distance and then gave up.

"All right, by George," he said. "All able-bodied men overboard!"

Elroy blenched visibly but you could see him meeting the challenge with Christian fortitude. Holding on to the gunnel he lowered his lavender stalks over the side. We saw him shudder and knew that his feet had found the bottom. Out in the eelgrass meadows the bottom was black mud, soft and squelchy as lard. His face changed as he began sinking and we watched him with scientific detachment as he went down. The mud, we knew, was like some hideous plum pudding filled with broken shells, live crabs, and other fauna. Jellyfish sometimes touched one's flesh like nightmare kisses and at intervals nameless creatures wriggled underfoot. All these experiences were reflected in Elroy's face, but meeting our eyes he put on his jolly Christian smile. Suddenly he gave a wild un-Christian yell and sat down with a tremendous splash—a great treat for us.

"All right?" asked Pop, helping him to his feet.

"I stepped on a snake, I think," said Elroy, whose lips were now light blue.

"Probably an eel," said Mum and burst into gales of laughter, in which we all joined. Then Dave, Aldie and I hopped over the side into the warm soupy shallows, where we were as much at home as the eel. Pop lunged ahead holding the painter, we hung on to the sides, dragging our feet in a very dishonest way, and Elroy lurched behind pushing. Mum and the Hideons sat in the boat. Elroy, because of his weight, sank down so far with each step that only his head was visible over the stern. Mum was obviously on the edge of one of her laughing fits and had on her wicked face.

Finally the water receded until it was only up to our ankles and *Mandarin* went aground. Pop jammed the oar into the mud and tied the painter to it. Elroy staggered over and tried to help Mum over the side, but this chivalrous gesture was ruined when he fell on his hands and knees. We all giggled and he said he thought he'd cut his toe. Mum gave a muffled shriek of mirth.

"Oh, we always get cuts out here," we said, but Elroy insisted on examining his wounds, and out of politeness Mum and Pop had to stay with him. We took off over the flats, splattering through hot little puddles, kicking up our heels, and sliding for long distances on the mud, which had a greasy, soapy surface and squeezed up between our toes like warm toothpaste.

It was dead low tide and all the flats were bare—a gray, lunar landscape where holes bubbled, miniature volcanoes hissed, and the feeding tubes of buried creatures bristled like tiny chimneys. In shallow lagoons clouds of minnows skittered about, and everywhere was the patter and starflash of shore birds. We could see their busy little forms, running like clockwork toys on the mud flats ahead. The big plovers stood tall among the smaller sandpipers and the yellowlegs were even taller. They stalked in the shallows, pursuing tiny fish, teetering on their lemon-colored stilts as though they had just learned to balance on them.

We scared up flock after flock—constellations of birds blinking on and off as they veered and wheeled in the sunlight.

Standing alone on the flat we heard the long "dear-dear-dear" of the yellowlegs, fleeing down the sky.

The gulls were harder to scare and padded ahead of us, croaking apprehensively, then exploded with wild white flappings. The flat, like a deserted battlefield, was strewn with dismembered shiners and smashed clams. Tank tracks of hermit crabs crisscrossed the whole area, with the centipede ribbons of clam worms. Where the gulls had been were splashes of bird lime and big webbed footprints, but where the sandpipers had run were necklaces of little stars.

Our best quahogging place was on the other side of the flat, where the soupy water was only a foot deep and eelgrass grew in widely spaced clumps. Here the mud was especially soft and squelchy, and all kinds of shellfish lived in the area. Scallops kept plopping up to the surface but the rest were invisible, and we proceeded happily to churn the place black. Presently I felt the exciting egg-shaped lump and reaching down into my footprint grubbed out a quahog, gluey with mud. At this point the grownups appeared with the Hideons in tow. Elroy was limping but a brave smile was pinned to his face. Pop was explaining to him the technique of quahogging and, ignoring Elroy's piteous glances, led him into the buffalo wallow we had made.

"Watch out for crabs," he said callously.

The sight of Elroy and his white city limbs was not edifying, so we went off to another place we knew. The incoming tide was sliding across the mud flats like a sheet of glass, and the buried population opened a thousand siphons to suck down tidbits fresh from the ocean. The water swirled warmly against my shins, the sun was hot on my back, and once more the magic of the place took hold of me. In the dry, aromatic air the golden grasses rustled above my head and the only other sound was the crying of plovers over the marsh.

When my pail was full, I went over and dumped it into the boat. The tide had floated her off and she rocked gently in the little waves. I picked out a good quahog, cracked it on an oarlock, and ate it still squirming, pink as a baby's tongue and tasting of the river and summer.

The next morning Elroy didn't appear at breakfast, and after Pop had seen him he went up to Synton and called the doctor. Elroy had a high fever and was, Pop said, one huge blister. With the callousness of the young we felt no sympathy for him at all and were glad to have him incarcerated and out of the way. We heard Pop discussing him with Mum upstairs.

"The man is an ass," he said. "I kept telling him he'd get a touch of the sun."

"Serves him right," said Mum. "Always talking about fellaship."

"Well, the poor chap has a lot of good in him," said Pop, who would have said the same of Rasputin or Jack the Ripper.

"He has not," said Mum. "I'll bet he signs his letters 'Yours in Christ.'"

"As a matter of fact he does," said Pop. "Man ought to be shot. Does the Church more harm than good."

It may be apparent by now that Pop did not conform to the conventional idea of a minister—a silver-haired fatherly character whose nice, dull sermons gave his congregation a chance to rest and sent them home to Sunday dinner calm and comforted. Nobody could relax for an instant during one of Pop's sermons, and they went home either seething with fury over what they considered his dangerously liberal views or in a white heat of enthusiasm for some new idea. The truth was he was a pioneer at heart, brave and adventurous. I sometimes think his talents were wasted in the pulpit. They were more suited to leading a wagon train across the prairies or carving a new nation out of the wilderness like his ancestor John Alden. He was a born speaker, so much at ease in the pulpit that he could jettison the sermon he had brought with him and preach a brand-new one more appropriate to the audience he saw before him. He had the sense of timing of a great actor but he spoke straight from the heart and often became so deeply moved by his own words that his voice faltered, then failed completely. At such times there wasn't a dry eye in the house except ours. Five minutes later he would be leaning on the edge of the pulpit telling a funny story about the Old Farm, and while people were still laughing he'd straighten up and deliver his point like a blow between the eyes. You never knew what he would do next. Even we couldn't help listening to him, and he spoiled us completely for any other minister, just as his church seemed to us the only church and all others faded imitations.

The church in Holyoke—the first one we remembered—had burned down when Aldie and I were very small and we were picked up in the night to watch the conflagration, which filled the whole sky with a hellish glow. This disaster gave Pop the chance to build a new church more like his idea of what a church should be, which was a Gothic cathedral. Like the monks in the heroic age of religion, he raised his church to the glory of God and spent a large part of his free time up on the scaffolding with the builders. He used to take us across the nave on catwalks one plank wide to see the carvings on the ceiling beams and explain the principles of the Gothic arch. We sat in on conversations with the architect, who had escaped from a German prison camp, and learned about the ancient art of stained-glass making from the expert who did the windows. When the church was done and Pop stood for the first time in his carved-oak medieval pulpit, it was a breathless and dramatic moment.

Sunday in the city was one of the high points of the week—not as good as Saturday, of course, but rich and colorful—a sort of pageant in which Pop played the leading role—a commanding figure in his gown and scarlet-lined hood. Following the service came Sunday dinner, with roast lamb and acres of white damask tablecloth. After that Sunday deteriorated with lightning rapidity and reached rock bottom at suppertime with shredded wheat around the kitchen table. At the Point in summer, however, the whole day was terrible.

CHAPTER SEVEN

Summer Sunday

ONE OF THE disadvantages of moving back into the Victorian era was that we had to go to church even in summer and also comply with the Sunday blue laws laid down by the Puritans in the seventeenth century. I'm not sure who was responsible for this but it was clear that when we were on the hill we conformed. The rule seemed to be that if something was fun you couldn't do it, but it wasn't all that simple. Sailing and swimming were forbidden as they were obviously too much fun, but so was *knitting*. It hardly seemed possible that there existed someone so misguided as to think knitting was fun so I asked Baba about it.

"Sunday is a day of rest," she said.

Knitting, she explained, was work and the Bible said no one should work on the Sabbath Day. Everybody was supposed to rest.

We had never considered swimming or sailing work but rowing seemed a lot of very boring work. Still, rowing was permitted on Sunday, although you couldn't use the rowboat for crabbing or eeling or anything worth doing. Possibly crabbing was work?

We had to walk all the way to church and back every Sunday and this was to rest the horses and the coachman who didn't exist.

"Why can't we go in the car?" we asked after one sweltering Sunday. "Why can't *we* have a rest instead of a lot of invisible horses?"

"Don't tell us we have to rest the Artful Dodger," I said to Pop, but he cleverly sidestepped the issue.

"They've always walked to church," he said. "It's one of those traditions." "They" meant Mum's family.

Pop himself seldom joined the hot, dusty group that trudged down the lane on Sunday mornings. He was usually off preaching at some elegant summer colony where everybody worshiped him and he had the royal treatment.

"You don't walk to church at Watch Hill, I'll bet," Aldie said to him.

We felt very bitter about going to church in summer and told Pop that we ought to have a vacation the way we did from school. We believed, I think correctly, that people didn't need as much religion in summer as they did in winter. We ourselves required none.

"Who needs God in warm weather?" Dave said.

"I'd rather have you than God," I said to Pop. We didn't trust God for an instant; you never could tell when he'd strike and we always blamed him for every bad thing that happened, and so did Mum.

"Guess what God's done now?" she would call out to us when some misfortune occurred.

If we had a spell of bad weather or ran aground out sailing or if Pop's glasses fell overboard—in fact, any time disaster hit— we'd all attack God (all except Pop, of course).

"God!" somebody always shouted. "Watch what you're doing!"

Pop would play along with this at first, but in the end he always rose to the bait. I remember one day after lunch hearing a crash in the pantry and a wordless cry from Pop.

"Guess what God's done now?" called Mum. "He's broken the bread plate."

The bread plate had on it a picture of Mr. Pickwick and his friends getting out of a stagecoach and Pop used to take it into the kitchen himself to protect it. That day he tripped and threw it across the pantry.

"*I* broke the bread plate," he said. "*I* tripped over the sill."

"That was God. He tripped you," Aldie said and pretty soon

Pop hit the ceiling and started explaining God all over again.

"God lets us make mistakes," he said. "He gives us choices and if we make the wrong choice we pay for it. He lets us learn by experience."

"Well, why doesn't He learn by experience?" Mum asked. "Why does He allow war?"

"He doesn't—*we do*," Pop said. "Gosh almighty, you're hopeless. Don't pay any attention to your mother. She's just teasing me. She's a better Christian than I am."

"I am *not*," cried Mum, who loathed this remark. "Stop driveling!"

We could easily imagine how God enjoyed watching us stumble down the lane on Sunday mornings. Hot and angry in our Sunday clothes and hard shoes we toiled through the dust in the wake of the grownups. In the early years Aldie and Dave wore white sailor suits, I wore smocked dresses, and we all wore long white stockings held up by garters. We slapped mosquitoes, kicked at stones, and said bad words to each other, words like "hips" and "belly"—real swear words.

The white dust got all over our Sunday shoes, and when we reached the main road somebody always moistened a handkerchief and polished them off, taking any spots off our faces at the same time. We objected violently to being washed with spit, but as long as we were little we had to submit.

From the village street we could see off between the white and silver-gray houses to the blue glitter of the river and the sea beyond the hayfields and stone walls. The air smelled of new-mown hay and roses, barn swallows dived and circled in the shining air, and gulls rode the wind, free and beautiful, while we had to go indoors and listen to what we considered a lot of nonsense. The waste of a lovely day made us seethe with fury, and by the time we arrived at the house of God we were hardly in a proper mood for divine worship.

The village church had a carriage shed behind it where a few horse-drawn vehicles could still be seen. Apparently everyone didn't believe in walking to rest the horses.

Inside, the church was painted pale green with varnished trim, and instead of pews there were rows of curious wooden chairs framed in iron and screwed to the floor. I can still see the pattern of holes in the plywood backs and the iron curlicue on the crest of each one.

The hours we spent in this place of worship were, I'm sorry to say, hours of absolute torture, because during the entire service we were half strangled with laughter. This was no reflection on the church or its members but simply the family curse at work. Pop's emotional temperament and Mum's overdeveloped sense of the ridiculous were a fatal combination and made us all dangerously vulnerable to the idiosyncrasies of our fellow beings. There was something about church that brought out the very worst in our characters. All those people sitting in rows staring straight ahead at a minister who usually had some peculiar mannerisms of his own were too much for our equilibrium. As minister's children, forced to attend church every Sunday, we were students of the human face and searched each congregation for diverting types. Churches seemed to be filled with weird-looking individuals, many of whom had nervous tics and sniffed, blinked, twitched, or grimaced all during the service.

The little church at the Point had a much smaller congregation than Pop's big city church but there was plenty of material for our research. One old lady who sat right behind us hooted off key during the hymns and I really dreaded the moments when she gave tongue, because from then on we were perfectly helpless. Our row of chairs shook all during the service and our insides became so knotted up with suppressed laughter that we nearly suffocated.

Another dangerous period in the service was the moment when, according to the Methodist custom, the minister gave one of his extemporaneous prayers. There was one young clergyman who would run out of things to say so he'd start blessing everybody he could think of. We listened carefully as he went through the members of the government of the United States from the President down, the members of the state government, and on and on, until he was blessing the local police chief, at which point we exploded into giggles. We behaved so badly that nobody would sit anywhere near us, and the whole congregation spent most of its time glaring at us in disapproval. Rock bottom was reached one historic Sunday when I was studying the back pages of the hymn book. It was a perfect summer day outside and through the open window near me came gusts of warm, sweet air and the whistling of meadowlarks. Far off beyond the fields I saw blue water with a sail moving across it. The precious morning hours were draining away, one by one, while the minister went on and on about "Gahd." In my despair I started going through the hymn book backward and so discovered a hitherto unexplored index of first lines. These were arranged in columns exactly an inch wide and the lines were cut off arbitrarily without regard for sense. It became immediately clear that even the most cursory perusal of them would be fatal. I began shaking at once, and then I found the line which sealed our doom. This was "It sweetly chee." Silently I passed the hymn book to Aldie and pointed. He in turn passed it on to Mum. There was a short interval while she struggled for control. Then she started shaking too, and the rest of the service was pure anguish for all of us.

"Sweetly chee" became a valuable addition to the family language and was used to describe Pop's expression of saintly, patient suffering which he assumed after one of his sleepless nights. It was also the name we gave to one of his saccharine female adorers, who scared him to death by laying her head on his shoulder and later trying to help him put on his rubbers.

Once we had found the index we were just so many ticking bombs, and shortly thereafter we were relieved of church attendance. I remember that for a while Pop taught us a Psalm each week and drilled us until we memorized it. As a result I have a headful of beautiful words that I wouldn't lose for anything. He also devised a substitute for church which was supposed to pass the time on Sunday afternoons. While Mum and the Hideons took naps Pop dragged us off somewhere and read aloud from a semi-religious book. This was almost but not quite as bad as church. We got through *Pilgrim's Progress* but it was rough going. I thought it one of the worst books in the whole world and have avoided it like poison ever since. I don't think even Pop liked it. We read most of it under an oak tree halfway up the shore of the river—a dull sort of place, good for nothing else.

One Sunday Pop took us up into the treehouse he had made in a big oak by the boathouse. It was a hot, muggy day, and after our gigantic Sunday dinner of roast lamb all of us were in a stupor. On this occasion Pop was manfully trying to get us through Dante's *Inferno,* a book which we felt had nothing to recommend it. Pop was droning on about the denizens of the various sections of Hell and he soon sank into a semi-coma of boredom. Before he realized what he was doing he read the great line: "The Devil made a trumpet of his rump."

That was the end of Dante's *Inferno,* and to this day that is the one line of the celebrated classic which sticks in my mind.

When we were down at the river on Sunday it felt queer. The boats, hanging at anchor with furled sails, were like the boats of people who had died. The sunlight was lonely. Our dock, the eel-grass, even the familiar rocks on the beach looked strange and sad.

Tink, unlike us, loved Sunday and had developed a special Sunday routine that took up nearly his whole morning. The chores still had to be done, so he put on a few clothes, his hat, and rubbers and went out to the barn. After breakfast he began the Sunday rites.

First he shaved, not only his face but his arms and legs, his neck and as far down his back as he could reach. Then, bleeding from a number of wounds, he ran a deep hot bath. He soaked a long time in his bath, diverting himself with his sponge, a real one that had a nice briny smell. After his bath he dressed in his Sunday clothes and polished his 'peckies, not only on all the towels, his bedspread, and handkerchief, but on all the other bedspreads upstairs. Then, with a pair of nail scissors, he trimmed the week's twills from all the chenille bedspreads. This entailed laying his head on the bed and squinting across the rows of tufts so as to spot some loose fiber against the light from a window. This he pruned off even with the top of the tuft. It was a time-consuming operation and the nail scissors became almost permanently imbedded in the flesh of his thumb and forefinger, but its completion gave him great satisfaction. Calm, clean, and refreshed, he went down to sit in the sun on the wide veranda steps.

It was lovely there on a summer Sunday morning, especially when the big lindens were in bloom. Three of them grew by the veranda and they thrummed and vibrated with bees, filling the sunlight with their lemon-honey scent. Each tree was a pyramid of pale golden blossoms that hung down like earrings under the heart-shaped leaves. These clusters shook with bees so that the whole tree seemed alive, humming one chord in its deep voice, a chord that never ended.

Sitting with Tink on the warm steps we listened to the voice of the lindens and absorbed some of Tink's Sunday peace. He basked in the sun like an old dog, happy in our company, in the drowsy sound of the bees, and in the heat of the wood under him. When Tink set aside a day of rest he rested. He remembered the Sabbath Day and kept it holy. If he felt like it he might walk to the river and play Hanky Wind Take, or he might "read" several pages of the Sunday paper. Then he sat with the end of his nose almost touching the page and his stubby forefinger following the lines looking for T's, his own initial, the one letter he knew, the only survival of Pop's attempt to teach him to read. Pop still felt the scars of this experience. He couldn't understand why Tink, who never forgot anything, who could, in fact, recite Baba's Christmas-card list, was unable to remember the alphabet. They had wrestled with it together day after day, sitting on the floor in one room of the cottage, but in the end Pop had to admit defeat— the only time he ever did. Tink, however, was quite happy with T.

On Sunday afternoons we had high tea at Synton, using the square ice-cream plates, which were pale green with pink corners, each with a different wildflower painted on it. I always chose pink clover or wild rose.

For tea Baba invented a special ceremony involving Whitman's Instantaneous Chocolate, which was kept in a blue-and-orange jar with gryphon feet. For this rite each of us was allowed to choose one of the many tiny coffee cups in the china cupboard and, using special little spoons with swastikas on the handles, mix our cocoa to a dark paste before Baba poured in the hot milk. Baba always made a lot of the swastika, which was one of her favorite designs, and she taught us the name very early. I'll never forget her indignation when Hitler picked *her* swastika for the Nazi symbol. You would have thought he had insulted her in person.

The end of a summer Sunday was always the same. We all congregated at Synton for hymns. Mum played the parlor organ, pumping valiantly and holding one chord until she could figure out the next one. This made it hard to sing in time, but I didn't want to sing at all as the hymns depressed me terribly. "Abide with Me" and "Jesus, Lover of My Soul" were so sad and lonely-sounding that I nearly burst into tears. If I could manage it I sometimes crawled under the big desk and looked at books. One of these was *The Rime of the Ancient Mariner* by Coleridge with illustrations by Gustave Doré—ghastly beyond words. The other was a dark-blue book about Indian massacres with colored pictures of Indians in war paint scalping people. When accompanied by the doleful howls of relatives singing "Abide with Me" these books were a living nightmare, and left permanent marks on my budding consciousness.

By the time the day of rest was over we were all exhausted, all except Tink, who knew instinctively what resting was and rested.

The Sunday blue laws continued to be enforced for more years than now seems possible and it wasn't until we were well on into adolescence that it occurred to us to rebel. We didn't even feel underprivileged, for the simple fact of being on the hill in summer was so enchanting that we never questioned the laws that guided that little kingdom. Then, too, we were as yet uninterested in the opposite sex, that is, in a romantic way, so we felt no need to go to the beach on Sunday morning when most assignations were made. We still viewed with disgust those of our contemporaries who went in for sailing dates on Sunday afternoons.

Ever since I could remember I had been treated as a sort of honorary boy by my brothers and their friends, and although I played with boys most of the time I had few illusions about the male. They were, of course, far more fun than girls but hardly the material for romantic love; I decided early to wait and fall in love with a man. On Sundays I could always go and look for birds with Pop. He had decided almost as soon as I was conceived that I was going to be his personal bird watcher. An ardent amateur ornithologist himself, he was always going off on bird walks with fellow addicts. However, this wasn't quite the same as having a built-in bird watcher right in the home. Mum had had the first shot at the post but she didn't have the temperament or the patience to stand still for hours staring at a black dot in a tree. She liked birds—they were pretty—but she didn't care what they were. What did it matter? This was a disappointment to Pop, who was a very romantic man and wanted to share everything with his little wife, but Mum wasn't a bird-watching sort of person. I got in on the ground floor by being born first, but Pop was fair and gave all of his young a chance. With great cleverness he used a method of teaching that appealed to our baser competitive natures, and as at meals he had a captive audience he chose those periods in the summer days to do the job. It was at the dining table in Snowdon that we were exposed to birds in a way that made it impossible to forget them, whether we wanted to or not.

CHAPTER EIGHT

Education of a Bird Watcher

ONE SUMMER MORNING before breakfast Pop came into the dining room with something rolled up under his arm. Removing from the wall a photograph of the Taj Mahal framed in perforated teak, he put up an Audubon Society chart, which showed a dead tree of improbable aspect, every branch of which supported several outsize birds. This tree overhung a stream and the scene had a dreamlike quality, gloomy and strange.

"Now," said Pop, sitting down at the head of the table, "there are a lot of birds on that chart—all birds you might see in summer here at Westport. We're going to play a game." The rules of this game were very simple. Pop pointed out a bird on the chart and we tried to see who could identify it first. Every meal thereafter was punctuated with screams of "indigo bunting" or "goldfinch" and the result was bedlam, but Pop believed children should be seen and heard at the table. As a way of enlivening a family meal and incidentally memorizing the names and field marks of birds, this game was unparalleled. Never as long as I live will I be able to forget the birds on that chart. I can see the very expression on the face of the rather truculent indigo bunting.

Birds didn't take with the boys, but this game infected me with a severe case of ornithological fever. Bird watching was not an acceptable form of diversion among my contemporaries, so I was forced underground in the city and had to lead a double life. But at the Point I was free to watch birds right out in the open.

Birds were only one aspect of Pop's grand plan for our education. His theory of child raising was to expose his five little towheads, as he called us, to everything except liquor, tobacco, and sex. To him a newborn baby was an empty vessel into which he and Mum poured as much joy, knowledge, and experience as possible during the child's residence in the home. This was to be insurance for the future, a bank account on which to draw in emergencies, solace in times of grief, and always a nest egg of happy memories to fall back on.

"You'll never forget this," Pop would say with relish. "You will remember it as long as you live."

He also prepared us for life's emergencies by teaching us many valuable skills, like rolling with the punch, vaulting fences, walking ridgepoles, skating on thin ice, and milking a cow with unerring accuracy into someone's eye. Once he showed us how to lean out over a cliff, supported only by an updraft of wind. If the wind had dropped we'd have been smashed to atoms on the rocks below, but the wind didn't drop. This was part of a course on How to Survive in the Woods, but I'm not sure where it fitted in.

One series of lessons had to do with Life on the Farm. In the winters we lived in the fertile Connecticut Valley, where great farms spread their patchwork quilts of fields and pastures. Here we saw all sorts of operations—sugaring-off, sheep-shearing, horseshoeing, pitching hay, teaming steers, butchering (but not sticking) hogs, apple picking, plowing, picking tobacco—everything in fact but taking the cow to the bull.

Everywhere we went we peeped into birds' nests, picked flowers, examined mosses and lichens, collected shells, watched bees swarming, dammed brooks and climbed trees, for Pop wanted us to know the earth. This was all part of what he and his friend, The Professor, called getting down to the roots of things, getting down to bed rock so you would have your feet on the ground.

The Professor, a pioneer in progressive education, was a rugged, handsome man, who walked like a cowboy and had laugh lines deep in his cheeks. He talked a lot about unfortunate city children who thought milk came out of a can. What they needed was a direct connection with the udder of a cow. We had had this valuable experience and so had Pop, who had milked many a cow on the Old Farm and preached his first sermon to a herd belonging to the president of Hamilton College, his alma mater.

Whether The Professor had himself been in contact with a cow's udder was not clear nor did it matter. The point he was making was that children should be in touch with reality—with farms, with the earth, with the birds and the bees in person, not in books. They should make things with their own hands, play music instead of just listen to it, plow the fields and scatter the seed, and so forth. He sometimes went slightly off the rails and had people treading out grapes with their bare feet to make *wine,* but Pop forgave him this as The Professor was a man after his own heart. He spent his summers at the Point, too, and loved the river and the salt marshes just the way we did. He was a member of the small minority who enjoyed swimming in the grass flats and he preferred to do this without a bathing suit. In this, as in so much else, he was way ahead of his time. Contact with Nature, like contact with a cow, must, he said, be direct. He said one of the best ways to be close to the earth was to sleep on it. Pop, who couldn't even sleep in a bed, said he believed in sitting still and keeping your eyes open, but they really meant the same thing.

When Pop and The Professor were exchanging views on the subject of life, bed rock, and roots they were worthless for all practical purposes. Mum, who never philosophized about life, just lived it up to the hilt, used to watch them with tolerant amusement.

"Books in the running brooks, sermons in stones," she would say.

My interest in birds somewhat interfered with my training as a lady botanist, but actually flowers and birds went together. A field full of daisies and buttercups was incomplete without the long, sweet whistling of meadowlarks and the bubble of bobolinks. Lady's-slippers belonged with the silver flute notes of the wood thrush, and it was impossible to imagine honeysuckle without humming-birds or thistles without goldfinches. When I went for flower walks with Baba we saw birds and found nests, and when I went bird walking with Pop we found all sorts of flowers.

A bird walk in Pop's company bore no resemblance to the decorous stroll with binoculars indulged in by elderly spinsters, as pictured by those who hold bird watching in contempt. We forced our way through thickets, trudged for miles across open country, waded in swamps, and crawled across sand bars on our stomachs. Together we searched the hill for nests and in August watched the shore birds pour in from their arctic nesting grounds. While Pop was busy studying I went out alone at all hours looking for new birds to add to my Life List—a thing all serious bird watchers have.

In the beginning I reported seeing some of the most amazing things—birds like the Bahama bananaquit or a passenger pigeon or something that had been extinct since 1863. I was considerably hampered in my research by lack of binoculars. All I had was a dainty pair of mother-of-pearl opera glasses that were out of whack to such an extent that they seemed to make things smaller rather than larger. In fact, I could see the birds better with my naked eye. Pop's binoculars were almost as bad; they often showed two images side by side, one slightly above the other. It was easier to go up where the birds were, so I spent a lot of my time in trees.

I also collected bird cards that the Dwight Baking Powder Company included in its packages to promote sales. The astonishing thing about these cards was that the birds were done by Louis Agassiz Fuertes, the greatest bird painter of the day, who had also done the illustrations in Forbush's *Birds of Massachusetts*. After we had accumulated a lifetime supply of baking powder the cards gave out, and I turned to collecting bird pictures of all kinds with special emphasis on photographs of nests and eggs, thus taking my first step toward a life of crime, for the best photographs of nests and eggs were in books and magazines belonging to libraries. In the beginning, though, I rifled only our own files of the *National Geographic* and *Nature* magazine.

Baba, who always encouraged us in any educational venture, allowed me to order from the Perry Picture Company every picture of birds' nests and eggs listed in the catalogue. They were all in color and I spent hours gloating over them.

Pop approved of this collecting at first, but then he decided that it had its dangers. Pictures—empty simulacra—were no substitute for the real thing, so he said he was going to take me out and show me how to "freeze"—that is, sit absolutely motionless in the woods until the wild creatures accept you as part of the landscape.

For this lesson we went down the river path to a place called The Tunnel, a kind of tube through the woods that looked like a set for a Tarzan movie. Honeysuckle and multiflora roses, escaped from Synton's garden, arched over the path and burst from the tree tops in fountains of blossom. Wild grape leaves covered the bushes so closely that under them it was nearly dark, and there were barbed-wire entanglements of greenbrier, canopies of poison ivy, and prickly mazes of wineberry canes, another runaway from Synton.

We sat down on a rock under a holly tree and Pop whispered instructions for freezing.

"Don't move. Don't make a sound. Just look and listen," he said.

As a member of a large brood I found these activities foreign to me and at first I found it very difficult. I kept feeling bugs on me: mosquitoes whined near my ear, ants ran tickling over my ankle. I itched all over. Then I began to notice things. In The Tunnel the light filtering through leaves was dappled green and gold, and every breath of wind shifted the pattern of sun spots. They flickered like butterflies or little birds, and some of them *were* birds but I couldn't see them long enough to tell what kind they were. Down on the ground coral-pink mushrooms pushed up the dead leaves with their heads, and Indian pipes, white as wax, grew from the brown mold in the shadows. I saw a thrush with eyes like a fawn slip through the maze of stems, then an emerald-green beetle landed in the sun on the path. Pop pointed to a tiny fern near my foot and whispered, "Ebony spleenwort."

I noticed the extraordinary sweetness of the air. It was

like pure honey but composed of many different scents. Honey-suckle and roses I knew, but there was something else that filled the air with a subtle perfume. Then I saw that under the roof of grape leaves were myriads of fuzzy pendants powdered with gold pollen that were undoubtedly the blossoms of the vine. This discovery alone proved how valuable freezing was.

Presently there were stirrings and rustlings around us. Coins of sunlight trembled as something moved among the leaf shadows. A chickadee flip-flapped down to inspect us, and a red squirrel started up—clicking and chattering like a little engine. Suddenly out on a twig came a tiny bird as vivid as a butterfly. His canary-yellow breast was necklaced with chestnut spots and his back was the gray-blue of smoke. I had never seen anything like him.

"Parula warbler," Pop breathed in my ear.

It was my first warbler. He had a worm in his beak and seemed very nervous.

"They nest in the usnea moss," said Pop, after the bird had disappeared.

The usnea moss was a great feature of our woods at that time and I knew it well. It grew in silvery festoons all over the oldest junipers and looked like a lot of gray beards hung up to dry.

Pop said that the parula turned up the tips of the moss and made a little purse like a small oriole's nest. In this the eggs were laid. I was utterly charmed.

From then on I did a lot of private freezing and tracked down all manner of nests for the pure excitement of the hunt, the triumph of discovery, and the first sight of the little cradle in its hiding place. Torn to shreds by briers, my hair full of juniper needles, I would at last part the sheltering branches and look down on my treasure. I found eggs like pearls, eggs like polished turquoises, eggs in all the pastel colors, some freckled with cinnamon or black, all arranged with points inward in a charming little basket or cup. One of my favorite designs was a chipping sparrow's nest that I found tucked snugly into the fork of a spruce branch. It was the size of a half baseball, woven of fine rootlets and lined with white hair. Here, arranged in a circle, were four small eggs, pale greenish-blue spotted with black and lilac. I gazed on it with the ardor that only a collector knows while the mother bird chipped in alarm close by.

Every day after that I made a house call and found her brooding her eggs, until she finally became resigned to my presence, almost bored. Then one morning she was off the nest, fussing around with a pale green inchworm in her bill, so I knew the babies had hatched. Peering into the nest, I saw that the eggs were gone and in their place was what appeared to be a pile of tangled earthworms. The minute I touched the branch four heads flew up like little yellow crocuses, and from the gaping mouths came a faint wheezing sound.

As the days passed I watched the babies change from ugly bags of skin to thimble-sized balls of brown feathers, big-eyed and appealing as kittens. I reported their progress to Pop, who proceeded to inflame my imagination with stories of bird-nesting adventures in tall trees, climbing after hawk's eggs, horrible moments when eggs carried in the mouth broke on the way down, and other stimulating episodes from his Tom Sawyer boyhood. At that time the ancient sport of bird nesting was an acceptable form of masculine diversion. Egg collecting was one of the popular hobbies, like butterfly collecting, that kept the nineteenth-century teenagers off the streets.

Mum's brother, our Uncle Basil, had also gone bird nesting in his youth and had a good egg collection, which he displayed in glass-fronted cubbyholes in his boathouse living room. I particularly coveted a large pointed sea bird's egg—pale blue blotched with chocolate—a little world with its seas and unknown continents. He also had a hummingbird's nest on a lichened branch, a tiny muff of fern wool shingled with lichens and bound around with spider webs. It fitted my finger like a thimble and felt as soft as cashmere. I like to think that there was a time in my life when I could have been made perfectly happy by the possession of a hummingbird's nest.

At the age of twelve I knew all the common birds by sight and had put my foot through the leaded glass window on our staircase landing, trying to scare English sparrows off my bird feeder. In those days only dedicated ornithologists had bird feeders and mine, which Pop built himself, was a sensation in the local bird circles. We had so many chickadees, nuthatches, woodpeckers, and blue jays hammering at sunflower seeds out there that Pop hardly got a wink of sleep from first light on.

So far I had gone bird walking only with Pop but now he became bloated with pride in my prowess and decided to expose his personal bird watcher to his friends. One summer day he took me along on a so-called bird walk with The Professor. When we were down in the woods The Professor held up his hand.

"Listen!" he said.

From the cool depths of the grapevine tangle the notes of the wood thrush floated up like silver bubbles rising to the top of a glass.

"Silence," said The Professor, "is a very important thing. Most of the world's problems would be settled if everybody learned to sit quietly in an empty room."

"Voltaire?" asked Pop, and they were off.

"The majority of people," said Pop, "are all but blind and deaf. Hardly anyone uses his five senses to the full."

"Drop a quarter on the sidewalk," said The Professor, "and they hear that very well, but they don't hear the sounds of the earth—the bird song, the frogs and tree toads, and the summer purr of insects in the grass."

Most people, he said, were only half alive and went around trying to "kill time." Time was life itself. The present was all anyone had. We each had all the time in the world.

After that one they never stopped talking for an instant, and although we had a nice walk it wasn't a bird walk. The truth was that the two philosophers couldn't watch birds together because they got sidetracked and went off into discussions about life. While they were absorbed in their analysis of man and his relationship to Nature the bird they were watching would get away. Pop must have realized this, for he now called in another expert—Uncle Smith Dexter, his favorite bird friend at the Point and one of our favorite people. We loved the way he looked—brown as an Indian with a cap of snow-white hair.

Like Pop, Uncle Smith was a minister and one of the saints of the earth. We believed he had no faults and I really don't think he had any. He had been in jail. Nowadays ministers and priests think nothing of spending a week or two in a dungeon but things were different when we were little. Uncle Smith had been arrested with H. L. Mencken on Boston Common during a protest march for Sacco and Vanzetti. He had spent an hour in jail, where they had taken away his belt and jackknife to prevent his committing suicide, and this incident coupled with a newspaper photograph of him being led away by the police gave him real status in our eyes. Pop, to his chagrin, had never been behind bars but had been called a Red by a prominent news commentator for preaching against the dangers of a closed mind—a great achievement but not, of course, as good as being in prison.

Uncle Smith kept his eye on the bird. He was making a census of the birds of Westport, so when he was out on a field trip he didn't allow life to get in the way of ornithology. You had to be really good on birds to go out with Uncle Smith, and one of my dreams was to see my name in his notebooks where the Westport bird records were kept. These notebooks were filled with local names, as many sightings had been reported by gunners, fishermen, and year-round residents. One of the lobstermen, well known to us, brought in reports of oceanic birds—gannets off remote ledges, kittiwakes, eiders, and other sea birds not visible from the shore. Uncle Basil and Pop were both mentioned in the notebooks and so was our hill, under its real and dull name of Eldridge Heights.

Uncle Smith very kindly consented to take me along on a projected trip to a marsh to see some snowy egrets which had come up from the South for their summer vacation. He even allowed me to look through his binoculars; I could hardly believe my eyes and drew back alarmed when the egret turned its dagger beak in my direction.

After this revelation I let it be known that the only thing I wanted for Christmas was a pair of good binoculars.

We spent that Christmas at Synton, packed into all the spare beds and cots. The hill in winter was very strange, stripped and bare in the sweet clean air of December. The sun was in the wrong place and the sea glittered with cold silver light. Dusk fell early, hanging like a blue curtain at the windows, and the house smelled of wood fires and kerosene lamps. A light snow fell while we slept and the next morning the river and grass flats were the blue and white of a Canton plate. In the woods the hollies shone with Christmas berries but the real wonder was the population of water-fowl. Great rafts of ducks lay out in the water and the day was full of their barnyard quackings. The marsh creeks were teeming with them and there was a constant coming and going. While we watched, Pop suddenly raised his hand.

"Listen," he said. "Geese!"

I heard them in the distance, a mournful chorus, so like a pack of hounds in full cry, and presently the squadron appeared in a gray wavering line. I turned my mother-of-pearl opera glasses on them but couldn't get them into focus and so missed the spectacle. Pop smiled significantly when I complained about this, so I knew right away that there would be binoculars under the tree.

Not since I had been given a real baby doll with a complete layette had I felt such pure ecstasy as when I opened that package and saw the leather case. Pop tried to open it for me but I managed to get it back and undo the catch. Inside, nested in blue velvet, was a pair of the most beautiful binoculars I had ever seen.

"They're Zeiss," said Pop, reaching for them again. "Look, I'll show you."

"I can do it," I said sternly.

Pop was worse than he had been with Bob's electric train and could hardly wait until the tree ceremonies were over to show me how they worked. Beside these superb instruments his old binoculars were as pathetic as my mother-of-pearl opera glasses. We went out on the porch to give them a trial run, and Pop was so excited that he nearly hung me by the neck with the leather strap.

After the tree we walked down the lane to do some more testing. Once when Pop had the glasses I suddenly saw what looked like a small snowball on the lower branch of a Scotch pine.

"Hey, look!" I croaked, for Pop had hauled up on the leather strap. "There's a bird right in front of me."

We went over and saw that it was a little owl with its head under its wing. Its breast was streaked with cinnamon and the feathers on its back and wings were russet and white, the colors of dead leaves in the snow.

"By cracky," said Pop, "it's a saw-whet owl. The smallest owl in the East."

The branch was so low that I was able to stroke the owl's back with my finger and he woke up like a kitten, unafraid and round-eyed. For a moment he gave us a golden stare, then slowly sank into a doze.

"Well, now, I think that's a record," said Pop proudly. "We must report this to Smith Dexter."

Uncle Smith, who was staying in the village for the Christmas bird count, came up to hear our story and said mine was the only sighting of this little owl in Westport. He would put me in his book. I had made it.

Uncle Smith said benevolently that to celebrate this milestone in my life I could accompany him and Pop to Gooseberry Neck to see the purple sandpiper. He spoke of this bird as though it were a personal friend with whom he had an appointment. I had noticed that real bird watchers talked this way and I was also aware that the purple sandpiper had a mystic significance in bird-watching circles. In the Christmas count recorded in a bird magazine called, I think, *The Auk,* this purple sandpiper always held a prominent place. Few publications had ever bored me as much as *The Auk,* or whatever its name was. It was worse than *Pilgrim's Progress.* However, here I was about to meet this key bird and join one of the famous expeditions that Uncle Smith and Pop usually went on alone. I knew, too, that Pop wanted me along so he could use my binoculars.

Gooseberry Neck was a treeless point covered with grass

and low bushes which at high tide became an island. It was one of Uncle Smith's special bird-watching places and apparently the winter residence of the purple sandpiper. From its windswept tip you could see a lot of oceanic waterfowl not otherwise visible from shore.

The next morning I put on my heaviest serge bloomers, wool stockings, leather jacket, and beret, for in those days no one had invented decent winter clothing for girls.

Pop had been outfitted by the U.S. Army for life in the trenches of France, so he was warmly clad in khaki riding pants, puttees, army boots, and some sort of khaki tunic. However, on top he wore a fedora hat and ear muffs.

Out on Gooseberry Neck the wind searched our vitals and I cowered behind the remains of a wreck while Pop and Uncle Smith combed the shore for purple sandpipers. Finally they summoned me. It was a solemn moment.

I don't know what I expected to see but I naturally thought it would be a purple bird—the rich purple of Baba's amethyst, maybe, something spectacular. The reality was a terrible letdown or perhaps I was too cold in my serge bloomers to appreciate what I saw. The purple sandpipers were stout drab birds, slate gray in color, with yellow legs. I quite realized their importance in my bird-watching career but I was unimpressed. Uncle Smith explained that the purple sandpiper's fame rested on the fact that it is the only sandpiper that winters in New England and, of course, that is something.

After we went back to the city Pop bought me a notebook —black with red leather corners and "Record" in gold letters on the spine.

"This is your field book," he said, "to record everything you see. You can keep your bird lists and flower lists here and any other interesting facts you want. It will help you observe clearly and you can live all those good moments twice. When you write something down you live it all over again. It will teach you how to use words well, too."

I opened the notebook and saw to my delight that the

pages were numbered, just like a real book. Filling my pen, I wiped the nib carefully and wrote down a date. Then I inscribed in my best Palmer-Method hand these words: "Saw saw-whet owl in lane."

There seemed to be something a little queer about the line but it was my first literary effort.

CHAPTER NINE

Warblers at Sunrise

ONE OF THE happiest by-products of my bird mania was that I became the chosen companion of Pop on his long walks after work or on early mornings in spring when the warblers were coming up the Connecticut River. Pop's bird companion in the city was a charming man called Aaron Bagg, whose notes can be found in Forbush and who was an amateur ornithologist of some distinction. He was very tall with a long nose and had the same gentleness of spirit as Uncle Smith and Pop. He and Pop had gone to France together in 1918 and ever since they had been close friends. Aaron Bagg owned the painting of the peregrine falcon by Louis Agassiz Fuertes and at that time in my life this set him apart from other men. That picture was in a *book*.

The arrival of the warblers in the first week in May is one of the high points of the year for all dedicated bird watchers, and the Connecticut, which runs from north to south in a nearly straight line, is on one of the great flyways. Aaron had taken Pop to several islands in the river where the warbler waves broke like surf on a beach, and here Pop proposed to take me for my first sight of this marvelous show. We set the alarm for five o'clock.

Getting up early on a spring morning is one of life's great free adventures that nothing can spoil. Between the last star and seven o'clock, when most people start the day, there are several hours of radiant sunlight and dew-washed air that are hardly used at all except by milkmen, farmers, truck drivers, and birds. A spring sunrise on a river with warblers is an experience so exquisite that it's hard to understand why so few people get out of bed to enjoy it. Pop and I were up before the sun. We were, in fact, up before the maids, which meant that the stove was cold and all the food hidden away in the pantry, that private domain of the cook. We sneaked down there like two burglars and poked around until we found the peanut butter, cut some slices off a home-made loaf, and made ourselves sandwiches.

We drove through the cool streets, munching our sandwiches. The city was empty and serene, but when we turned off into the woods the trees were alive with little wings. The new leaves were just unfurling and in the spring sunlight they glowed like shavings of gold and copper. Pop stopped the car and turned off the engine, and at once the dawn chorus of bird song took over the world. Then we got out.

"There they are," said Pop. "Listen."

I stood still and heard them. The woods were filled with thin wiry voices, alarm notes like struck crystal, zeeps, the flirting throb of wings close by. Pop explained that the warblers had been flying all night and had landed at sunrise to feed.

"Wait till you see them on the island," he said, so we went on to where the woods ended abruptly at the top of a cliff of sand known to the city's children as the Sand Bank. Below us the river glittered over its stones and we saw the island like a basket of feathers floating in the shallows near shore. This island was really just a large sand bar where willows had taken root, and in early May these were a green-and-gold mist of new leaves and catkins. We got there by sliding down the sandbank, jumping a few channels, and walking along strands of pebbles. In the rosy sunrise light the place had a magic look, as though it existed only at dawn in spring, and as far as I was concerned that was true. I have never seen so many warblers. All the time we were on the island they poured through the willows in such multitudes that the branches looked decorated as if for a Christmas party. I remember one small tree full of magnolia warblers and another where we saw at the same time a flock of black-throated blues, myrtles, black-throated greens, black-and-whites, and a Blackburnian. Yellow warblers were already starting nests—handfuls of silver plant floss in the forks of bushes. Pop and I were beside ourselves and for the duration of the warbler waves we went out every day.

Once a rose-breasted grosbeak sang his rich song from the tip of a poplar, and for the first time in my life I focused my binoculars on the famous rose-pink triangle. Another morning in the rain we saw a scarlet tanager and a treeful of Blackburnian warblers, their flaming orange breasts glowing through the drizzle like hot coals.

The pure happiness of those young spring mornings on the river with Pop has never left me, and rather than miss anything I get up at sunrise the year round, a practice that annoys my children and has caused me much trouble when visiting strange houses, where I nearly starve to death before breakfast.

Because of the blight of school I had no hope of seeing the warblers go over our hill at Westport. The Connecticut River was all very well but hardly in the same class as the Westport River. Still, there seemed no way to remedy the situation and I resigned myself to my fate. Then a real miracle occurred. I was removed from school and sent to Synton for six weeks beginning in mid-April and continuing right up to the first of June. I had stayed there with the family after Christmas and in what was laughingly called spring vacation but alone, no. We had never seen the Point in late April or May as school, with typical malevolence, saw to it that we were back behind bars before the real spring weather even started. We left the hill when nothing was in bloom but skunk cabbages, and now I was to see it all—primrose time, daffodil time, apple-blossom time, lilac and violet time; I could hardly believe it.

This incredible bonanza took place exactly a week after I had stolen a picture of a rose-breasted grosbeak's nest out of a library book, and the reason was that, according to the doctor, I was outgrowing my strength. This was a common ailment of the

period and meant you were run down and had to take iron and a
ghastly viscous substance called Maltine. My own diagnosis is
that I was haggard with guilt and fear that my crime would be
discovered. The announcement of my release gave me the first
peace I'd known since the return of the library book. For a week
I had lived in hourly expectation of arrest, and the sight of a
policeman made me feel quite faint. I even resorted to prayer,
which hitherto I had found useless for all practical purposes.

"Please, God," I whispered into the darkness, "don't let
them arrest me and I promise never to steal again."

Almost instantly God delivered the goods. Not only did
He save me from a prison cell but from school, which was virtually
the same thing. On top of that was the royal gift of a whole
spring at the Point, a treat so stupendous that I had never even
hoped for it. After this I wouldn't have been surprised if He
had anointed my head with oil, the way He kept doing to people
in the Bible.

With God responding like a slot machine when you hit the
jackpot I was a little worried about the effect of other prayers
I had offered up in moments of abandon. Would the whole
school burn to the ground as I had frequently requested? Like
all normal children of the period I loathed education and considered all teachers my natural enemies, as indeed some of them
were. The one whose name led all the rest was my Latin teacher,
probably the crossest woman the world has ever known. I won-
dered nervously whether she would now drop dead since I had
often prayed for this to happen. However, Shinola—for so we
called our enemy—was in rude health and also livid with rage
at being balked of her prey. She predicted with her witch's
cackle that I would flunk Latin. It will come as no surprise to
cynics that I not only passed Latin but completely escaped de-
tection and still have in my possession the picture of the rose-
breasted grosbeak's nest. What kind of a moral lesson this is I
shudder to think, but since that time I have understood perfectly the
statement that the wicked shall flourish as the green bay tree and
have observed that crime often pays very well. I also believe that

every child should be given a free spring before he is grown but have no hopes of getting this across to the educators.

When I look back on my spring at Synton I realize that I learned more in those six weeks of freedom than I learned in two years of Shinola's classes.

On my first evening alone at Synton Baba, Aunt K., Tink, and I sat by the fire in the drawing room and discussed plans.

The room was still in its winter arrangement, with the red oriental rug instead of the blue summer one and the copper coal scuttle full of cedar logs. The firelight flickered in the polished brass and copper vessels from India—there was a whole table of them—and in the glass doors of the tall mahogany bookcase, where the best calf-bound volumes were kept. The kerosene lamp with its yellow china shade made a circle of radiance around us, but off in the corners it was almost dark. In the shadows I could see the glimmer of gold where the biggest Buddha sat in his lacquer shrine and the glitter of the beetle wings on the embroidered hanging over the hall door. Near it was the white keyboard of the parlor organ. On the walls loomed giant etchings of cathedral interiors, a vast picture of unidentified maidens moping among ruins, another of choir girls singing, and a sepia photograph of Wells Cathedral. Synton ran to cathedrals, which I supposed had something to do with my grandfather, the president of Union Theological Seminary.

In one corner I could see the gilt frame of "The Last Gleam," an original masterpiece, whose canvas was entirely black except for a slit of orange. "The Last Gleam" was depressing enough in the daytime but at night it was far from reassuring to one about to go to bed by candlelight.

Around the fire it was delightfully cozy. Baba was in her rosewood armchair on one side of the carved oak fireplace, Aunt K. was in her big rocker on the other. Lad, the dog, was curled like a doughnut in his basket, and I sat bolt upright in the straw fireside chair from the Orkney Islands. Tink sat flat on the floor by the fire picking twills off his sweater. The sixth member of the group was on the mantelpiece—a china figure of a man in a red fez and bloomers, pouring water out of a pitcher into a large jar. For years I had believed him to be a statue of my grandfather, and in a way I still felt he was, since he had the same kind of mustache.

"Well, dear Jan," said Baba, her head cocked on one side like a brown-eyed bird, "we must think about your program."

Our family doctor, who was responsible for my free spring, had, to my disgust, outlined a health program which I was supposed to follow. I had to take iron in the form of a rusty-tasting medicine, eat two eggs for breakfast, and drink a lot of rich milk. I was supposed to get a lot of fresh air and exercise and had to take rests after lunch and before supper. While I was resting I had to "act like a vegetable." How was I supposed to do that, I asked? Which vegetable—a carrot, a pea, a Hubbard squash? Baba said she thought a cabbage would do and that she would read to me while I was resting. We would start Jane Austen.

I was to sleep in Baba's dressing room, which had one door into her bedroom and another into the servants' wing. This meant I could get out as early as I wished without disturbing Baba. Aunt K. was up at the crack of dawn and I intended to get up with her and help do the chores. All my Old Farm blood thrilled at the thought. Like Pop I thought the smells of hay and manure among the best in the world.

Aunt K. began to nod very early in the evening and Tink kept falling asleep. Every time he succumbed he sagged forward until his head hit the floor between his feet. The thud of his forehead on the wood woke him up enough so that he sat back, but he was down again in no time.

Baba was as alert as ever, but she finally said it was bedtime and we all went upstairs together, Tink walking in his sleep. I was glad we went together as I was scared to go alone. One aspect of moving back into the nineteenth century was the darkness of a house without electricity. Baba disapproved of electric light—"so glaring"—and Synton had only kerosene lamps and candles. Now we each took our candlestick out of the butler's pantry. Mine was blue enamel, shaped like a saucer, with a curly handle. Even remembering it scares me. We blew out the kerosene lamps and slowly climbed the ornate oak staircase to the second floor. The candles gave out a wavering glimmer that left the corners in darkness but threw huge moving shadows on the walls.

In the upstairs hall there was a terrible picture—some sort of etching—of dead horses in the snow. I can still see the bottoms of their hoofs and the dismal landscape, like the Russian steppes, that made up the background. This picture hung beside the bathroom door, making it even more frightening to enter that sanctuary after dark.

Synton's bathrooms were plunged in gloom even in the daytime. They were paneled in varnished matched boarding, and even the john seats were brown. The tubs were enormous but the water came out of the faucets in such a miserable trickle that it took hours to get even an inch of depth. My grandfather had always taken a cold bath every morning, part of the South austerity program that anyone with Scottish ancestry will recognize. You weren't supposed to be too comfortable. Beds were either hard as the floor or like hammocks. My cot in the dressing room was a cross between a hammock and a banana, but I knew better than to mention that.

After I was tucked in, Baba blew out my candle and stood in the doorway.

"God protect you, dear Jan," she said. "Happy dreams."

She and Aunt K. talked back and forth while they were getting ready for bed and this was reassuring as well as informative. As I floated between sleep and waking I heard interesting fragments. So-and-so had bobbed her hair. Somebody else had been seen on the village street wearing *socks*—horrid. Dear Mr. Eddy looked so well and handsome. They would take some flowers there tomorrow, and so forth. So the night went out peacefully and, of course, in the morning everything was safe and wonderful again.

Rajah started shrieking before sunrise and woke me just as the clouds were beginning to turn pink. I lay and listened to the dawn chorus of birds; choirs of robins caroling in the treetops, catbirds and brown thrashers garrulous in the thickets, song sparrows bubbling from the garden, and chewinks shouting, "Drink Your Tea!" all over the hill. I listened hard but there were no warblers.

It seemed about a hundred years between Rajah's first screeches and the time Aunt K.'s footsteps sounded on the stairs. I spent some of it memorizing the furnishings of Baba's dressing table—the pin tray painted with violets, the baroque silver fittings for a lady's toilet, including a pin cushion full of long hatpins and a hair receiver, an object now happily obsolete. Right over my head was a picture of Mum at eleven, wearing a topi and getting up on an elephant. There was another of her, very pretty at sixteen, standing with Aunt K. and Pop in a tea garden up in the Himalayas. On the extreme right of the picture was a native wearing a turban—"our bearer," Baba said. It was on this lecture tour to the Orient that Pop had become engaged to Mum.

Back at Union Seminary, as soon as he had recovered from the iron-bar episode, he began helping Mum with her homework and in no time at all he was down at the Point helping her push boats through the eelgrass. When she was fifteen my grandfather went on his second lecture tour to India and asked Pop to go along as his secretary and as a sort of royal equerry to Baba and the family. This he did, and from then on he never looked back. They were married when Mum was nineteen.

We were brought up on India. We were told bedtime stories of lepers screaming for baksheesh, of fakirs on beds of spikes, peasants making patties of cow dung, Baba trying to eat with chapattis—a kind of Indian pancake—and cobras crawling up drains into bathrooms or dropping on people from ceilings. There was one bedtime story about bats and flying foxes swooping into Mum's bedroom and one about a tarantula getting under the matting in Pop's room and making a crunching noise like the footsteps of a burglar or murderer. Once in Simla Mum and Pop had been attacked by a band of monkeys which chased them down some hill, and we saw slides of these very monkeys. We also saw slides, made from family photographs, of maharajahs riding on elephants, the Taj Mahal, natives playing flutes to cobras, bodies burning in the ghats by the Ganges, and "our bearer." I can't say these tales or slides made me want to go to India. In fact, the reverse was the case, but they did give our lives a glamorous extra dimension. The very word "India" had a magic power on the hill, and we knew far more about it than we did about the United States. I think I could have driven an elephant myself, we had seen so many slides of them, with their mahouts, hauling logs and bathing in rivers. We had cut our teeth on elephant goads and sampled the contents of the betel-nut chewers kit at a very early age.

I lay there in bed listening to birds and thinking about India while the pink faded from the sky and the sun blazed up behind the spruces.

At last the moment arrived and I flung off my covers, put on my clothes, and slid out into the servants' wing. The servants' staircase opened into the pitch-black labyrinth of corridors and storerooms—the inner heart of Synton and a real hellhole. I shot through there like a scalded cat and flung open the kitchen door.

Sun poured in from the two east windows, turning to gold the clouds of steam from the teakettle. The big black stove snapped and crackled, and the whole place smelled of wood smoke, geraniums, and oatmeal, with a faint overtone of kerosene. Aunt K. was striding around clattering pots and pans, stirring up the cereal, and watering plants. There were flats of seedlings in the sunny windows—rows of little green bowknots—the whole summer garden waiting to be set out.

"Oh, what a day!" said Aunt K. "Have some fresh bread. It's over there on the breadboard."

As usual there were a lot of things going on in the kitchen. A carton of ducklings were peeping behind the stove, and a pair of guinea pigs were whistling in a cage by the plants. Aunt K. said darkly that they were supposed to be the same sex but by the way they were acting she had her doubts. After a while we took the garbage pail for the hens and went out into the morning. The air was cool and sweet, scented with hyacinths. Spider webs were spun all over the trees and bushes, and at this hour they trembled with their load of dew. Birds were singing, bees buzzing in the peach trees in the little orchard. Under them a mother hen clucked to her brood of primrose-yellow puffballs. Here Tink caught up with us and looked proudly upon the little family. Aunt K. scooped up one of the chicks and handed it to me. It felt light and soft as a warm powder puff. Tink took it, and cupping it in his hands he kissed it tenderly on the end of its bill.

"Cutie," he said and returned it to its mother.

When chores were done we walked back through the chilly, golden air and Tink proposed to me. I accepted.

Breakfast was as elegant as usual, and my fresh eggs, eaten with a silver spoon, tasted better than any eggs in the world.

Over the blue Canton china Baba discussed the days prospects. It was immediately clear that the training of the lady botanist was in order, but first came the morning routine of the lady. This began with washing the breakfast dishes in the butler's pantry, but they weren't dishes, they were the "silver and glass."

Baba carefully explained to me that this was proper for a lady to do. Ladies always washed the silver and glass. Sometimes they did it right at the table, but she preferred the butler's pantry because she could look out on her bulb bed—now bright with daffodils.

"Why do they wash just silver and glass?" I asked.

"Because the servants might be careless with them."

"Don't ladies wash the dishes?"

"No, no, that is the servant's job," Baba said.

As she was actually washing a plate at the time and Aunt K. was clearly visible in the kitchen scrubbing pans, this was difficult to make convincing. Still, Baba managed it.

After the silver and glass Baba took off her violet apron and put on her rubbers, which were kept under the hatrack in the front hall. Then we went out on the big veranda and got the flag out of the sea chest. It was an enormous American flag made of proper bunting, Baba explained. It must *never* touch the ground, just the way the Bible must never be put under any other books. She bundled its red, white, and blue up into a huge ball and, picking up her long skirts to keep them out of the dew, headed toward the cairn—a large structure made of granite boulders that stood out in the huckleberry field beyond Synton's lawn. It had been built in 1897, and every summer morning of his life my grandfather had gone out before breakfast and raised the flag. Now Baba did it for him.

To reach the circular platform on the cairn you had to climb a ladder with flat steps so close together that you could hardly get a toehold. Baba gathered up her heliotrope skirts and went up it like a queen, the flag in her arms. I scrambled after her and we stood for a moment looking out over the world. We could see the blue wall of the ocean on the southern horizon and the water tower across the harbor. All around us were the thickets of berry bushes, covered with little bells and laced with greenbrier. A faint, winy fragrance rose from them.

"A blue day!" said Baba with a smile. "Well, up with the colors!"

I unwound the halyards from their cleat on the flagpole, and while Baba held the flag I snapped the clips into the grommets. Then we stood back, and when I pulled Baba loosed the folds of bunting until suddenly the whole flag was free, red and white stripes unrolling into the sunny air and all the stars visible. I pulled it up to the top of the pole, fastened the halyards and watched it play in the breeze. For a full minute Baba and I stood there looking up in silence. Then she came back to me, her eyes familiar and gay again.

"Northeast wind," she said.

Following the flag raising Baba sat at her desk writing letters in her elegant, illegible scrawl, and then I helped her move the flats of seedlings into the windows where the sun was. We turned each one so the little plants would grow straight, and Baba told me what they were: calendula, petunia, cosmos, zinnia, lettuce, cabbage, broccoli, and marigold. The list went on and on. They seemed to me perfectly charming lined out on the dark earth, and I loved the different greens—the blue green of cabbage seedlings, yellow green of lettuce, and bright Irish green of parsley.

Some flats were not up yet and had panes of glass over them. We peered at every one.

"Look," said Baba. "My columbines are up," and I saw tiny bluish fists pushing aside crumbs of soil. I had never seen seeds coming up in the house before. It was a magic thing.

After this we walked in the gardens, where the English primroses were out in butter-yellow bunches by the path and pale pink carpets of little square flowers spilled out over the flagstones. The cool air was full of the musky scent of many daffodils.

"Moss pink—phlox subulata, say it!" Baba commanded. It was the pink carpet.

"Moss pink—phlox subulata," I repeated, quite unaware that I was speaking Latin. I had no difficulty at all doing this and never once connected the flower names with the insane gibberish taught by Shinola in school.

"See this daffodil," said Baba, bending over a clump of fat double ones, yellow as scrambled eggs. "One of the oldest known. Van Sion."

I looked at Van Sion with respect.

All over the garden daffodils and tulips held the sun in their cups. In the little triangles and squares where vegetables grew were spring onions, radishes, and rosettes of young lettuce.

"Peas," said Baba, pointing to a long ruffle of leaves.

I liked the garden in its spare May dress. Everything was lower; the steeples of delphinium and hollyhock were missing. Where I walked in summer chin deep in petals was space. There was a lot of rich chocolate earth visible, and some ancient urge rose in me to dig it up, to plant seeds.

"Bleeding heart. Dicentra spectabilis," said Baba, setting the loop of valentines swaying with the tip of a gloved finger.

"Bleeding heart. Dicentra spectabilis."

Baba was just explaining to me that all daffodils were called *narcissus* when she interrupted herself.

"Look, look—a flying violet," she cried, and there was a little butterfly, powder blue, feckless and gay, dancing over the myrtle bed by the cottage.

"I wish I could plant something," I said.

"You shall. It's time we started you on a garden," said Baba. "The cottage beds will be yours."

I wanted to start at once but first we had to do the flowers for the house, one of a lady's most important jobs. I gathered a big bunch of daffodils and Baba collected some primroses and blue hyacinths for a centerpiece.

"Now you choose a flower for the bud vase," she said. "Just one, the most perfect."

After some thought I chose a slender spray of small deep-yellow blossoms that smelled like bananas.

"Ah," said Baba, pleased. "Jonquils. Remember, *these* are the only jonquils. Never, *never* call a daffodil a jonquil!"

"I won't," I said quickly.

Indoors we went over the vases and chose the right ones for our bouquets. The jonquils went in a bud vase to stand on the Empire card table in the drawing room. Baba explained that the Japanese hardly ever used more than one flower or branch in an arrangement. She then put on her work clothes—an old silk coat, a panama hat, and gray cloth gloves—and got her parrot-nosed clippers and her hoe from the shop. It was time to clear her trees.

On our tree-clearing operations Baba did some good hard labor, hauling down greenbrier, clipping off bushes, and pruning the little trees themselves. All over the hill were sample trees and shrubs sent her by the Arnold Arboretum for experimental purposes, and she kept them in excellent shape. In the process she did some vigorous hoeing on the road. Pop had put in a lot of thank-you-ma'ams for draining the steep places, but she said they were too rough. Thank-you-ma'ams, in case you didn't know it, are substantial bumps built across steep sections of a dirt road to prevent its washing out. They also send the passengers of a car through the roof unless the driver goes slowly. Pop had once caused Baba to hit the ceiling of our car, crushing some things like black snakes which graced the crown of her hat. Ever since she had been against thank-you-ma'ams.

"Greatle better to smooth them out," she said, hacking away.

("Greatle" was Baba's word for "great deal.")

When we had scraped most of the thank-you-ma'ams into the ditch we went down into the brook woods and found a whole colony of white violets on the green plush moss by the brook. I learned the name of the little ferns that clothed one of the big rocks—*polypody.* Then Baba saw a flat stone she wanted for her rockery so she picked it up and we went home.

"I like to get up a good perspiration," she said surprisingly. (Ladies couldn't say "sweat.")

This whole operation involved so much physical work that I found it hard to understand how ladies could do it. If they could work on the road why couldn't they wash dishes or cook?

At my rest that day we read Jane Austen—a book called *Pride and Prejudice,* in which there were so many ladies talking about being ladylike that I was utterly disgusted. The men were appalling and seemed to have no jobs. All they did was ride horseback and pay calls. There was a lot of talk about whether or not somebody was a gentleman.

It was some time before I could figure out what a gentleman was, but finally I realized that one of his virtues was he never *did* anything. Baba's father was a gentleman and there was a miniature on ivory of him leaning against a mantel with his hands drooping like lilies. ("He had very distinguished hands.") You could see the blue veins in those white hands, and what with the simper on the lips and the Pendennis coiffure the effect was quite powerful.

"What did he do?" I asked respectfully.

"He did not have to do anything," said Baba. "He was a gentleman of leisure."

"You mean he never went to work?" I asked in amazement. "Where did he get money?"

"He was very comfortably off," said Baba, a little stiffly. "Ladies do not discuss money, you know."

It appeared that the gentleman of leisure was just like the gentleman in *Pride and Prejudice.* He rode horseback and paid calls.

"Every morning at ten o'clock, James, the groom, brought the horse Beauty around to the front door and my father went for a ride. Beauty was a very spirited horse," said Baba proudly.

We went on to discuss the Jane Austen ladies. I said I found them silly. Why were they always worried about being proper?

"Because ladies must learn to behave properly," said Baba. "If girls aren't trained in the right way they are rowdies and no man wants to marry a rowdy."

Rowdies, she said, played with "rough boys" and were "loud."

"Loud?" I asked.

"They talk too loud and laugh in a loud, vulgar way—'The loud laugh that spoke the vacant mind,' " said Baba.

"Oh," I said.

Ladies couldn't whistle either.

> Whistling girls and crowing hens
> Always come to some bad end,

said Baba gaily.

Ladies, said Baba, always carried a clean handkerchief. Their white gloves were always spotless. It was important that they wear gloves and wide-brimmed hats when in the sun to keep their skins white. A true lady had pretty hands—soft and white to show that she never used them for rough work. Their long hair was their "crowning glory." Aunt Sis, Baba's elder sister, had been able to sit on her hair, and Baba showed me a photograph to prove it. It was part of a set that Uncle Scott, Aunt Sis's husband, had ordered taken of her.

"Of course, this was for Scott only," said Baba, a little flustered, "but I think it is proper for you to see it as it is quite decent —if a little—a—"

She handed me a sepia photograph presumably of Aunt Sis, but all you could see was a great tent of hair and the heels of a pair of shoes.

"Why did Aunt Sis want to sit on her hair?" I asked, but Baba didn't reply to this silly question and put the photograph away.

I had no wish to sit on my hair but Aunt Sis, whom I adored, was undoubtedly the most enchanting and pretty person I knew. She had been a belle of the Hudson River Valley and had been called the Beautiful Mary Boyd. She was also merry and gay and wore heavenly clothes of silk and velvet, in shades of apricot and gold to go with her auburn hair which in the daytime was wound into a shining coronet of coils and braids. When outdoors she carried a delicious frilly parasol and was swathed in diaphanous veils and gloved to the elbow. She always smelled sweet and sparkled with jewels and was the best argument for being a lady I knew. However, the price was too high. I still wanted to be Robin Hood, and at that moment I really was a sort of outlaw in the Sherwood Forest of the hill.

Following my rest Baba changed her dress for an afternoon costume of some richer material. This, she explained, was in preparation for callers and afternoon tea. While waiting for the callers she rested on her Empire sofa and read the paper, and I went out with Aunt K. and started my garden. She gave me tools and some packages of nasturtium seeds with gorgeous orange and yellow pictures on them.

"There," she said. "All yours."

With the soft spring sun on my back and my knees in the new grass I went over the earth in my beds until there wasn't a lump or a pebble in it. As I crumbled the clods in my fingers a faint clovery sweetness came from them. The little blue butterflies danced by and I lost all track of time. Gardening seemed to me the perfect pastime. I poked holes in the earth with my finger and dropped a big wrinkled seed in each one until my packets were empty. Then I impaled the packet on a sharp stick, which I set in the ground the way Aunt K. did when she planted anything. It was utterly satisfactory, and I sat back on my heels to look at my work. I was glad there was *something* ladies could do that was fun.

That evening Baba read aloud to me from *The Secret Garden,*

which was a great improvement over Jane Austen. Afterward
while I read to myself she looked at a novel to see if it was suitable
for the library which she and Aunt K. sponsored in the village.

Apparently it wasn't, for she tore out pages at intervals and
threw them in the fire.

"Horrid!" she said.

"What was it about?" I asked.

"Never mind," said Baba, pursing her lips.

"No, never you mind!" said Tink virtuously. "Siskusty, dear
Jan!"

He had been waked by a bonfire of several pages and obviously knew what was going on.

The warblers came on time. I saw the yellow palm warbler
in the brook woods one day when I was down there picking violets.
When he came I was among the alders by the brook where the
white violets grew. The brook sang along between green velvet
banks, making silvery chinking sounds over miniature waterfalls
and a rustle like taffeta skirts where it ran over pebbles. This water
music always drew the birds, especially warblers, and presently
I heard the feeble "wissa-wissa-wissa-wissa-wissa" of a warbler's
voice, the first since the previous summer. In a moment or two
the yellow palm with his chestnut cap appeared, wagging his tail
up and down exactly as he was supposed to.

A few days later the big waves of warblers began pouring
through. One morning I woke when my window was still full of
stars, and against the eastern sky the twin spruces were like
pagodas of ebony. I lay and listened for the first notes of the
dawn chorus, one of the loveliest experiences in life, which most
people sleep through.

As the stars faded a robin gave a sleepy chirrup and others
answered him. Then a catbird caterwauled from the lindens near
my room. I got out of bed and knelt by the window. In the east
the rosy light welled up, touching the rows of little clouds until
they looked like flamingoes in flight formation. Bird after bird

burst into song, and then through the full-throated, silver-piped symphony I heard the warblers coming in. Dropping down the sky they signaled to each other in wiry insect voices, and in no time they had joined the chorus—buzzing, sizzling, zeeping, and chippering as they began to feed.

When Aunt K. and I went out to do the chores the trees and bushes were full of yellow flirtings and exciting flashes of blue and orange. In the stillness before the breeze rose the air shimmered with insects, gnats whirling in some mystic dance, flies of all kinds, a million gauzy wings caught in the low sunlight. These were the warblers' breakfast.

The worst thing about warbler watching is that you have to spend so much time craning your neck at black specks in the treetops. I solved this by going up in the trees myself. I practically lived in Baba's spruces, where I had a secret hideout. This was a special hammock-shaped branch about halfway to the top, where I used to lie and rock in the breeze.

A branch had broken off during the winter, leaving in its place a spicy, prickly green cave, full of sun, with a curved branch to lie on. The wind hummed in the needles; the great tree sighed and breathed out fragrance. I could hear birds warbling, Aunt K.'s hens crooning, the surf on the beaches going "hush-hoosh" very softly in the distance. It was an ideal perch for watching birds, and the whole tree with its wide platforms of needles, its inner thickets, and sunny outer slopes was like a private mountain or forest to me and its other inhabitants. Warblers, who love evergreens, searched the branches for food, probing, peering, snatching, and making quick flycatcher sallies into space after insects on the wing. Sometimes one came so close I could see the filmy edges of its feathers and the stiff hairs around its bill.

Once each day I took Snowdon's key and went out on my upstairs porch. I didn't like the lonely sunlight in the empty rooms but it was all right on the porch because the trees were full of life. You can't be too lonely outdoors, I've found. Some of my best friends are chickadees. Perched on the broad railing overlooking the river woods I waited with my binoculars at the ready, and presently the warblers arrived. I could see them in the woods below me, playing tag and diving, twirling in pairs high in the air, zeeping angrily. Entranced I watched them, recognizing the dazzling black, white, and gold of the magnolia, the smoke-blue and yellow of the parula, and the elegant white shirtfront of the chestnut-sided. The baby oak leaves were like snippets of chartreuse silk and pink velvet, as tender and soft as the wings of newly hatched moths. They made an exquisite setting for the warblers with their tropical colors. I think it was the beauty of these miniature birds rather than their identification that charmed me. A redstart hovering under a branch like a great black-and-orange butterfly, a yellow warbler among the rose velvet grape leaves or a Canada, ash gray and daffodil yellow, probing among the green-gold oak catkins—all these bright little vignettes were unforgettable additions to my bank account of memories. I still have them—as vivid as they were that spring.

I was pleased and surprised that the male warblers in their breeding plumage looked exactly like their portraits in Forbush, whose warbler plates I knew by heart. I spent hours poring over Pop's bird books, with their beautiful paintings by Louis Agassiz Fuertes, so I really knew the warblers almost as well as Pooh and Piglet.

Day after day I pursued my warbler studies. I really worked hard. I deserved an A+ in Warblers and if you can get a B.A. degree in Advanced Poultry and Chick Sexing, which you can, I don't see why you shouldn't be able to get credit for Warblers.

Botanically I was in good shape, too. My garden was up and I had dozens of spring-flower entries in my notebook.

As for my qualifications as a lady I'm not so sure. Before I left to go home I had a final lesson on behavior at a public function. Part of a lady's training was to say "prunes and prisms" just before entering a room. This arranged one's mouth in a pretty shape. Baba stood with her neat head on one side, her bright brown eyes fixed on me and her lips forming the shameful words.

"Now, dear Jan, let me hear you," she said afterward.

There was a moment's pause while I wrestled with my rowdy

old nature. Then, because I loved Baba, I did it.

"Prunes and prisms," I muttered.

"Now, now, chin up, stand straight. Again!"

"Prunes and prisms."

"That's better. Once more."

"Prunes and prisms."

Once you got into the room with your mouth all pursed up you had to curtsy to the guests if you were a little girl. Otherwise you bowed. Curtsying was so embarrassing I could hardly stand it, but I consented to hold out the legs of my bloomers and bob up and down, hitting the floor in back of me with my toe.

Physically I was in excellent health; the program had worked. Now I had to go home.

Back in Latin class Shinola was teaching my classmates to sing a foul song called "I'm Forever Blowing Bubbles," which that malignant woman had translated into Latin. When her eyes rested on me she gave a harsh laugh.

"Have a good vacation?" she shouted.

I looked at a bust of Julius Caesar and remained silent. Ladies don't go in for vulgar wrangling in public.

Fortunately the school year was almost over and I passed out of Shinola's sphere forever. We went back to the Point as usual, and I was able to preside at the first flights of many of my former nestlings. I also discovered to my delight that many of the warblers I had seen in the spring were nesting right on the hill. A prairie warbler sang his tremulous scale from the tip of a juniper by the path to Synton and I later found the nest beautifully lined with the coppery stems of one of the mosses. Pop spotted a black-throated green's nest in our white cedar, and we kept a stepladder there for daily checkups on the eggs and nestlings. It was clear that other warblers were nesting in the woods, and I spent hours crouched behind bushes trying to track down the nests.

Aldie made scathing remarks about my activities in this line.

He ridiculed my clothing and said nobody liked girls who were interested in Nature.

"Why don't you cut your hair?" he asked. "You look just like a campfire girl."

That summer he seemed irritable and restless and complained that his head kept hitting the ceiling of his studio so he had to paint out on the porch. I couldn't figure out what was the matter with him, but it finally turned out he was just growing up and was, in fact, way ahead of me. He talked about girls and much to Pop's alarm began doing sketches of naked women. What's more, they were *good*.

CHAPTER TEN

Art and Agriculture

ALTHOUGH DAVE AND I had several irons in the fire and were un-decided as to our final choice of career, Aldie had never once deviated from the course Baba had chosen for him. It became in-creasingly clear that he really had talent as well as the artistic temperament, and Pop was out of his depth. He had given the boys special instruction in the use of tools, how to throw a ball, how to swing a scythe, and other skills essential to the develop-ment of the male. Dave was an apt pupil, but although Aldie was an excellent athlete he could hardly drive a nail and spent most of his time at his easel. Pop was afraid he wasn't getting enough fresh air and exercise, as he seldom went swimming or sailing with us. Aldie let it be known that he hated water and didn't even like taking baths—just like a real artist in a garret. He had out-grown his studio in the cottage and shifted his operations to his bedroom. As a result his privacy, so essential to the artist, was at an end, and everybody in the family could see what he was up to. It now became apparent that he had stopped copying old masters and doing pretty little studies of the hill and the sand dunes and was painting human figures, starting with himself, the only avail-able model he had. After several self-portraits he consented to do a portrait of Pop sitting in his Morris chair reading. This was an amazingly good likeness although Pop complained that his suit looked as though he'd slept in it.

"That's the way all your suits look," said Mum. "That's what I keep telling you."

Pop tried to get Aldie to paint a portrait of Mum, but Aldie said he didn't like doing portraits. One morning shortly after this I met him on the stairs in hand-to-hand combat with the gigantic Sistine Chapel screen, which he was trying to drag up to his room. This hideous monstrosity was a sepia photograph of Michelangelo's masterpiece framed in golden oak and mounted on an all-but-immovable base of lead. We had loathed it all our lives and often sustained quite painful injuries falling over the base.

"What are you doing with that?" I asked amazed.

"I'm going to use it to study anatomy," he said, pausing to mop his brow. "Real artists have to learn where the muscles and things are, and at art school they draw from nude models. All I've got is the *Geographic* and this."

"The *Geographic*'s better than this thing," I said, peering at a heavy-set female with biceps like a prize fighter. We had all spent hours riffling through the *Geographics* for photographs of natives wearing nothing but a string of beads or in some cases a conch shell, very uncomfortable looking.

Aldie said the *Geographics* weren't art and the screen was. He added bitterly that the only naked women he'd ever been able to see were some he'd spied on over the tops of the bathhouses, struggling into their bathing suits or putting on corsets.

"Once I saw The Fiddle," he said, shuddering.

"Serves you right," I said as I had suffered considerably from this aspect of the boys' research.

He then showed me a portfolio of sketches he had made— detailed pencil drawings of arms, legs, bottoms, heads, hands, and a lot more bosoms. Pop would have been horrified that a pure young girl had looked on such sights but I found them very instructive and quite beautiful—a lot better than Michelangelo's.

"Hey, these are great," I said, "but you'd better not let Pop see them."

"Do him good," said Aldie.

Shortly after this interchange Pop strolled into his son's room to admire the canvas on the easel and saw a drawing of the female bosom lying in full view on the bureau.

"What's this, fella?" he asked, using a dear-old-dad form of address.

"Don't you know?" asked Aldie.

"Look, boy," said Pop, frowning. "I asked a simple question."

"It's a detail of a nude," said Aldie.

Pop said he didn't like to see "this sort of thing" in the home.

"The real test of this sort of thing," he said, "is whether you would want your mother or your sisters to see it. Can you imagine your mother or your sister posing like that for an artist?"

"Holy cats, Pop," said Aldie. "What's that got to do with it? What if they did see it? They're women and they know what they look like. Anyway, what's wrong with the human body? It's beautiful."

"Some things are supposed to be private and that's one of them," said Pop. "There's such a thing as decency."

"You mean you think the human body is indecent?" asked Aldie.

Pop, as he usually did with Aldie, had fallen into a trap of his own making. He quickly changed his tactics.

"I suppose you'd like to see everybody going around with no clothes on?" he asked. None of the older generation at that time could use the word "naked." When they were forced to refer to this regrettable condition they said delicately that there was "nothing left to the imagination."

"Look, Pop," said Aldie, "I copied this off the Sistine Chapel ceiling that you had right down in the living room where everybody could see it. It's crawling with nudes. Adam hasn't a stitch on. Neither has Eve."

"That's different," said Pop. "It's the ceiling of a church. Those are biblical scenes." But he was confused.

"What's the difference between a naked woman who's supposed to be Eve and any old naked woman?"

"You know perfectly well what I mean," said Pop, who clearly had no idea what he meant himself. He was in another trap and he knew it.

I think Mum must have talked to him about Aldie's anatomical studies or else he had decided on a more positive approach to the problem. He asked why Aldie didn't paint a nice picture of a square-rigger like the *Charles W. Morgan* or do the view from the upstairs porch. He had always wanted a painting of the view. But Aldie said the view had no composition and anyway he couldn't paint things other people wanted. However, he did paint a picture of the boathouse because a rich guest said he'd give him twenty-five dollars for it. Pop was delighted and asked why Aldie couldn't paint him a picture of the boathouse, but Aldie said he couldn't paint the same thing twice. He then did some beautiful beach scenes, but he almost always managed to insert a nude figure into the picture. Sometimes it was himself sitting naked on a camp stool painting a tiny canvas of the same scene. Pop said he wished he would just once do a seascape without somebody's bottom in it. Every now and then he thought there was one and then he'd see a tiny nude woman way off in the distance or a little naked man peeking around a tree. Finally he gave up. Assuming his poor-old-geezer pose he said he was just a country boy, just a farmer from the sticks, and knew nothing about art.

"That's right, you don't," I said, for it was true.

"You are not a country boy," said Mum sternly, "and you're not a farmer either. You lived on a city street in Utica and your father was in business." But Pop liked the picture he was making of himself and began to improve the role by dropping his g's.

"I don't know what things are comin' to," he said, "but I know what I like."

Aldie uttered a wordless cry.

"I'm not ashamed to admit," said Pop, warming to his work, "that I enjoy a pretty landscape, sumpin' you can live with in the home. Your mother and I love the old masters and pictures that mean something to us." His voice broke.

"You mean like Hope by Watts?" asked Aldie.

"Hope" by Watts was a sepia reproduction of a nineteenth-century painting which showed a lightly clothed female playing a harp while perched on top of the world. Her eyes, if I remember rightly, were bandaged and on the whole I think it was the worst picture I ever saw. It hung in our upstairs hall.

Pop sidestepped a discussion of "Hope" and said he meant things like "The Sistine Madonna" or "The Monarch of the Glen" by Landseer. Or, he added, the picture over the fireplace.

"Now there," he said, "is a beautiful thing."

The picture over the fireplace was a French railway poster showing two white-trunked birch trees in golden autumn leaf. There was a pool strewn with fallen leaves and there was a small ivy-covered church in the background. Pop had brought it back from France after the war and even Aldie hesitated to criticize this sacred object, which somehow symbolized the Point and summer. Still, when I now looked at it, I realized that instead of being the most beautiful painting in the world it was just a French railway poster. I didn't know much about art, but close association with Aldie had infected me with the collecting fever, this time of what the family called "art pictures." Aldie and I had rival collections and my exposure to the Perry Picture catalogue while assembling pictures of birds and their nests had opened up a rich vein of reproductions—all sepia, unfortunately, but with an intoxicating list to choose from. The most coveted treasures, though, were the Medici prints, beautifully and accurately colored, which could be bought in the large sizes as well as in the cards sold by museums.

That summer Baba had forced Pop to drive us up to Boston to the Museum of Fine Arts, which was our first art museum and a revelation. Pop had a rather grim time, as he ran into a car in Copley Square and nearly sent Baba through the windshield. While he was talking to the police we sat in the car in front of the public library, and a man with a fascinating form of elephantiasis came over and collected a quarter from Baba, presumably for the privilege of looking at him. The combination of this incident and the fact that her son-in-law was in the hands of the police caused Baba to assume her most austere, queenly pose, and as she was already in full city regalia she was an awesome presence in the Artful Dodger's front seat. By the time we entered the museum's portals she looked exactly like a miniature Queen Marie of Rumania, and the uniformed officials all but salaamed before her. We had the royal treatment, and the whole affair gave the world of art and artists an aura of glamour. Right there I began my art collection by purchasing the entire postcard set of Puvis de Chavannes's murals, which Baba greatly admired. Pop trailed after us like some sort of lackey, tired and depressed by his tussle with the law and Baba's remote manner.

Later in the summer he organized an expedition to New York, where he took us to the Frick Collection and the Metropolitan—a major coup. At the Metropolitan I saw a painting by Alma-Tadema called "The Pasha's Grief," which portrayed a dead tiger lying on an oriental rug strewn with rose petals and with a turbaned character, no doubt the pasha, weeping by its head. Every hair of the tiger was painted clearly, and you could see every vein in the rose petals. I thought this a great work of art, but luckily I had also fallen in love with the Winslow Homers and Breughel's "The Harvesters" with its golden wheatfields and all those men in codpieces lying under trees. Aldie and I bought an enormous number of colored postcards in the shop by the door, although "The Pasha's Grief" was unfortunately not among them. When we went home we told Pop that the pictures which covered the walls of Snowdon and Synton were not art. We even attacked the steel engraving of "The Cricketer" in Synton's dining room and, worse, "The Charge of the Scot's Grays" over Baba's sideboard. We took down a lot of the sepia pictures of cathedral interiors and Highland cattle at Snowdon, but I am happy to say that both Pop and Mum put up a spirited defense of their tastes and rehung every one.

"This is our house," said Pop firmly, "and we'll hang any dad-gasted thing we feel like," but he admitted humbly that where art and artists were concerned he was completely uneducated. He was very proud of Aldie and tried hard to learn what "these modernistic fellas" were trying to do. He bought a huge book on the history of art and studied it faithfully, but every time he found a picture he liked Aldie would say it was no good. The truth was Pop loved sentimental pictures that told a story and were as clear as colored photographs, or inspirational master-pieces like the one of Sir Galahad and his horse by (I think) Burne-Jones. There was a really ghastly picture by Holman Hunt of Jesus, wearing a crown of thorns and carrying a lantern, called something like "I Am the Light of the World," which made Pop croak with emotion. In the end he managed to learn a few simple facts about the artists' tools and the various media in which they worked. Here was something tangible he could get hold of, for he loved and understood all good craftsmen. After a while when he went up to bed he would say, "This is a drypoint etching of R. W. on his way upstairs," and the next night it would be a lithograph, a woodcut, or a pastel.

Where Aldie was concerned Pop was like a mother hen who has hatched out a wild goose and is watching it take to the water. In this trying period he was greatly comforted by Dave, who loved to work with tools and was already an excellent carpenter. Better still, he wanted to be a farmer just as Pop did himself. He wore overalls and a farmer's straw hat and showed a healthy interest in manure, that cornerstone of agriculture. Together, he and Pop pored over seed catalogues and planned a huge vegetable garden that was to be a miracle of fertility, fed with compost and well-rotted manures of the best quality. Pop found a farmer with a team of horses and a plow and watched, radiant with joy, while the silver plowshare turned back the sod and revealed the good earth, brown and rich as chocolate cake. His joy was momentarily dimmed when the plow crashed into a boulder the size of a sperm whale and the farmer gave vent to some very earthy expletives. A stone expert was called in and after a short period of tapping and listening to the boulder he split it into a thousand pieces with a few well-directed blows. Pop was in ecstasy—here was what he loved most in the world: an old-timer who knew his craft. The removal of the boulder left a crater in the garden which Pop and

Dave filled with garbage, compost, and manure. It subsequently proved to be the richest spot in the garden, and Pop used it over and over in sermons as an example of how a disability could be turned into one's greatest asset.

When the garden was finally planted and the seeds came up in ruler-straight rows it looked just like a picture in Dreer's seed catalogue. At one end were the shining fountains of young corn with the broad tents of summer squash at their feet. At the other end were the staked tomato plants and in between orderly rows of carrots, beets, parsley, radishes, and lettuce, beautiful to look upon. There was a whole section devoted to potatoes and there were two long trellises of peas. Pop and Dave were out there all the time hoeing, weeding, thinning, and dusting with rotenone, the only insecticide they used. They had a bag of cow manure soaking in a barrel on the front lawn; it smelled to heaven and made an ideal breeding place for mosquitoes, but they loved it and kept dipping out jarfuls to admire the color. When in June the garden was well up, they fed it drinks of this brew and claimed the plants doubled in size overnight. In fact Dave was progressing by leaps and bounds toward his career as agricultural missionary to India as Baba had planned. Aunt K., who had given him the freedom of the barn and chicken house, claimed that he had said to her, "My life is a straight road with India at the end," but nobody really believed this and Dave hotly denied having said it. What he did say morning, noon, and night was that he had to have a thing called a Planet Junior, a sort of hand plow or cultivator with two handles and a wheel in front. Never in my whole life did I hear anyone talk so much about anything as Dave did about that Planet Junior. He had found it in Dreer's catalogue and the name Dreer was constantly on his lips. It was Dreer this and Dreer that and then more about the Planet Junior until Aldie and I nearly lost our minds.

"For Pete's sake, shut up about Dreer's," shouted Aldie one day when Dave had been lecturing on the subject all during dinner, "and if I hear you mention that Planet Junior again I'll go out and rip up all your lettuce."

Dave's method worked, however, and finally Baba gave him the Planet Junior.

Pop was nearly as bad, and the two of them could talk for any amount of time about the virtues of Golden Bantam corn as opposed to Country Gentleman. Pop was absolutely maudlin about the garden, and he loved to go out before the noon meal and pick the vegetables for the day. He liked to have one of us along so he could reminisce about the Old Farm and philosophize about life in general, especially the joy of working with the earth and growing your own food. I was usually the one who volunteered because I felt exactly as he did about the garden. On sweet June mornings with the gulls calling from the river and the clean clothes billowing like sails on the line nearby, he and I would pick peas, twisting off the light grass-green pods and dropping them into our basket and every now and then splitting open a pod and eating the peas too tiny to cook. Later on when it was hotter we would pick beans and the yellow crookneck squashes hidden under their umbrella leaves. The first corn—which Pop called "green-corn" in one word—was a major event and so was the first ripe tomato, warm from the sun, but the best fun was digging potatoes. Every hill was like a cache of buried treasure, and we gathered up bushels of Early Rose and ate the little "pig potatoes" for lunch with butter and parsley.

Dave was not, however, as single-minded as Aldie and ran an eel business on the side, peddling eels to all his relatives and selling any crabs he caught to city people for bait. This was not his first business venture. Back in the city he had set up a leaf-mold company, using our compost heap, an old baby carriage, and Bobs, who was a great asset when Dave was trying the soft sell on the old ladies of the neighborhood. As most of his clients were Pop's parishioners and Dave gave the impression of being small and innocent, he netted a fortune—$35 to be exact.

I sometimes helped Dave with his eel business, usually in the humble capacity of rower. Now that Aldie was shut away in his studio so much of the time I missed his raffish, amusing company and the reckless, even dangerous, projects he originated. It was a pleasant surprise to find that Dave, instead of being the nuisance we had thought him, was a merry creature, ready for any adventure that came along. I began helping him with the chores up at the barn and learned a lot about the care and feeding of hens.

Pop was proud of Dave's business acumen as well as his farming skill but his education was, Pop felt, lopsided. He never read anything but Bailey's *Manual of Gardening,* which didn't count as a book, and two others: *Under the 4H Flag* by somebody or other and *Adrift on an Ice Pan* by Sir Wilfred Grenfell. Aldie and I read everything we could get our hands on and Pop read aloud to all of us every evening, but Dave just reread *Adrift on an Ice Pan* and *Under the 4H Flag.* We all went to work on him and finally Aldie and I persuaded him to try an Edgar Wallace mystery story, whose name escapes me. It was not an attractive book, being printed in microscopic type on very cheap paper, brown and flaky with age. For some time Dave frowned over this volume and we thought he was reading it. Then he spoke.

"Listen to this," he said. " ' "It's of your own choosing," said the man with the withered arm.' ' "It's of your own choosing," said the man with the withered arm.' It says that fourteen times in the first chapter. Boy, this is some book. ' "It's of your own choosing," said the man with the withered arm. ' "It's of your own—" ' "

"Shut up!" yelled Aldie.

"All right, you look," said Dave, holding out the book.

We looked and it was amazing. He was right. Naturally this finished that book for him, but the man with the withered arm and his words, "It's of your own choosing," passed into the family language. On one dreadful occasion a guest announced at table that he had a withered arm and was greeted with screams of laughter, but this was the only result of trying to get Dave to read. Pop shelved that idea for the moment and started him building a model yacht. In no time at all Dave became so revoltingly nautical that Aldie and I could hardly stand going sailing with him. He wore his naval officer's cap every waking hour, laying it on the floor beside his bed at night and putting it on the minute he woke up. Evidence of his three conflicting careers have been preserved in a photograph of him standing in his vegetable garden wearing his officer's cap and holding an eel (cleaned) in his mouth. Eventually, however, his honeymoon with the Planet Junior lapsed into a humdrum relationship, the market for eels became saturated and his business folded up, and instead of Bailey's *Manual of Gardening* he read copies of *Yachting,* which he had requested as a birthday present. Beside the boats pictured in this slick magazine even our beloved *Hawick* looked small and unimportant. He said we ought to get a Beetle Cat like the people at the Harbor. Pop said he was sorry to see this trend; we didn't realize how lucky we were to have any boats at all. He was a poor man and we were already living above our income. Most ministers' children didn't have a summer place to go to but had to stay and swelter in the cities.

"Uncle Smith's a minister and he has a summer place. His kids have two sharpies and he has a seagoing sloop," said Dave, who had a one-track mind.

"They have a bathhouse at the beach, too," I said, more as a scoring point than in envy.

"How did bathhouses get into this?" asked Pop. "Are you trying to say you want me to rent a *bathhouse?*"

I denied this unfair accusation. The last thing we wanted then was to get involved with the young of the summer people. I had once or twice been invited to go swimming at the beach club by an adolescent summer person who was my age. She had no brothers, talked about boys all the time, and was clearly boy crazy. It had been very dull compared to our sailing picnics, bird-watching trips, hunts for bootleggers' hideouts and beach-combing orgies. Even Baba's annual expeditions to the Sand Hill Property, although not calculated to send the blood coursing through the veins with excitement, were more interesting than that.

CHAPTER ELEVEN

Beachcombers and Bootleggers

THE SAND HILL PROPERTY which Baba owned was a lovely wide strip of dunes, forest, and marsh, reaching from high-water mark on the beach to the river on the inner side, and including Liniken Island—twelve acres of salt marsh and upland where Captain Kidd was reputed to have buried his treasure.

Baba organized her safaris to the Sand Hill Property with special reference to the blooming time of the wild orchids and marsh rosemary and the ripening of the beach plums. The orchid expedition took place in July and was one of the major floral anniversaries I celebrated with Baba during those enchanted summers before the hurricanes, when pitch-pine forests still stood behind the dunes and the old cranberry bogs shone in the cool green shadows where now there is nothing but hot sand and summer cottages.

For her Sand Hill expeditions Baba chose a blue day when the wind was in the north and the sea sparkled in the sun like a great blue-and-silver pond. She would announce her plan at the after-breakfast summit conference and we would go in two conveyances: Baba, Aunt K., and I in the phaeton and everybody else in the Artful Dodger. I went in the phaeton because I was training to be a lady botanist and had to pay attention to wildflowers instead of just horsing around in the sand dunes with my brothers. We trotted down the main street, across the bridge and down the old shore road, built when the village was over in the dunes.

Then we would park Gyp and the phaeton in the beach-plum bushes and walk through the pines, over the sand hills to the beach. Baba, dressed as though for a trip to Boston, hat, gloves, and all, inspected the beach-plum crop, commented on the condition of the trees, and took a census of the wildflowers in bloom. She always pointed out the hudsonia that grew in heathery clumps in the hollows, the dusty miller with its gray velvet leaves, and the seaside spurge, which spread on the sand lace mats, round as dinner plates or silver dollars with pink stems and tiny green leaves all growing from one taproot. In one place the wild cranberry stitched patterns on the sand and over half-buried timbers the beach pea looped its garlands. Before retracing our steps we would climb the highest dune and look off over the sea to the islands. Then we stared down at the private beach, just to the east of the property, where summer people lay around on the sand or disported themselves in the surf. We watched them with the suspicious curiosity of Indians observing the white man trespassing on his private hunting grounds. Sometimes we spotted an individual wearing a horrid bathing suit, and once we surprised a loving couple closely entwined on the sand—a most instructive sight. Tink and Baba were outraged, although Aunt K. and Mum gave vent to most unsuitable giggles. Pop said he'd like to give that young man a piece of his mind.

On the way back we stopped the horse by a cranberry bog to pick cattails and hunt for the wild orchids—the rose pogonia or snakemouth and the arethusa or dragon's mouth. The bogs were full of the polished dark green leaves of cranberry vines and the little orchids grew on the banks—magenta pink with open snake faces, mysterious and sinister.

Down on the salt marshes was the calopogon, another small orchid, which Baba had invested with a mystic significance. Its violet-pink blossoms on almost invisible wiry stems looked like a swarm of butterflies in the fluffy grass. The visit to the Sand Hill Property ended with a call on the calopogon colony, where we picked one or two sprays for the bud vase.

In late summer Baba made another expedition to the Sand

Hill Property, but this time she came by water, landing on the shore of Liniken Island, where the marsh rosemary grew better than anywhere else. All along the top of the beach were smoky clouds of it, each plant like a miniature tree hung all over with little blue bells. Baba picked several large bunches, which she dried for winter bouquets.

The final excursion was in September, to harvest her beach-plum crop for jelly.

We ourselves visited the bathhouse area only before breakfast on blue mornings, when Pop or Mum would drive the car down onto the beach and go humming up the whole length of it, with us riding the front mud guards or sitting astride the hood. We were often out on the sand when the sun was just climbing out of Buzzard's Bay. A rosy light flushed the lines of crumbling foam and the smooth breasts of gulls. At that radiant hour the beach was still strewn with the treasures of the night. The life guards had not yet raked the private area, so there was often a half-buried beach towel or a red pail left by the summer people. We looked at them as archeologists look at remnants of another civilization, for we were not then aware that we were summer people ourselves.

In the early morning the beach was all ours, and on the whole golden expanse no other human figure moved. The only living things we wanted to see around were gulls and shore birds. At sunrise the sand was still damp and the last high tide had left its freight of tumbled seaweed, shells, and man-made junk, a scalloped flounce stretching up to the blue haze at the harbor. Anything could be there—notes in bottles, whole oars, bailers, rare shells—it was never the same twice. As a family we were inveterate scavengers, dump pickers, ash can searchers, and explorers of abandoned houses, but we were beachcombers first and foremost. There was something particularly romantic about flotsam and jetsam—objects delivered by the sea and left on the clean sand for anyone to find. Scoured by salt water, smoothed and polished by the waves, bleached silver or chalk white by sun, some of these treasures had been traveling for years, antiques of the Atlantic that had suffered a sea change. The bones of a dead bird had become delicate carvings in ivory, bits of broken bottles were transformed into pebbles of frosty aquamarine and emerald, and pieces of wood into abstract sculpture.

Pop and the boys practiced the grosser form of beachcombing, collecting firewood, timbers, cable spools, old deck chairs, and similar heavy articles of salvage. The sight of a perfectly good board on the beach went to Pop's head like wine, for he had a passion for wood, possibly inherited from his ancestor, John Alden, master carpenter of the *Mayflower*.

Mum gathered shells and Irish moss, a rubbery species of seaweed that when boiled with milk made a tasteless white blancmange. We ate this with sugar, and although you couldn't really like it, it was part of the family tradition and summer.

I collected shells primarily, and other cast-off possessions of the creatures of the sea: skates' eggs like purses of black plastic, the thin beige celluloid cases of baby horse shoe crabs, fragments of coral, crab claws, the round porcelain boxes of sea urchins, and sand dollars, each with its five-petaled flower pattern like marble disks etched by a lapidary. My favorite shells were jingles—translucent glittering things shaped like rose petals and colored gold, silver, orange, and pale lemon white. We used to call them "Venus toenails" and Baba strung them together in long ropes to hang against window panes. The bright jingles lay among gentian-blue mussel shells and scallops, boat shells, moon snails, arks, and angel wings. Every now and then there would be a big whelk standing above the small shells like a stranded teapot.

To contain my treasures I used to select one of the big clamshells that lay all over the beach like abandoned dishes. Blue, gray, cream, russet, white, or striped these shells were heavy as hotel china, armored for life on a surf-pounded shore. Horseneck was always strewn with them.

On north days when the wind was off-shore the sea was still, a floor of celestial blue jelly just firm enough to hold the lobster boats that moved across it without a sound. On these mornings the shell windrows contained all kinds of fragile things laid unbroken on the sand, and the waves left exquisite patterns in seaweed, floating out the hairlike fronds and withdrawing so softly that the rosy branches stayed perfectly spread as though still growing in the undersea gardens. I used to collect these pieces of living lace and, imitating the action of the waves, float them out in a dishpan and mount them on stiff paper so I could keep them forever. There was magic in this—preserving something that was almost all water— veins and capillaries of pink gelatine that one hour in the sun could destroy.

While Pop and the boys staggered along the high tide mark dragging their loot I would wander alone at the foam's edge, watching the newest offerings spin shoreward among the bubbles and settle on the blue glaze of reflected sky like little stranded boats. I was happy in my solitude, at one with the day.

After Baba gave me my microscope I discovered a new aspect of beachcombing that was like something out of *Gulliver's Travels.* One delicious blue morning after a storm I was strolling as usual on the edge of the water when I noticed fields of multicolored particles, sweepings of the sea's floor, too small to identify. There were also streaks of raspberry pink which seemed to be a special kind of sand. As the possessor of a microscope I now saw a chance to examine these fragments, so I scraped up a shellful of the colored particles as well as some of the pink sand and took it home to examine. I was by that time accustomed to the magic of the lens, but when I peered down at this slide I was thunderstruck. On the glass were piled handfuls of square-cut diamonds mixed with amber beads and uncut rubies—the spilled contents of a Spanish jewel chest. I checked the slide with my naked eye and there was nothing on it but sand, the stuff we walked on. The next slide was a drift of tiny shells, some like pink butterflies but most of them minia- ture, translucent versions of the ones in my collection, perfect and unharmed by the tumbling waves. Every slide was heaped with treasure, but without my microscope these miracles of beauty were just colored dust. It was a fascinating experience. I felt like a female Gulliver in Lilliput or like one of those characters in a fairy story who are given a magic eye.

We always left the private beach before anyone else appeared, for we didn't go to the beach to see people but to get away from them. Anyway, for our purposes the bathhouse area was worthless after dawn, being all cluttered with bathers, prostrate forms smelling of suntan oil, old ladies sitting in deck chairs, lifeguards flexing their muscles or raking, and family clutches huddled under umbrellas or spread out around picnic baskets, Thermos bottles, and beach toys. At the fashionable swimming hour we went to the beach by water, landing at the upper end on Sandy Beach, which we considered our personal property. A really nice guest was worthy of a Sandy Beach sailing picnic, something we didn't undertake for everybody, as it was a major operation.

Guests were bewildered when we organized a trip to the beach. The road to Horseneck was clearly indicated by signs, the traffic thereto was impossible to ignore, and on every trip to the village or post office cars full of happy bathers could be observed returning from their morning at the bathhouses. However, when we went to the beach we headed downhill to the boathouse, bowed down under picnic baskets, bathing-suit bags, grills, and other junk. After loading this gear into *Mandarin* we rowed out to *Dehra,* transferred the impedimenta and ourselves, made sail, and spent the rest of the morning trying to get through the grass flats, across the tide rip in the boat channel, and over the mussel beds to the river side of the beach. Here we pulled the boats up and everybody went into the dunes to put on bathing suits, bent double behind clumps of goldenrod or in extreme cases lying down in the grass.

We swam in the channel just off the inner beach, *not* in the surf of Horseneck proper around the corner. Pop then built his fire, and the enchanting smells of wood smoke and charred meat filled the air. While this was going on we all pursued our various projects—beachcombing, hole digging, castle building, or bird watching, as the case might be. We hardly ever saw another human being.

From the breakwater, on whose wide stone platforms we had our picnics, we could look down the whole length of Horseneck. A violet mist always hung over the breakers, and far down the sand was a confetti-colored mass which revealed the location of the bathhouses. Every now and then a gay fragment from this drift of confetti detached itself and came up the beach into our territory. We regarded these persons as trespassers, pure and simple, and watched them guardedly until they went away. Who did they think they were? I felt particularly concerned for the birds who nested right on the open sand. A least tern colony occupied an alcove in the dunes, and their beautifully camouflaged eggs lay in hollows between the dunes and the high-tide mark. Olive-tan, splotched with chocolate, they blended perfectly with the sand and bits of sun-dried seaweed. The terns milled over the place like a flock of white butterflies, and when any intruder approached they dive-bombed him, screaming their harsh war cry. The Cities and even the beach walkers from the bathhouse area were too dumb to get the message and flapped beach towels at them, chased them, and trampled all through the nest area. I hated the people who did this with a fierce, primitive hatred.

Near the breakwater the dunes were lower and the sand loose and deep as snow between fountains of beach grass. Here the piping plover hid his nest. Ash gray, the color of dry sand, he ran like a little ghost, his sweet call sounding from all sides as he signaled to his babies. Once I spotted two infinitesimal shadows racing across the sand and only after hard concentration did I see the twins themselves—each a pinch of fluff with a bright eye in it propped up on yellow matchstick legs. I felt responsible for them, so small and precious, and anyone who strode heavily through the nesting ground seemed to me an enemy. Having been made aware since birth of the creatures that shared the earth with us, I didn't realize that most people didn't even know they were there.

This attitude toward the summer people was partly the result of living up on the hill like a highland clan in its glen. Also, ministers like our grandfather, Pop, and Uncle Basil spent so much time tending to their flock in winter that they needed a respite from people, a time for recharging their batteries, seeing their families, and just plain resting. We, however, were not ministers.

A good example of our antisocial point of view is an episode that occurred on a Sandy Beach picnic when Tink was along. As we sailed toward our usual landing place Dave and I saw the head of a man swimming just offshore in our swimming place. We happened to be in *Hawick,* our small sharpie, and the rest of the party were laboring along in *Debra*—an awful vision, with human bodies, dogs, and dunnage covering every surface. Presently the man in the water sighted us and made rapidly for shore in the lee of a small grass flat. When he crawled up on the beach we saw to our delight that he was naked. Wriggling like a snake across the sand he disappeared behind a clump of goldenrod. We were entranced.

"Don't tell anybody," Dave said. We didn't. We all landed and took our swim. Pop built his fire and cooked the steak, and we sat comfortably on the warm sand and ate it. At last Pop stood up to stretch and then he gave an exclamation.

"Somebody's left his clothes here," he said in surprise.

"Oh, has he?" we said innocently. "I wonder where he went."

"He must have gone swimming," said Pop, who could put two and two together as well as anybody. "Gad, I hope he didn't drown."

"Gee, maybe he did," we said, but Pop's quick mind was working on the problem. He began to look around and naturally discovered the poor creature lying with chattering teeth behind the goldenrod.

"My dear sir," we heard Pop say, "this is terrible. I do apologize. We had no idea anyone was here."

He gave the man his clothes and sheltered him with a towel while he dressed. When our victim left he looked darkly upon Dave and me, but we returned his gaze calmly, untroubled by guilt. People who trespassed on our beach deserved what they got.

We paid for this callousness in a way as in the confusion Tink had disappeared. For the rest of the afternoon we searched the beach, combed the sand dunes, and Dave and I walked all the way down to the bathhouses hunting for him. He always thought it exquisitely humorous to run away from Pop. When we returned empty-handed, so to speak, everybody was gathered in a bunch by the boats, scared blue. Suddenly we heard a muffled squeak like somebody laughing with a hand over his mouth. This was exactly what it was and there was Tink lying behind the identical golden-rod clump that had sheltered the naked man. He had been there for two hours, but it was clear he thought the time well spent. Our reactions had been very gratifying and he was in fits of laughter.

As we grew older we ventured alone into the sand-dune coun-try in our endless hunt for bootleggers' hideouts. At the Point the years of Prohibition were romantic and full of excitement. Certain lobster boats, we were told, were rum runners and went out beyond the three-mile limit to collect cases of moonshine or rum—the two were synonymous—from steamers that waited there. Every night people heard the trucks rumbling down to the shore to pick up the vile stuff. Blinking lights were observed—signals from boot-leggers on land to rum runners at sea—just as in a smuggling story by Sir Walter Scott.

Heaven knows what we would ever have done if we had come face to face with a real live bootlegger, but hunting for their hide-outs gave our walks the spice of danger that Aldie, especially, re-quired in any project. He and I had read *The Royal Road to Romance* by Richard Halliburton, an unconventional character who swam in the Taj Mahal's pool *naked* and lived a life of high adventure, usually in defiance of rules and conventions. We didn't have much to work with but we did the best we could with boot-leggers and the wild landscape of the dunes.

The geography of the world of sand was very confusing, for there were so many fan-shaped amphitheatres, curved golden drifts starred with bird prints, and secret hollows, round as bowls, with a russet flush at the bottom where the amber sand grains had settled. Beach grass ran in waves under the bright sun, and on the back of the big dunes it looked like silver fur. In the hollows out of sight and sound of the sea we would stand still and listen to the throb of crickets in the grass and the beating of our own hearts. Sometimes we got so scared that we had to climb to the crest of one of the big dunes, from where we could see the water. There, standing with our bare feet in the top twigs of buried oaks, that the dune had conquered, we would reassure ourselves with the familiar panorama that spread out below us. To the south was the sea full of the blue and white of the summer day; to the north the river and the salt marshes stretched inland in a maze of creeks; and on each side the dune country rolled in waves of ivory and green, pathless and austere.

Even in the heat of our Richard Halliburton phase, I became fascinated with the life of the dunes, evidence of which was written on the sand as on new-fallen snow. Because we had to look out for the tracks of boots (bootleggers naturally wore boots and leggings) we noticed all sorts of other tracks—the charming necklaces of mouse footprints, the asterisks of horned larks and song sparrows, and the long dragging tracks of crows. We saw the circles drawn on the sand by the tips of grass blades—as precise as those drawn by a compass, and we studied messages left by centipedes and spiders. I began to copy these prints into my field book, a practice which filled Aldie with disgust.

"What do you think you are, a girl scout?" he asked. "If you don't look out you'll turn into an old-maid nature lover."

This depressed me but it didn't stop my doing it. Aldie, at intervals, expressed an interest in the bathhouse area and actually made friends with a girl in a white rubber bathing suit. However, he made no efforts to change the status quo on the hill; he just moved on to fresh fields and pastures new. After a while he went to Labrador with Dr. Grenfell (the author of *Adrift on an Ice Pan*), an adventure more in his line than gate crashing the bathhouse society. Dave and I were the pioneers who finally dragged the family off the hill and into a bathhouse, but I doubt if we would have succeeded if we hadn't had help from outside, possibly from God, as it was in His field of jurisdiction. Pop accepted the post of Dean of the Princeton University Chapel, and the structure of family life was shaken to its very foundations. Not only would we move out of New England to *New Jersey,* a state whose exis-

tence we barely recognized, but we would go to the Point in June
on the Fall River boat. We had nothing against New Jersey except
that it seemed incredibly flat and the woods looked all wrong. The
area around Newark with its pig pens and burning dumps left
much to be desired—everything, in fact. But Princeton itself was
beautiful, and that, after all, was where we were going to live, not
the Newark dumps. As for the Fall River boat, this was pure gravy.

Ever since we could remember Pop had been approached by
scouts or spies from other churches and educational institutions
looking for a new minister, president, dean, or whatever. It was as
though Pop were a debutante ready to be married off. Once he had
rashly accepted a proposal from Rochester, New York, and the
movers were practically backing up to the door when the board of
deacons persuaded him to stay and save them from the Holy Ghost
of the moment, who wanted to take over.

One spring Sunday Pop came home and said both Yale and
Princeton had been in the back row. Delegations of tall tweedy
men filed into his study and I suppose he must have accepted
Princeton, but I was delirious at the time with measles. Everybody
had measles and 231 Oak Street was indistinguishable from a lazar
house.

At some point during this upheaval Pop received a copy of
the *Daily Princetonian*, the university newspaper. In the photo-
gravure section was an oval picture of an elderly man unknown to
us and under it the words "Dean Wicks, newly appointed Dean
of the Chapel, preached here on Sunday."

"What in Sam Hill?" cried Pop, staring at this vision.

"That's a great picture of you," said Aldie. "Just great."

"How did you manage to preach in Princeton and here at the
same time?" I asked him. "Nice work."

"Hey, will all of you let a man get a word in edgewise,"
shouted Pop. "I'll have to call Duffield and find what this is all
about. Holy Caesarea Philippi, I wonder who that old geezer is."

"It's you, can't you read? 'Dean Wicks, newly appointed
Dean of the Chapel,'" said Dave, pointing.

"Now, think hard," Aldie said. "You know how you are. Maybe you actually did preach there but somehow went in the wrong body. You never know what you have on."

"That's right," said Pop. "I'm an ass, I know. Ask your mother," and he went off to telephone. Presently he returned and said that by some amazing fluke the university had invited a minister called Wicks from a small town out West to come and speak at the Princeton Chapel. Highly flattered but mystified the man had come and preached.

"Intelligent bunch they must have down there in Princeton," said Aldie. "They have your address, they've *seen* you, and what do they do? Track down some unknown character on the boundaries of civilization. Good thinking. Can't wait to go there."

Pop was considerably upset by this experience but soon forgot it in the cataclysmic period that followed. The whole house was dismantled while upstairs the measles raged and Mum sat by beds reading aloud and sponging foreheads. Finally, she went down to the Point with most of the family and one of the maids. As the last victim of the measles I was left in the city with Pop and a nurse, and after a dim interlude creeping around in a darkened room I recovered and we drove to the Point.

That summer was one of the bluest and most beautiful in the memory of all on the hill and it went on and on through a golden autumn, for we never left. We had no place to go. The university was supposed to be building us a new house—Pop's dream house and a copy of the New England farmhouse he'd always wanted—but according to the unwritten laws of carpenters' unions it wasn't ready on time; in fact, it wasn't ready until after Thanksgiving, so for two whole extra months we stayed on at Westport, sleeping under piled blankets at night and keeping warm with open fires and the coal stove. For the first time we learned what after Labor Day was like and enjoyed the always intriguing experience of seeing what happened at the Point when we weren't there. Once Labor Day was over the family rules for summer ceased to function. It was no longer obligatory to go swimming in the morning and sail all afternoon. We could sail all morning and swim any time or not, according to our fancy. Like my free spring some years before, this enchanted fall was one of life's bonanzas, a gift of time, most precious of all commodities. It was a magic interlude between the old life and the new, as far as I was concerned between childhood and growing up. It was many years before I recaptured the un-clouded joy of those Indian-summer days.

CHAPTER TWELVE

Beeline

A NEW SEASON IN A FAMILIAR PLACE is as exciting as a journey into a foreign country. Because I knew the spring and summer by heart I found these autumn days rich in surprises and discoveries. To see autumn color on our hill and in the marshes, to watch the leaves falling and the waterfowl flying in for the winter was endlessly fascinating.

These mornings were full of twitterings as migrating warblers came through the woods and the chickadees and kinglets gathered to spend the winter. Blue jays gobbled acorns in the oaks, whose leaves slowly turned a deep rose color. When the mornings were windless the polished water reflected the soft colors of the woods on both shores. This in itself was like a strange dream; all the bunched green forests we knew so well changed to raspberry pink. I had seen such miracles before through the stained-glass windows on Victorian staircases. Before sunrise the river was like a pink mirror where all the fishing herons were reflected upside down. Sometimes there were as many as thirty great blues standing with outstretched necks in the shallows watching for fish or crabs. Several times, through my binoculars, I saw one catch a sizable fish, at least six inches long, that flashed blue above and silver below. Tinker mackerel, I believe they were, because we got them ourselves in the fish market.

Every morning when the dew had dried on the grass and the chores were done we took our walking sticks and swaggered off into the world. These sticks were derived from the quarterstaffs of Robin Hood as well as those rakish poles with bandana bundles tied to them which people in fairy tales slung over their shoulders when they went forth to seek their fortunes.

We were happy vagabonds, free of school and all the dismal commitments of dancing class, music lessons, and Junior Choir, dressed like bums in our favorite old clothes and content with our own company. The sun would melt the frost out of the day by eleven, so the noons were like warm honey, golden and sweet. Before four the crispness would come back and the sunsets were wintry. Mum, who had learned to cook by then, made us little suppers that tasted wonderfully good, and then we'd build up the fire and draw our chairs up close around the kerosene lamp while she read Joseph C. Lincoln aloud. Every night was the same, and we eventually got through the complete works of this New England hero.

We slept like logs after all that walking and woke up to another breakfast of oatmeal, boiled eggs, and homemade bread toasted, the routine breakfast of those with Scotch forebears.

We had never walked much in the summers except on the beach. If you have to swim in the morning and sail all afternoon there's not much of the day left. To go *inland* away from the water was almost as painful to us as going to the city. Anyway, summer is too hot for walking. There are mosquitoes and horseflies and poison ivy; the countryside is choked and smothered in leaves, the bunched trees puff up like green featherbeds, the distances shimmer with heat waves, and the whole idea of land is stifling. Only the Cities and those odd types who go to the mountains in the summer are content to be inland on a blue day. In the fall, though, conditions are ideal for walking; the ground is dry and firm, the colors of the country spectacular, and something in the air makes you tireless. At the Point going inland was one way to get out of the wind which blew up every afternoon to a near gale. Sailing was all but impossible and it was too cold to swim, so we started walking. A whole new world opened up for us of inland pastures unexplored, cowpaths leading us into little dells where springs kept the grass green, or up onto moors where nothing grew but junipers in great heathery circles.

Out family temperament being what it is, we couldn't simply go for a *walk*. We had to turn it into something else, preferably something involving risk. Pop, on one of his weekends from being Dean of the Chapel in Princeton, invented the beeline.

Our family had over the years invented a great many games as well as corrupted those invented by others. Crennis, for instance, was a form of tennis played with croquet mallets and balls, probably the most dangerous game of any in our repertory. Porchie, a game for males only, was played with the rung of a chair and a softball on the porchie court (the veranda), and finally had to be abolished because Pop said the house was being destroyed. Sline, using the round covers of cracker tins, was later patented by some low character under the name of Frisbie. But the greatest of all our inventions was the beeline. It could not be patented because it required no equipment and the only comparable activity was the Marine Corps training program.

One of Pop's Old Farm stories was about lining bees with Uncle Duane during his summers at Paris Hill. This involved catching bees in matchboxes, marking them with a dab of red paint, and releasing them from several different points. Since the honeybee always flies in a straight line, the place where these lines intersect is the bee tree or hive. We toyed briefly with the idea of doing this, but it turned out that all that matchbox-and-red-paint stuff was unnecessary as the lines of the local bees intersected right over Synton—in the gable over the maid's room, to be exact—and finding the hive was childishly simple. All you had to do was stand in the maid's room and listen to the bees roaring around overhead. The house was full of them, people got bitten, and finally Baba decreed that the swarm should be removed. Part of our education that fall was observing the eviction and the removal of sixty pounds of comb.

The bee man, who seldom shaved and was reputed to be a Harvard graduate, came at dawn with his equipment and climbed up to the gable. We took up our stations nearby and were there to receive every washtub full of honey and comb that he lowered to the ground. The fresh white combs of that June's clover honey were my particular undoing. They came down almost intact, and we broke off big hunks that bled all over our hands. To bite into that delicate geometry was irresistible, and after a while we were sticky from head to foot and smelled like the perfume counter at Bonwit's. Pop, as usual, spent hours talking bee talk with the Harvard graduate, and we all watched the displaced bees zooming about in angry confusion. It was October and naturally they were upset at having to move out just when they had gotten all snug for winter. I forget the end of the story, but it seems to me that the bee man put the queen in a hive and eventually captured the swarm. Much more vivid in my mind is the first trial of that greatest of family sports. Instead of lining bees, Pop suggested that we ourselves go on a beeline, not to find a bee tree but just for fun. Because it was October and the summer's heat over, all the conditions were perfect, and from then on the common walk was a real adventure, full of hazards and new experiences.

The rule for a beeline is simple. Starting from Point A you go straight across country to Point B, *never* turning aside for so much as an inch to bypass any obstacle, however formidable. We were committed to climbing trees, going over or through buildings, crossing bodies of water, invading private property, galloping through fields inhabited by bulls (probably mad), and pressing onward regardless of wind, weather, hunger, exhaustion, time, tide, or human interference until the goal was reached.

Two people are the ideal number for a beeline, although when Pop was around he took along as many of us as he could round up. A beeline with Pop was always memorable, and on one of the first he plunged directly into the woods to the north of the house, where the greenbrier was like a barbed-wire entanglement. We climbed over a couple of oak trees, fought our way through thickets, and finally burst out into the open.

"By the great horned spoon," said Pop. "This is heading straight for Old Howland's front yard."

We were a couple of fields away from a little white farmhouse and as we looked Old Howland himself came out the door with a pail and went over to his well.

"Come on," said Pop, starting over a stone wall. "We'll ask him for a drink of water."

The well was in one of the old white-painted well houses with a round window of black iron lace in the side. Old Howland greeted us rather sourly, but after Pop explained that we were lost and thirsty he softened slightly and cranked up the wooden pail. Then he gave us each a drink from a blue enamel cup. I remember how the sun quivered in the cup and how cold and fresh the water tasted after our struggles in the underbrush. After we had left Pop said it was important to experience real thirst in order to appreciate a drink of water. He was right because I've never forgotten that one.

Farther along our line we came to a pasture full of cows. This was nothing to Pop with his training on the Old Farm.

"Cows are stupid," he said, climbing over the bar-way. "They're more afraid of you than you are of them." (People always say this about animals, I notice, even rattlesnakes.)

"Just speak to them," said Pop, advancing on the herd. "C'boss, C'boss!" he yodeled. This, we knew, was cow talk from the Old Farm.

The cows regarded us balefully, then swung around as one cow and lowered their giant heads. Several of them pawed the ground and bellowed in a very hostile way.

Pop had not remembered our three dogs, who now flung themselves into the foreground, shrieking hysterically.

In the resulting stampede the thunder of hoofs and the bawling were just like a cowboy movie. We all went over the stone wall like birds, breaking all records for the broad-jump. When we had caught our breath Pop said it reminded him of the time he had been chased by a bull and cleared a six-foot fence.

"It's the adrenalin that does it," he explained, mopping his face.

I saw what he meant on a subsequent occasion when he and I went on a beeline across the unknown country near Barney's Joy.

This enchanting beach of white sand faces south on Buzzard's Bay and we had always wanted to explore it.

" 'Private Property,' " Pop read off a sign. "Well, let's see what happens."

Nothing happened for a while and we presently found ourselves in an old pasture partly grown up to blueberry bushes. A stout wall of squared granite ran along beside us, and over it the head of an enormous red bull rose and glared at us with inflamed and bulging eyes.

"That's a Jersey," Pop said calmly. "Much the fiercest of all bulls."

As we walked along the bull paced beside us, breathing stertorously over the top of the wall and once giving vent to a low, menacing bellow.

"Hello, old boy," said Pop. "He's just curious, you know. He's more afraid of you—"

Suddenly, bang, the wall ended and there we were face to face, practically nose to nose, with the bull.

It was then that I learned about adrenalin. Pop rose straight into the air and soared over a large blueberry bush and I, hardly aware of any effort, did the same. We landed running and all Pop's training (Run on the balls of your feet, Get into a regular pace, etc.) paid off. As he skimmed over a rock Pop shouted that bulls charge with their eyes shut.

"Just—sidestep," he gasped.

When we had vaulted another stone wall we stopped and looked back. The bull, deprived of our company, was eating grass in a bored way. Pop said to remember that bulls gore sideways and if their horns are long you can lie flat in a trench or manure gutter and they can't get at you.

"Thanks a lot," I said.

"Uncle Duane had a bull go for him in the barn," said Pop, "and he lay right down in the manure gutter and stayed there. Never had a scratch."

"Why didn't the bull step on him?" I asked. "He could have trampled him to a pulp."

Pop said he'd never thought of that and maybe lying flat wasn't such a great idea.

When Pop was not there Dave and I went on a beeline almost every morning while Aldie worked in his studio. Our favorite line went crosscountry from our hilltop to the town landing at the foot of the street, for we had discovered the charm of approaching the familiar village through its back yards, where there were barns and workshops, whitewashed privies buried in blossoming clematis, and little lanes hidden from the main road. This line combined a variety of terrain; it began in deep woods, crossed some neglected fields full of goldenrod and asters, and went through the yard of a little empty farmhouse near the river shore. Sometimes we sat in the sun on the porch to rest before tackling the marsh and the living hell of greenbrier and blackberry canes that stood between us and the lower pastures of the village. Roses had grown across the doorway of the farmhouse and honeysuckle had practically obliterated the privy. Phoebes had built nests under the eaves, and there was a robin's mud cup on one windowsill. In the neglected fields were all the wild creatures that live off the beaten track. Once, jumping a stone wall, I dropped into a covey of quail. And then there was the day of the fox and the owl.

Dave and I, that October morning, took our quarterstaffs and struck off through the woods, coming out on the old wagon road that wound downhill between clouds of asters. I remember that the air was full of the glistening parachutes of milkweed silk and thistledown as well as the ballooning threads of traveling spiders. It was what Thoreau calls a "gossamer day," still as a dream, smelling of bayberry and wild apples. There was an old orchard down there where we used to pick crab apples that nearly took the enamel off our teeth. On that gossamer day we came on a fox sitting in the road. He jumped up when he saw us and loped off down the wheel rut, nose and tail drooping like a tired little dog on his way home. His black paws made no sound and seemed hardly to touch the earth. He moved with the boneless, thistledown lightness of an angora cat. I remember being surprised that he was not red but pale gold with black points, and his brush was full and fluffy, nearly as wide as his body. He made no attempt to hurry and was obviously not the least bit afraid of us.

Presently the wagon road left us and curved off downhill. We climbed a wall and saw the deep October blue of the river and below us the marsh, glowing like a bed of coals where the high-bush blueberries grew and burnt orange where the salt grasses had turned. There is something medieval, heraldic, about the colors of a New England fall, and all that splendor made us feel like Robin Hood and Little John going forth to play a merrie prank on the Sheriff of Nottingham. The sumacs hung like battle flags over the stone walls, berries spattered the thickets with strings and clusters of lacquer red and coral. There were fringed gentians growing in the hollow at the edge of the marsh—such blue you could imagine the monks making for the Virgin's robe, grinding lapis lazuli.

These glories drove us to excesses of silliness and daring, and as I remember we rode cows for a while. I can't honestly recommend this as a sport, a cow's back being like a knife loosely covered with a fur rug. After this we popped milkweed pods, setting free shining clouds of silk. We also pinched cattails to make them erupt into handfuls of stuff like kapok—buff tipped with cinnamon and deliciously soft in the hand. While we were thus engaged, an enormous bird rose up out of the grass below us and floated silently to a sumac bush nearby. We knew enough about birds to recognize him—the great horned owl, which does most of his flying at night and sleeps by day. This one must have been after mice down in the grass but he was like all owls in the daytime—incredibly tame and helpless. Now he remained quite calmly on his perch, which was so low that we could look directly into his eyes. He sat nearly two feet high, his ear tufts erect, his glassy yellow eyes staring out from the curious facial discs, cinnamon colored in his case and composed of feathers as fine as velvet. An owl's eyes are immovable, so he had to turn his head to see around him. He had a most unbirdlike expression. Like the eyes of cats and goats his were blank, but the ears and the cruel hooked beak gave him an angry feline look.

We walked right up close enough to stroke him and so were able to admire in detail his wing's buff and chocolate markings, the delicate barred feathers of his breast and the creamy "gloves," the texture of fur, that covered his feet to the talons. Kelt, our old dog, was with us and his abrupt arrival caused the owl to flatten his ear tufts, clack his beak, and fan his great wings in Kelt's direction. After a while he floated off the sumac to a fence post, but so sun-dazed was he that we were able to run full speed to the village and bring back Uncle Smith Dexter, who was making the fall bird census. The owl gave him stare for stare, and after Uncle Smith had completed his notes, the owl closed his eyes and appeared to sleep. So we left him as untroubled by us as the fox had been.

Now the salt marshes had come into their own, and we found their red-gold meadows of salt hay and network of creeks ideal beeline material. Walking on the marsh was like walking on a spring mattress—the cowlicks of matted grass on the rubbery floor of peat very comfortable underfoot. Then, too, it was amazingly beautiful, the ruddy grasses being sprinkled with con-stellations of marsh asters, small as snowflakes and faintly pink. Marsh rosemary grew in miniature forests, cloudy blue with blos-soms, and along the edges of the marsh itself the seaside goldenrod was spectacular, its heavy yellow plumes weighed down with bees. To make the whole thing perfect there were the creeks, which added just that touch of risk necessary to a respectable beeline. Beyond the place where we had seen the owl was a little inlet called Hulda's Cove, with an ancient stone causeway to the far shore. Our line, however, just missed the causeway, making it necessary for us to launch an old boat that had been quietly rotting in the bushes for several decades. Its planks were dry as tinder and the cracks between the floorboards so wide that the water spouted up in fountains. Paddling with one of the thwarts we managed to reach the other shore just as the boat settled on the bottom, which naturally made our day.

Bodies of water were our favorite hazard, and each one presented a fresh challenge. Aldie specialized in beelines that crossed water; an ordinary line was too tame for his reckless nature.

Probably the most satisfactory coup in the beeline records was pulled off by Aldie and me on an Indian-summer day. We had the fantastic luck to come out on the shore of the river in the midst of a group of unknown people in wading. Ordinarily we didn't require audience reaction but for this feat we welcomed it. Without looking to the right or the left, without a moment's hesitation, we waded, fully clothed, straight out from shore until we disappeared beneath the waters of the deep channel. It was a bit difficult staying under so as to give the impression that we were walking on the bottom. Actually we swam under water to the marsh island in the middle of the river, where we allowed first our hair, then, inch by inch, the rest of us to rise dripping from the depths until we stood on solid ground. We then walked across the marsh, descended solemnly into the channel on the far side, and after another session under water emerged again on the opposite shore of the river. The response of our audience could not have been more rewarding. They were either running about shouting and pointing or standing transfixed with amazement, staring after us.

Later in the season, when the leaves had fallen, we took a long line to Adamsville, the village at the head of the river. It was a splendid event and we managed to hit four brooks and any number of salt creeks. Most of the way was through unexplored uplands, which for generations had been landscaped by cows. The veteran beeliner knows that some of the best walking in the world is through grazed land. Following a cowpath, we crossed a brown brook on a small causeway, and soon found ourselves on a moor high enough to give us a marvelous view of river and ocean, blue and sparkling between violet clouds of bare trees. November at the Point is very like early spring in northern New England, and when the wind is offshore the water has the sleepy, simmering look of summer. From our knoll we could see the pods of ducks feeding out by the grass flats and great rafts of Canada geese cruising against the wind, their long necks invisible under water.

The only trouble with cow-landscaped territory is that it is full of cows, and on this line we had made the mistake of taking along three dogs: our own Kelt, a puppy called Skippy, and Greyfriars Bobby, a mongrel that belonged to Aunt K. Dogs on beelines are always a hazard because of cows, chickens, cats, dogs, and other domestic fauna. We were always dragging them off by the collar while they made hoarse, gagging sounds of protest.

Our journey through cow country was very tiring. Aldie had the two older animals tied to his belt and sped over the ground in giant leaps and bounds. I toiled in the rear carrying the puppy, which was passionately eager to roll in cow manure. As we approached Adamsville the dangers increased and we began to run into people. There were some characters in rubber boots in wading —we always seemed to meet people in wading—and they had a dog. The creek where they were was directly on our line, so we gauged its width by eye and decided we could jump across. Aldie just made it and then turned to catch Skippy, who was small enough to throw. My pitch was low and Skip landed in the water, with me close behind him. After this it wasn't much use trying to look decent for our entry into the town. I wrung out my hair and beret but this made very little difference. In any case, when you are wearing serge bloomers with the elastics around your ankles there's not much you can do. I do remember pulling the bloomers up above my knees in preparation for entering civilization but bloomers are bloomers. They don't do anything for you.

"Boy, do you look awful," said Aldie, but he was in a genial mood, mellowed by air and exercise.

It was lunchtime in Adamsville, whose white houses slept in the noon sun. Like tramps or Indians, we came to it from the marshes, through stone-walled hayfields and pastures to the back doors of barns and manure piles. One of the dogs (G. Friar's Bobby) got into a pig pen whose occupants screamed like train whistles. There were four more pigs and a little furry cow in one barn, and we fed them all generously from a barrel of mash. A narrow lane led up from the fields to the gristmill, where a rhythmic chunking announced that grinding was in progress. The back door was ajar so we went in and watched. Everything inside the mill was dusted with white flour. The floors were polished smooth by generations of grain bags, and the sweet smell of crushed corn filled the air. The miller poured the white kernels into a wooden chute over the millstones and it came out a chute at the bottom as the famous johnnycake meal.

There were geese asleep in the road by the millpond when we went up toward the village to Miss Debby Manchester's to buy food. This was the country store where the Adamsville cheese came from and where they carried everything from lamp chimneys to straw hats for horses. Dear little Miss Debby, so old she looked transparent, sold us a wedge of cheese and some crackers out of a glass-fronted box and gave us two of her big soft molasses cookies.

We took this loot over behind a stone wall and ate it in the sun, assisted by the dogs. It's hard to explain how intensely satisfying such a picnic was—a gypsy kind of picnic or a Robin Hood feast. Purged by fresh air and exercise, wet, dirty, ravenously hungry, we reaped the reward of all beelines—heavenly exhaustion and complete well-being.

On the return trip I fell into a mud hole in the marsh, and the dogs stampeded somebody's cows, but we arrived home by tea time and ate a whole plate of English muffins.

The Professor sometimes went on beelines by himself and would decide to combine this exercise with a call on Pop. Every now and then he'd claw his way through the greenbrier and emerge onto our lawn, bleeding from various lacerations but delighted with his woodsman's skill. Then he and Pop would discourse on the importance of getting off the beaten track, roughing it on your own. Once they went on a beeline together and no one was surprised when they got lost.

"Books in the running brooks, sermons in stones," said Mum pityingly when they finally came crashing through the underbrush.

Thanksgiving at Synton shattered all tradition but traditions were being shattered all over the place that year. After Thanksgiving we drove to Princeton in a downpour of rain. The Newark dumps with their leaping fires looked exactly like Hell and Mum said so. We arrived at the new house after dark, and we were all so depressed that we decided we hated it. The golden days of fall seemed like a happy dream and the present was nothing but rain, rain, rain, cold, and the strange red mud of New Jersey.

CHAPTER THIRTEEN

The Old Order Changeth

MY FIRST DAYS in Princeton were so appalling that even remembering them makes things go black before my eyes.

To begin with, Pop forced me to ride a bicycle to school, actually routing me up Prospect Street, where the Princeton eating clubs are, across the campus and down Nassau Street to Miss Fine's, where I suffered tortures among the young sophisticates of my year. All of them had their hair up in a bun, all of them wore lipstick and had been attending Princeton dances since the age of thirteen. All of them had captured a student to squire them around. I learned at once that no respectable Miss Fine's girl would dream of going within miles of the campus, for if you did you were greeted with wolf whistles and shouts of "Fire!" In order to get back home that day I took a route around the campus so circuitous and complicated that I got lost and it was dark when I staggered in the door at last.

"I won't ever ride my bike again," I said fiercely, "and I'm throwing away my glasses and this rotten leather jacket. And, Pop, a girl there lived at the house where you stayed and she said you told her I watched birds and drew pictures of tracks in the sand!"

"Well, you do. I'm proud of you," he said.

"I'll never do it again," I said. "You've ruined me."

"That's nonsense," said Pop. "Anyone would be glad to know a nice wholesome girl interested in Nature."

"Wholesome! Nature!" I screamed. "The last thing anyone wants to meet is a nice wholesome girl interested in nature. I wouldn't be seen dead with one myself."

"I told you," said Aldie.

"Shut up!" I yelled.

Dancing school was pure horror. There was one girl there who was only thirteen and she looked like a divorcee of thirty. All the boys fought to cut in on her, including Aldie.

"What do you expect?" he said. "She's a hot number."

Dancing school, ghastly as it was, was nothing to the freshman reception at the president's house, where Mrs. Hibben in violet lace and silver slippers introduced the girls of Miss Fine's School to the freshman class. My sufferings at this festive affair were intense. Mum, having been engaged at sixteen, knew nothing about the problems of adolescence, and I had been sent to the freshman reception in a smocked dress and low-heeled shoes. I was forbidden to buy a lipstick or use powder and wore service-weight lisle stockings.

"You are still our little girl," said Pop when I complained about this, "and you don't need lipstick or high heels to make you attractive. There's nothing a man likes better than a fresh, natural girl."

"You mean all they want is a sister, a friend?" I asked.

"That's right," he said.

"Well, let me tell you something," I said. "You're crazy."

The boys didn't seem to mind Princeton and, of course, Pop loved it. He had a luxurious office in the great Gothic chapel and a secretary called Miss Shunk, whom we referred to as S. Hunk. He reveled in his title and had writing paper made with his own letterhead.

Dave, who had fallen in love with a springer spaniel, persuaded him that a man in his position should have pure-bred dogs. Our old Kelt had been run over—just one more depressing thing about Princeton—and Pop bought a springer puppy with a kennel name a foot long. We renamed it Ogden, which first became Oggie, then The Egg. The Egg was a monomaniac on the subject of squirrels and ate part of a window frame trying to get at one. In protest against this new trend I acquired from the Animal Rescue League an adorable creature like a gray-blue mop which we named Graham, after Graham McNamee, the radio announcer, despite the fact that she was a female. Graham soon became The Grail and proved to be slightly insane, too, as she ate buttons and caught nonexistent flies. Still she was brighter than The Egg.

Before the year was over I saw I'd have to find myself a student to escort me to Miss Fine's dance. One afternoon when Dave and I were sitting in a ditch by the driveway cracking butternuts a freshman came up to the house to see Pop. He was good-looking and wore a nice tweed coat, and I decided he would do. Dave and I accosted him, and in no time at all I had maneuvered Mum into asking him to supper. He was taking engineering and talked about nothing but gear shifts, but he was a gentle soul. He must have been hard up, too, for he took me to the Engineering Ball, one of the most horrible experiences of my life, as I was stuck with him the whole time, and whenever the music stopped we went in and looked at gears.

Escaping to the Point in June was heaven, and to make the occasion even more enchanting we left from New York on the great *Commonwealth,* the most luxurious ship of the old Fall River Line. It was our first ocean voyage and no vessel since has even approached it in glamour.

We left Princeton in the afternoon with the Artful Dodger loaded to the Plimsoll mark with baggage, dogs, and human freight. When we arrived at the dock in New York the magic of ships was in the air. Ocean liners loomed up against the sky and every now and then the heart-shaking bellow of a whistle proclaimed the sailing of one of them. Gulls rode the wind over the baggage sheds and we smelled the rank, salty odor of the harbor, the breath of the sea. Mum and Pop, as seasoned travelers, were drunk with nostalgia and babbled of arrivals and departures in foreign ports. Every time they heard the penny whistle of a tugboat or the moo of a great ship about to sail they spoke the names of long-dead ships—*Ivernia, Saxonia, Princess Alice,* and the most romantic of all, *Leviathan,* the ship that had brought Pop home from France during the war.

The *Commonwealth* lay alongside her pier dripping water and making those hissing sounds that steamers make in docks. Her tiers of open promenade decks gave her a lacy, top-heavy look like one of the old Mississippi steamboats. We looked up in awe at the lifeboats swinging on their davits, at the wheelhouse with the gold-lettered name plate under the windows and her two black funnels smoking gently against the late-afternoon sky.

Pop drove the Artful Dodger across a wide gangplank into the bowels of the ship; then he came back and we all went aboard.

"It's just the same," said Mum, happily. "Nothing's changed." We had come full circle and were now back in the nineteenth century with Mum, a plump little girl in one of those white ruffled dresses, running down the red-carpeted corridors ahead of us, looking over our shoulders into the vast gilt-framed mirrors, and gazing through our eyes at the pretty French ladies in oval frames, the gold-and-white paneling, and the gas fixtures of the elegant nineties.

White-coated deck stewards finally shepherded us into our staterooms. Our parents had the bridal suite and we were allotted bunks in smaller staterooms, compact little snuggeries, crimson carpeted, whose paneled walls were thick with decades of shiny white paint. When all our suitcases were stowed Pop said we would now make a tour of the ship. On the upper deck we were nearly lifted into space when the whistle went off. The call of "All ashore that's going ashore!" echoed around the corridors and we ran to the rail to watch the casting off of hawsers, the withdrawing of the gangplank, and the widening of the green strip of water between us and the wharf.

The romantic voyage down the river and under the bridges to Hell Gate was a marked departure from the old rut of the Artful Dodger's back seat. We stood entranced while the towers of New York retreated into violet haze, and then we went down into the engine room, for Pop always wanted to see what made things go and talk to experts about their craft.

We opened a door and stepped out of the windy evening into brilliant electric light and a curious busy silence. Below the spidery metal stairs were flying rods, shafts, wheels, and pistons, all in motion, and a giant scarlet elbow—some sort of crank that went up and over, up and over, just missing a man with a handful of cotton waste who stood at its head. There were glints of polished brass, and the red glow of fire boxes, and from the darkness beyond came a steady rushing roar. The *Commonwealth* was a side-wheeler and the great red cranks were turning the wheels.

Pop was in ecstasies and we stayed down there for ages while the engineer explained how everything worked. Young men, stripped to the waist, were stoking the fires, and one, his face shiny black with oil, delicately rubbed the sleek golden shafts, turned little handles, and examined gauges with a kind of tenderness as though the whole working complex were a pet animal that he loved.

It was rough rounding Point Judith, and the ship creaked and groaned as the seas hit her. I lay in my upper berth wondering if I was supposed to be seasick, but the next minute I woke to stillness and the sounds of a city. We were in Fall River.

We had melon for breakfast, bacon and eggs, piles of buttered toast, and other luxuries. Pop discoursed on the amazing simplicity of our new mode of travel, and Bobs washed his hands, face, and neck in his finger bowl.

Shortly after this adventure Pop met the press, and our reputation fell alive into their merciless hands. We had been sitting around the living room trying to decide who was going sailing with whom when two reporters showed up to interview Pop. We saw them coming, and by the time they reached the front door Pop was alone in the living room and the rest of us, including Mum, were lying on the floor in the kitchen.

"I refuse to see them," said Mum when Pop came bleating to the door, "and you be careful what you say. Remember it will all go in the papers. No blubbering about the home, now."

"Eye Guy," said Pop. "They will want to see my wife. Come on."

"Never," said Mum from the floor.

Pop flumped off and for two hours sat on the veranda with the reporters. We peeked at them periodically and Pop seemed to be in full spate.

"I hate to think what he's saying," Mum reported.

She was right to be alarmed. In the Sunday paper there was a double-page spread of photographs. "Dean Wicks plays with his dogs. Dean Wicks and his ship model. Dean Wicks tells of his plans for Princeton's new chapel, etc., etc."

"Gawd, Father," said Aldie. "Listen to this, you guys."

" 'Dean Wicks, his fair hair blowing in the wind—' "

"What hair?" asked Dave.

"Now cut that out," said Pop.

" '—fair hair blowing in the wind watches his son sailing in their boat, *Dehra Doon*.' Oh, brother."

"Let me see that," I said, snatching the paper. There was a feature article of great length, and it was filled with appalling evidence of Pop's artless confidences.

"Oh, no!" I shouted. " 'Dean Wicks, on the porch of his summer home, patted his dogs, The Egg and The Grail—.' Now you've done it. Robbie, forget the job. Try to get back your old one."

"How could you?" cried Mum. "The Egg and The Grail! The Princeton people will love that."

"Now look, dearie," said Pop, "the papers like the human touch. Their readers want to know what a man's home means to him," he croaked. "And, anyway," he added in a sensible voice, "their real names are just as bad—Ogden and Graham. How can you explain why a female animal should be named after Graham McNamee, a radio announcer?"

"Don't explain. It's none of their business," we said.

When Baba saw the paper she pointed to a photograph of Pop's head which was a blurred mass of ink. His nose was jet black and the expression on his face was one of leering malevolence.

"One would think it a criminal face," she said, and really it did look exactly like those photographs of most wanted persons you see in post offices.

After this episode we guarded Pop very closely from anyone remotely connected with the press. Our first year in Princeton had made it clear that he would have to be educated in the ways of the great world. In the super-sophisticated circles of Princeton he was as innocent as an unborn child. Even .we knew more than he did about vice, and we hardly knew anything. The situation was serious and we intended to devote the summer to his training.

As for me I saw that unless steps were taken Pop would destroy any chances I might have of surviving in a man's college town. Safe at the Point, I began right away to make myself over.

My hair, hitherto a curse, now proved a blessing as bobbed hair was out, long hair in. However, you had to put it up, either in two buns or a doughnut at the base of the skull. Somehow I got hold of some blond celluloid hairpins, and with much anguish skewered my hair in a circle on the back of my neck. Every time I thought I had it right a thing like a paint brush stuck out from the center of the doughnut, and after it was all in place I hardly dared move or it fell down again, hairpins rained over the floor and slid down inside my clothes—very trying.

I then purchased a stick of Roger & Gallet's pink pomade, with which I decorated my lips. I even bought a compact.

Clothes had, of course, to be dealt with. I threw out all bloomers and long stockings and forced Mum to buy me some white duck sailor pants with bell bottoms and dozens of buttons with anchors on them. I got socks. I got a tight-fitting jersey bathing suit that made Pop avert his eyes with weary despair.

"This isn't you," he said sadly.

"Yes, it is," I said. "Who do you think I am, anyway—Alice in Wonderland?"

Unfortunately we were still free from vices of any kind and now set to work to remedy the situation. Prohibition was still going on and the wickedest thing you could do was smoke. Parents were always promising their children gold watches if they didn't smoke until they were twenty-one, and stories went about of evil public-school kids who smoked behind the barn. Pop said over and over that he didn't want us doing any experimenting behind the barn, but the barn seemed to be merely a symbol. We didn't have a barn and the only thing behind Synton's barn was a manure pile. Still, Pop continued to say that he didn't worry about us doing anything behind the barn because he trusted us.

"What did *you* do behind the barn?" we asked him. "You seem to know a lot about what went on back there."

It finally turned out he meant smoking cigarettes. Nobody in the family used tobacco except Pop's father, Gumpkie, a bewitching man, who smoked cigars and wore a derby hat. However, it was made quite clear that he had only taken up smoking after Pop's mother died. He had never smoked in the home because she didn't like it, and Pop had never smoked at all.

One day Dave and I in a burst of daring bought a box of cigarettes called Headplays. The box was a foot long, with a picture of a horse on it, and the cigarettes were a foot long too, and were supposed to be cut into short lengths with scissors. We scorned such paltry stratagems and each lighted a Headplay a foot long.

Looking back on this experience I wonder if Headplays were made of tobacco. They tasted exactly like burning horse manure and there was that picture on the box. Possibly they were horse manure? Frankly, I have never in my whole life tasted anything as foul—they were so horrible you had to take another puff to believe it—and with much gagging and choking we smoked them down to our fingers.

"Boy," said Dave, "I smoked corn silk once and it was better than this. Aldie said he smoked some calking out of that deck over at Catamaran." (Catamaran was the name of Uncle Basil's house.) "We might try it."

The calking, which we pried out of the cracks and wrapped in newspaper, nearly took the lining out of our throats. It was like inhaling a blow torch.

"I don't think I want to smoke," I said, reeling away from the scene of our excesses.

"We've got to get real cigarettes," said Dave.

Oddly enough, Pop was going through much the same experience. He was so charmed with his role of Dean of the Chapel and squire of a country estate that he began carrying a cane when he took the dogs for a walk. The idea of a country squire strolling over the estate with his springer spaniel at his heels appealed strongly to his dramatic sense, but something was missing—a good, straight-grained brier pipe, polished like a horse chestnut, with tobacco mixed to one's own formula. He bought one and spent most of his spare time trying to light it or choking until he was blue on the smoke. He burned holes in his clothes and there always seemed to be a fountain of sparks coming out of the bowl of his pipe. One day we realized he was blowing out, not in.

"Look, Pop," said Aldie, "that's not the way you smoke. Suck *in*."

Pop took a deep drag and exploded into loud barking.

"Don't drag the whole pipe down into your lungs," said Aldie as we dispassionately watched his paroxysms. "Just puff gently."

"Dad-gasted stuff tastes so vile," wheezed Pop, as with streaming eyes he mopped his brow.

"You'll get used to it," said Aldie, but Pop never did and finally carried the pipe around only as a prop.

We hadn't made much progress in training Pop for life among the fleshpots of Princeton but then we were severely hampered by our own lack of experience. However, help was on its way.

A crisis arose in the kitchen department, where The Fiddle suddenly went off the rails and started wearing a khaki sweater and a skating cap to wait on table. One day when Mum rang for coffee she brought in a nickel-plated alarm clock, and after she'd retired muttering to herself we all exchanged glances.

"Gone off her rocker, finally," said Pop.

Mum said it was no more peculiar than the things Pop did like pouring cream onto the table instead of into his coffee cup or putting his glasses on the floor and rocking on them.

"We're not talking about the old man," said Pop. "We're discussing The Fiddle and I say it's time we had a change. Just because somebody talks with a Scotch accent we don't have to live with her forever."

Also, he went on to say, it takes away a man's appetite to hear dissertations on disease at the dinner table. The day before we had heard about a woman whose intestines were as big around as your thigh in places, no bigger than a pencil in others.

"Not the sort of thing a man in my position can afford in the home."

Shortly after the alarm-clock episode The Fiddle left of her own accord, a merciful release, as no one would have dared fire her.

Pop was not Dean of the Chapel for nothing and now took charge of the matter. He had been on some sort of employment board in Princeton, and before Mum could catch her breath he had hired a combination cook-butler who was to take the next train to Providence.

"A butler?" said Mum, wide-eyed. Pop said he had been butler to some elegant family in Princeton. He was black and his name was Bruce. It's hard to believe that there was a time when that name of power was unknown in the home.

Bruce arrived in due course and proved to be a handsome, middle-aged man with a wide, flashing smile and a laugh that would melt the heart of a stone.

The first meal he served was dinner, and to wait on table he wore tails and a white tie. The service was impeccable, the food ambrosia. Never having experienced correct handling of dishes we were on the verge of giggles out of sheer amazement. When Bruce retired to the kitchen Pop said, "I can't have him wearing those clothes. I'm a simple man and we can't live on that scale."

"Why not?" we said. "He's great."

"He's great, all right," said Pop, "but no white tie and tails."

Bruce was crestfallen at this news but was allowed to wear starched white jackets, which became his uniform. The sight of his kind dark hand in its white sleeve would be part of our meals for years to come, but we did not of course know it at the time. After the first week, though, we knew who ran the household. Bruce.

He told Pop what he could eat and what he couldn't eat. He instructed Mum on correct service as known in the upper echelons of Princeton society. When he answered the telephone he didn't just bellow, "Hello!" the way we did; he said, "Dean Wicks' residence." He told the boys about women and warned me against the perils of the world of men.

"You're too young to know, Miss Jan," he said severely, "but most men are up to no good. No, sir!"

I wasn't in much peril from men at the Point. In fact, I never saw any that weren't related to me except from a distance. Aldie was no help as he had a job and a Model T car named Bertha, so he was hardly ever around. Dave, though, was, and he and I examined the situation. Dave had his eye on a girl with bronze curls, and I had spotted a young man whose looks appealed to me. Both were summer people. Both went to the private beach club. Clearly, this was the best place to start. We, too, were summer people and anyone could rent a bathhouse.

I forget the exact sequence of events here, but at some point Dave and I made an inspection of the bathhouse area at swimming time (10:30 to 1:00). There we saw many members of our generation enjoying the surf, sunbathing, and consorting with persons of the opposite sex. Clearly we were about a hundred years behind the times as far as social mores were concerned, and a lot of work had to be done. For one thing we must at once join the human race, and Dave and I initiated a program of parent education.

"Why don't we have a bathhouse like everybody else?" I asked at dinner that night.

"Well, we like the privacy of our own bailiwick," said Pop, "and anyway, I can't sit around in the hot sand like that. It gives me a touch of the sun and bothers my old knee."

"You don't have to go," we said, "but we could."

Pop said summer was the time to spend in the home with the family. It was a time to be together.

"Look, Bob," said Dave, for by now we called him anything that came into our heads, "we might like to see somebody we aren't related to. Like girls."

Pop said we must realize that if we hired a bathhouse we were taking a big step. "You will move out of the home into another world."

"Well, why not?" I said.

"The next thing it will be joyriding in fast cars and staying out until all hours and worrying your mother out of her wits."

"Oh, Pop," said Dave, "all we want is to rent a bathhouse, not a saloon. For Pete's sake."

In the end we rented a bathhouse and the next thing we knew we were going to Saturday-night square dances. We even went sailing with members of the opposite sex. Talk about Dionysian orgies! Why, sometimes I even went to a movie in New Bedford. However, Pop had been right—things would never be the same again. Instead of wandering free as birds on the wild reaches of the upper beach we haunted the bathhouses, watching for a certain dark head or a special bathing-suited figure, without which the beach was a desert. We were in bondage. We thought we were in love.

Even at Synton change was taking place at a dizzy rate. Baba had bought a car—a Buick—and Aunt K. had learned to drive. The first time she was turned loose with a license she took Mum and Bobs for a ride and suddenly drove off the road into a field, ending up against a tree.

"I just forgot the horse wasn't out there," she explained.

Now that they had a car Baba, Aunt K., and Tink drove all over everywhere, and each day Baba thought up a feature to give purpose to the drive. They took fresh eggs to shut-ins, vegetables and flowers to those without gardens, called on everybody for miles around, and had a wonderful time.

In Synton itself Baba took one more step into the twentieth century and put in electric lights. It was difficult to believe this when you went in there, as the place was, if anything, darker than in the old kerosene days. I remember when I went up to be shown the new miracle.

"Look, dear Jan," said Baba, "I've had the old lamp converted to electricity and you see if you can tell the difference."

She pulled a chain that now hung down under the yellow china shade of the big brown lamp on her table. A dim orange glow lit a circle of mahogany below the shade, hardly affecting the rest of the room.

"Now look at this," said Baba proudly and snapped a switch on a chased-brass temple candle that had a small shade affixed to a minute bulb.

"Just like candlelight," said Baba, looking fondly at the glow-worm illumination on Aunt K.'s desk.

Upstairs, though, she had really triumphed. Between her large bedroom and her dressing room, where I slept on visits, was a narrow strip of wall, and here a light fixture had been set with its bulb shielded by a frosted-glass shade like a Canterbury bell. Baba went over and switched it on. The murky gloom of the two rooms was hardly changed at all.

"No horrid, vulgar glare," said Baba. "You'd think it was a kerosene lamp."

"That's right," I said. "You would."

As if this were not enough Baba caused a road to be cut through the woods to the river to Catamaran, Uncle Basil's house. You could drive down it in a car, but it was almost impossible to drive back again. Still, it was a road.

Baba then built a set of bathhouses for Aunt K. and Tink and bought them a new rowboat. It was much smaller than *Mandarin* and was, of all things, painted yellow and called *Sunlight*. This was a radical step in more ways than one. Tink now had a boat of his own and could take off alone any time he wanted to. The new boat was light and easy to row and Tink could practically lift it out of the water with one gargantuan stroke. I never saw any human being who could row as fast as Tink. His oars churned like paddle wheels, and his boat planed through the water with a bow wave like a steamer. He went foaming around the bay in circles, laughing and singing, happy as a clam, but once in a while he'd feel gay and would make a break for the wide open spaces. Then somebody would have to go after him and bring him back. Once he took off for Adamsville and Pop, wearing a wet bathing suit as he had been in swimming, had to chase him in *Mandarin*. When they returned Tink looked depressed.

"Now, no more!" Pop was saying in a stern voice. "If you want to be my old chum don't do that again. Gad, I'm half dead."

Tink explained that he couldn't help it. He had felt gay and made a mistake. Shortly afterward he did it again and was heading for the harbor mouth when Aldie cut him off by taking a short cut through the grass flats.

Everywhere was change. Even in Snowdon things were all different. Pop, who was going through a phase of thinking he wanted to retire to the Point, had bought some stoves and caused Will Brightman, the town carpenter, to cover the pine-board walls with sheet rock, thus providing ideal housing for armies of mice, squirrels, chipmunks, and other fauna. A large new kitchen was built, and part of my room was stolen to make a bathroom, but we must go back a bit in time to trace the course of this radical change in the plumbing system.

CHAPTER FOURTEEN

Water!

IN THE PRIMEVAL ERA of washbowls and pitchers Pop somehow managed to keep pace with the family demand for water without breaking under the strain. However, by the time his brood numbered five the subject of plumbing became an obsession with him. He spoke of a flush toilet the way the knights of old spoke of the Holy Grail and, being a resourceful man, thought up all kinds of ways to beat the system.

The system, if you remember, was for him to carry all our drinking water from Synton in two French milk cans, as the water from our cistern was said to be teeming with germs. A black pump delivered this lethal liquid to the kitchen, where it was used for washing or bathing. The pump was the only piece of plumbing in the house, and other human needs were cared for by a two-hole privy in the wood shed.

Pop attacked first the problem of drinking water. Baba's artesian well was practically a shrine on the hill, being the only source of the precious fluid. She served it like the Cumaean Sibyl, and the pump seemed to us a kind of altar where Baba and Pop worshiped all summer long. They used to descend into the subterranean cavern where it lived by a flight of slimy steps, and once they were inside their voices echoed like the voice of the oracle.

One day Pop said that if he carried those blasted milk cans much longer his arms would be pulled from their sockets. He had a plan, he said, which could be put into effect in a matter of hours.

"Only a man of genius," he said, "could have conceived of anything so brilliant and yet so simple. You see before you an oil painting of that man."

"Well, what is it?" we asked.

"It's a hose," he said proudly. "A plain rubber hose obtainable at any hardware store."

"A real genius would have thought of that years ago," Dave said, but Pop said he didn't want to hear any remarks from the floor.

We went and bought what seemed like several miles of black hose, and Pop spent a happy day threading it through the thickets of huckleberry and poison ivy, finally attaching it to some fixture in the sacred recesses of Synton's pump house. Tink, who had observed every move with interest, now let it be known that Baba wasn't entirely swept away by Dear Robert's invention. Still, she never said anything herself, so we let it pass. Pop got a spectacular case of poison ivy and went around covered with calamine lotion, but he was so pleased with himself that, except for staying awake all night, he hardly noticed it.

The water from the hose was often hot from the sun and tasted like rubber but we soon got used to that. Pop now turned his attention to the more basic aspects of plumbing. The privy, he said, could no longer cope with the rush of traffic in the home.

"There are so many dad-gasted women and children storming the place after breakfast," he said, "that a man has no alternative but the woods." Also, he said, The Fiddle spent a large part of the day in there.

Pop's solution to the problem was a radical new invention called a chemical toilet. This vile object had as its main feature a pail the size of a hogshead. Modesty forbids me to go into detail here, but the traffic was so brisk that Pop had to make a steady series of trips into the forest with the thing and soon reached his threshold of tolerance for this activity.

"Gadzooks," he said one day, staggering away from what was known as The Pit, "I feel like one of those Chinese coolies we used to see in Shanghai."

"What coolies are those?" I asked.

Mum said they carried the nightsoil out to the gardens every morning in two pails, one on each end of a yoke.

"Slop, slop, slop," she said. "They always trotted."

"Boy, I'm glad I didn't have to eat stuff out of those gardens," said Dave.

"Maybe what you need is another pail and a yoke," I said to Pop.

"What I need is another unit," said Pop. "I'm going to build myself a private cell in the garage."

This he proceeded to do and, except for falling off the scaffolding during its construction and nearly breaking his leg, he achieved his goal with no serious injuries. Unfortunately, a wren decided to nest in a corner of his new facility and used to attack him whenever he went in, but he said it was a small price to pay for a private john. He took some magazines up there and said he was a different man. This happy interlude was, however, of short duration. The pail duty came close to breaking his spirit.

"I am supposed to be a minister of the gospel," he said, "not a walking sewer. There must be a better way to handle this thing."

After some concentrated study he found it.

"Once more," he said at breakfast after a sleepless night, "the man of genius has thought of a plan."

The plan was an extension of the hose idea and went as follows: The hose would be attached to a new kind of pump, which in turn would be connected by pipes to a tank in the attic. By shutting off the pump's normal spout the water could be diverted into the pipes and thus pumped upstairs to the tank. The power was supplied by the human arm, and at first this seemed a minor item.

"With a tank in the attic," said Pop happily, "we can have running water and a flush toilet upstairs."

"You don't mean you're building a real *bathroom*?" we said.

"That is precisely what I do mean," said Pop.

The new bathroom was carved out of my room, thus eliminating a knothole into the former maid's room, which had provided occasional diversion on rainy days for those interested in anatomical research. It was a howling success but was hard to get into as Pop used to lock himself in and read. There was a low story in circulation at that time called, "Father, Are You Shaving?" That's all I can tell you about it, but we developed it to include a crescendo of knocking on the bathroom door—a crescendo that started with a mere tap and ended with a thunderous assault on the panels, both fists and feet being used. Aldie split one panel from top to bottom in one round of "Father" and Pop said his functions were permanently impaired.

"Well, if you don't like it, give somebody else a chance in there," we said. "Talk about The Fiddle! You're twice as bad."

"No respect for the old man," said Pop. "A figure of fun, a mere clown in the home, that's yours truly."

The next summer things were slightly improved, as a second bathroom was built off the new guest room by a rich guest, who said he'd have to give it to us in order to survive his visits.

Pumping water into the tank came to be a terrible ordeal, and the minute anybody discovered the tank was empty he escaped from the house as quickly as possible. It wasn't hard to tell when the tank was empty as the john wouldn't flush and nothing came out of the faucets but an obscene hissing sound like the last gasps of a dying serpent.

I'm sorry to report that most of the pumping devolved on Pop, but in the honeymoon period he was so delighted with his bathroom that he didn't seem to realize it. Then all of a sudden he got the message, and from a sprightly vigorous pumper he was transformed before our eyes into a poor old geezer, crippled by overwork, barely able to totter into his chair.

"Eye Guy," he said, massaging his shoulder, "why is it that nobody's ever around when the tank runs dry? Nobody except R. W.?"

"Because you like to be an early Christian martyr," said Mum accusingly, and Pop said he washed his hands of the whole thing.

However, from this moment on the hose system began to fall apart.

The water, after a while, acquired a new and strange flavor. Not only did it taste like hot rubber, it tasted of something else.

"I think it's sewage," said Dave. "Maybe the pipes are mixed up and we're drinking out of the john."

"It tastes fine to me," said Pop, shuddering.

"Your taste buds are paralyzed by all that medicine you take," I said to him. "Anyone who keeps munching Bell-Ans and soda mints has no tongue left."

Somebody else said it tasted like fungus; someone else said rotted garbage; so finally Pop hoisted himself into the attic to explore. Bent double under the rafters he groped his way over to the tank, and we heard him hit his head twice on beams and swear. At last he turned his flashlight into the tank and there was a short silence.

"There's a dead rat in here," he said.

After this frightful episode nobody drank much water, and at the same time Tink's spy reports indicated that Baba would be pleased if Dear Robert dug his own well. With hardly any trouble at all Pop persuaded himself that this was his own idea.

The well man arrived with his equipment at the beginning of the next summer and was there, it seems to me in retrospect, until Labor Day. Possibly the time was shorter, but for weeks the clanging thump of the drill went on and on until we accepted it as we accepted our own heartbeats. Pop said he heard it in his sleep, and it made sermon writing almost impossible.

"Just preach old ones," Aldie said. "No one will notice."

"Probably not. Probably not," said Pop. "Why should they?" He was very discouraged by the well man, who said he had been through two ledges so far and not a drop to be seen.

"One place I drilled," he said with ill-concealed relish, "I went down five, six hundred feet, cost the guy two, three thousand bucks and never got water at all."

"Is that so?" said Pop and flumped back to the house.

"I'm a ruined man," he said. "This fella's bleeding me white."

"He can't help it if he doesn't hit water," Mum said. "You told him to drill there."

Luckily they hit water soon after that, and the beautiful stuff was running at six or more gallons a minute. Pop was jubilant. The water proved to be pure and celebrations were in order. The hose to Synton was eventually gathered in and our own pump installed in a cement cavern above the well. It really looked as though all our troubles were over, and for a long time they were. Then came the famous summer when the well went dry.

On our hill the summers were so much alike that the family had developed its own dating system. Mum dated everything by the births of her various babies. She would refer to the summer before Dave was born or the summer after Targ was born, and that fixed it in her mind, since it didn't really matter what was going on in the outside world.

Pop used the cataclysm system and spoke of the summer we had five flat tires on the way down or the summer the dog bit the ham man. The summer the well went dry, however, was a milestone that no one ever forgot.

In the course of time Uncle Basil had taken over the hose system and attached one to our pump to supply his house at the river. This meant, to put it baldly, four toilets on one well, to say nothing of all those women and children washing dishes, brushing their teeth, cooking, bathing, doing enormous laundries—the whole idea made Pop's head swim. He used to sit and estimate the astronomical number of gallons that were being pumped out of his well by his pump. We could hear the pump start up the minute anyone in either house turned on a faucet or flushed a john, and at the sudden throbbing from the top of the hill Pop would give an anguished cry.

"There it goes again," he'd shout. "Dad-gast it, they'll pump the thing dry at this rate."

"Look, Robert," Dave said, "the well man said we were using the water of an underground river coming from New Hampshire, for Pete's sake."

"How in Sam Hill does he know it's from New Hampshire, just tell me that?"

"It's his job," I said.

"And what difference does it make whether the blasted river started in Timbuctoo? It's being drained. The way people in this family use the bathroom you'd think there was something wrong with their pipes. And why does anyone need baths down here? We go swimming every day."

"Oh, Pop," Aldie said. "Relax. Try to think of something besides water. There are other sides to life."

It was a dry summer, the driest in living memory, and people went around saying such and such a well that had never failed since the eighteenth century had gone dry. Pop became really alarmed, and then one morning we heard him shout from the bathroom.

"It's dry!" he bellowed. "I told you. Now maybe somebody will listen to the old man."

We went in and watched him turn the faucets on and off. A few drops of water and some sand came out.

"Sand!" he yelled. "We've hit bottom."

The terrible word went around the hill like wildfire, and presently the culprit, who shall be nameless, appeared and said nervously that he had a confession to make.

"I left the toilet running all night," he said in a miserable voice.

Pop didn't bother with recriminations. He simply laid down the law.

"No baths. No laundry," he said, "and nobody is to use the johns for anything but serious business. The woods were here before flush toilets. What was good enough for the Indians is good enough for you. Also, *don't flush* until absolutely necessary!"

"Why Father," I said. "What a foul idea. Hardly nice in the home."

"You heard me," said Pop. *"Don't flush!"*

"O.K. O.K.," I said.

From then on Pop seldom left the house and nobody could approach a bathroom door or turn a faucet without his knowing it.

"Don't flush!" he would shout and the unfortunate person would start back as if bitten by a snake.

Every now and then one of us would absent-mindedly push the lever, and at the sound Pop would give a wild cry.

"Who's that?" he'd yell. "Get out of that bathroom. Now!"

As far as we could tell he stayed awake all night listening for the heartbeat of the pump and at breakfast would give a rundown on the number of times it had gone on. The well had filled up enough to provide a minimal amount of H_2O, but it seemed to Pop outrageous that individuals were capable of sneaking into bathrooms in the middle of the night.

"I heard the pump go on at three-fifteen!" he said once. "Now who in Sam Hill was responsible for that?"

We would all indignantly deny any part in the affair.

"We sleep during the night," I said. "We don't sit outside the john door with a gun across our knees."

"Well, I distinctly heard the pump at three-fifteen and again at five and six."

"Maybe somebody's got the green-apple quick step," I said, but Pop didn't think it was funny. He, himself, he said, went outside before bedtime, and there were articles called thunder mugs which had served mankind in the past and were as good as ever. Our collection was intact. He hoped Basil had not rashly disposed of his.

The well gradually returned to normal but Pop never quite did. The experience had been too traumatic. The throb of the pump at odd hours always upset him, and he couldn't rest until he had figured out who the guilty party was.

Besides these earthshaking changes in the plumbing system there was the change in our system of communication. We got a telephone—on a party line, something new to us. There were three other parties on the line and we could listen in on the conversations of a series of unknown voices, mostly female. Their conversations were far from exciting, being composed of long reports on what somebody else had said, recipes, or discussions of disease, but we listened anyway. Sometimes they went on so long with one party telling what she said and the other one saying, "Ayah," that Dave would lift the receiver and yell, "Shut up!" However, Pop frowned on this practice. There was no privacy whatsoever as the telephone was right in the living room, and everybody used to sit around listening, giving advice or asking who it was. This was particularly trying for Dave and me, since we were making a determined attempt to live our own lives.

The minute the telephone rang every person in the house made a dive for it. Pop would leap from his chair, Mum would come trotting out of the kitchen, I would jump downstairs two at a time, while Dave galloped down the lawn. Whoever won sat on the sea chest, covering his free ear with his hand to shut out the babble from the group.

"Who's that?" Mum always asked over and over, while Pop shouted, "Is that for me?" and the rest called out things like "If that's so-and-so let me talk to him" or "That's for me; I'm expecting a call."

The victim usually had to cover the mouthpiece with his hand and hiss to everyone to shut up.

Dave and I were particularly anxious at lunchtime because we were always hoping one of our new friends from the beach would ask us to go out sailing on their big boats. Every afternoon a procession of tall white sails went down the channel heading out to sea, and on the decks below were the lucky people who had been asked to go that day. We used to watch them through the glass to see who they were, and we longed to be aboard. Pop and the boys had gone out in other years but I wasn't asked because, they said, I was a girl. Now, I hoped, I'd be asked *because* I was a girl, but in the end I was asked because I was a bird watcher. Uncle Smith invited me to go with him and Pop on their annual sail to the island of Penikese to see the tern colony.

CHAPTER FIFTEEN

The Islands

THE ISLAND of Penikese is one of the Elizabeth Islands, lying between the mainland and Martha's Vineyard. The islands were discovered by Bartholomew Gosnold in the seventeenth century and named after Queen Elizabeth. In Gosnold's time they had forests of beech, cedar, and sassafras, but all the trees are gone on Penikese now, leaving fields of soft russet grass patched with clumps of bayberry, sweet fern, and wild roses, where song sparrows nest. At one time there was a leper colony there, at another time Louis Agassiz established a school, but nothing is left of either except some cement foundations. The tern colony at that time occupied most of the land around the harbor on the sheltered side. Every July during the nesting season Uncle Smith invited Pop to sail out there with him on his sloop, the *Spindrift*. Aldie and Dave had gone along on a special trip with a bird-watching English divine called Canon Raven, but I, who was the bird watcher in our family, was not asked. I was at that time plowing through a gigantic book by Frank M. Chapman called *Camps and Cruises of an Ornithologist,* in which Mr. Chapman was constantly landing on islands that were knee deep in young birds and eggs. As an ardent bird nester and amateur ornithologist, I considered this state of affairs ideal, and I felt that I was being discriminated against. I wanted to go to sea and explore the islands, which now seemed as romantic as those in the South Seas.

During the pea-green years of boating, when we sailed the river in our sharpies, the sea was comparable to the wide world, the grownup world, into which we peered at intervals with mixed emotions. Beyond our flats and mussel beds, beyond the familiar channels and sand bars, lay that great slow-breathing expanse where we were forbidden to go. I'm sorry to report here that we went anyway but not very far, as we had a healthy respect for the tides that boiled and eddied through the harbor entrance. Up against the Point of Rocks there was a back eddy where we could see the giant kelps weaving and writhing in the green depths. When the wind was against the tide, the swells piled up on the ledge by Half-Mile Rock and broke in a swirl of foam on the rocks below the blinker. After a gale they broke right across the harbor mouth and no boat could go in or out, but on a still morning when the wind was offshore, flattening the waves, the whole expanse twinkled in the sun like an inland lake. Blue and gentle, it drowsed under the summer sky, and at its far rim were the islands, the color of ripe grapes. There were windless days when they floated in the air above the horizon, unsubstantial as lands in a fairy story, and weather breeders when they loomed so close we could see the purple shadows in their folds. There was no question in my mind that these islands bounded our Point world exactly as a stone wall bounds a field. Distance gave them a special enchantment as it did to ships at sea. From the flying bridge of our porch the vessels that moved slowly across the horizon seemed to exist in a realm of perfect silence and peace. Six-masted schooners leaned to a breeze we couldn't feel or hear. Rarely, we saw a square-rigger rising like a white tower out of the violet haze, and once every summer the New York Yacht Club went by, scattering sails from Newport to Cuttyhunk. We knew they were headed for Edgartown on Martha's Vineyard somewhere out of sight over the curve of the world. We used to see plumes of smoke from invisible steamers below this curve, and sometimes there was a smokestack poking up over the edge. I used to picture the islands covered with palm trees and natives like the islands in the *Geographic*. Later on, of course, I realized they were not like that and except for the settlement on Cuttyhunk the islands were inhabited only by birds, sheep, and Boston Forbses. Of these I was most interested in the birds.

We had islands in the river which up until this time had satisfied our explorer's appetite. Some were simply rocks rising above the green-gold levels of salt marsh; others were high enough to support small groves of oaks, horribly framed in wreaths of poison ivy and greenbrier. On the stony little beaches grew clumps of long silky grass, seaside goldenrod, and asters, all sewn together with morning glories. In late August the goldenrod bloomed in heavy yellow plumes, and near it were little groves of marsh rosemary, blue as the sky.

Ospreys nested in dead trees on several of the islands, and on one—called Mysterious Island—lived a bunch of characters from the House of David who, according to legend, refused to cut their hair until the second coming of Christ. As a result of this rash promise they were all like walking haystacks, and spying on them was pretty daring. Now the river islands seemed tame, mere hells of poison ivy splashed with osprey droppings. Even the beards lost their sinister appeal.

Dave and Aldie went to the islands several times. When the *Wanderer*, the last of the New Bedford whalers, was wrecked on the rocks off Cuttyhunk, Pop took the boys out on the little steamer. Did they take me? No, they did not, but they took my precious new binoculars. When they returned they had the *Wanderer*'s teak helmsman's rack and several pounds of copper spikes, but Pop had left my binoculars on the beach, where they were covered twice by the tide before he went back and got them. This episode made me feel very bitter about men and their high-handed ways. The last straw was when Uncle Smith took them all on a cruise in the *Spindrift*. They came back burned brown as Indians and babbling of romantic little harbors at dawn, lonely beaches of white sand where they swam naked as the natives in the *Geographic,* and meals eaten on deck after a sunset landfall.

"Why can't I go on a cruise?" I asked angrily.

"Now, dearie," said Pop, "this was a man's affair. It's rough out there and you might be seasick—"

"You were," said Dave.

"I was not," cried Pop indignantly.

"Then why were you bright green? Why did you keep eating crackers?"

"I felt a little queasy, yes," said Pop with dignity, "but that's beside the point. The main reason she can't go along is that the *Spindrift* has only one cabin and she's a girl."

"The main reason is there's no john," said Aldie, "just a pail."

Pop held up his hand.

"There's no need to go into detail—" he began.

"—and we couldn't go in swimming raw if you came along," said Aldie.

There seemed to be no solution to this apart from changing my sex, but later, apparently, Uncle Smith had a change of heart. Either that or he improved his plumbing facilities.

The Penikese expedition couldn't be planned in advance because of wind and weather. An island day had to be a blue day with a gentle morning breeze changing to southwest in the afternoon. On an island day the houses across the river looked pinky-gold in the early light and the oak leaves shone like silver. The sea was cornflower blue with no whitecaps, quiet and serene. In the stillness the loon laughter of the gulls sounded clearly from the river.

The *Spindrift* had no auxiliary engine, so we had to be sure the wind would hold. Uncle Smith knew his weather, though, and he and Pop would consult over the telephone.

Finally the right kind of morning dawned. Pop went out on the porch to check and shouted, "This is the day the Lord hath made!" and burst into his yodeling act. Uncle Smith called soon after breakfast, and we assembled our gear, took the binoculars, several boxes of saltines against seasickness, bacon, eggs, and home-made bread for lunch, and *hats*. In those days all the grown-ups wore white duck hats with green under the brims to cut the glare and prevent sunstroke. Now we had to wear hats, too, sailor hats or mildewed antiques from the sea chest at Snowdon or old felt hats of Pop's.

Out on the boat we helped Uncle Smith stow the gear in the cabin, take off the sail covers, untie the stops, and haul up the sails. We loved the *Spindrift*'s cabin, our first experience of the snuggest of all human habitations. It wasn't much of a cabin compared to the ones we knew later, but it had portholes, and when you were inside you could hear the liquid chuckle of water against the planking and the creak of timbers as the boat heeled over in the breeze. Nobody dared stay there very long because it was well known that going below at sea made you green. Getting green was the most terrible disgrace anyone could imagine, even worse than missing a mooring.

On that lovely morning the *Spindrift* tilted to the light breeze and headed out into the blue-and-silver hush of the open ocean. I remember the lift of the first swell under her bow, the sudden sensation of deep water below us. Twelve miles out on the horizon lay the islands, and this meant two or more hours of sailing—long enough to lose touch with the land behind us, to get the sun-soaked, blue-drowned feeling of a day at sea. We passed the Spindle two miles out and looked through the glasses at the cormorants drying their wings. We heard the bell buoy coming up, and left its chiming behind as we sailed into the zone of the hooter. The lightship loomed ahead, with *Hen and Chickens* printed boldly on her hull. We waved to the crew high above us and they waved back, grinning.

All the way out terns passed us in steady processions, one line headed for the mainland and the fishing grounds, the other going like us to Penikese. These all held silver fish wriggling in their bills.

The common tern is one of the most beautiful birds alive —streamlined, graceful, exquisitely colored. The pearl-gray back, snowy belly, and aristocratic black-capped head are set off by a bill of bright coral and orange feet. Uncle Smith and Pop used to spend half their time trying to distinguish between the common tern and the roseate, both of which nest on Penikese. The roseate's bill is black and its feet vermilion, but its loveliest feature, visible only at close range, is the flush of pale sea-shell pink on its breast.

We anchored in the lee of Penikese, dropping the hook into forests of eelgrass, where the water had the aquamarine clarity of ocean currents. As we took down the sails the terns rose up in a white, screaming cloud exactly like the snow in those paperweights that whirls up when shaken. They boiled out into the harbor, and the noise was such that we had to shout over it. As we rowed in they began diving at us, shearing off just before their bills struck us in the forehead. Any war movie showing planes strafing a road or dive-bombing a ship will give you the idea. Their cry of anger is "Kuk-Kuk-Kuk-aow," very like a machine gun, and it was quite something to be the target of several dozen at once.

The curved beach where we landed was made of small pebbles, that rustled in the wash from our oars. At the high-tide mark was a line of dried eelgrass and driftwood, beyond grew clumps of seaside goldenrod and beach pea, and the pale pink wild morning glories hung their deceptively fragile garlands over everything. A hill of green-gold grass rolled up to the sky, and the terns seemed to pour from its crest like smoke from a volcano, a blizzard of birds exactly as pictured in *Camps and Cruises of an Ornithologist*. As I stepped out onto the pebbles I stood still and savored the moment. The polished air was scented with bayberry and wild roses, and all around were space and blue water. For the first time I felt the island magic.

Pop and Uncle Smith made a beeline for the upper beach and, as protection against the dive bombers, filled their hats with seaweed. It drooped about their faces like the dyed and frizzled locks of elderly ladies with wigs, but they were quite unaware of their hilarious appearance.

"Tuck it in, Pa, for crumb's sake," I said. "You look like an old lady."

"I don't give a hoot what I look like," said Pop. "A bald-headed man has to be careful on this island."

"Watch out for eggs and chicks," said Uncle Smith, who resembled a depraved duchess in his seaweed wig. I looked and saw with astonishment that eggs lay all around us—in shallow depressions in the seaweed, on the sand, in the grass, and more were revealed as angry mothers flew up. These eggs were beautifully camouflaged, their color varying from deep olive brown to pale greenish tan mottled with chocolate, and I hardly dared take a step for fear of crushing one. Frank M. Chapman would have felt right at home.

The caretaker of the sanctuary, who lived in a little house back from the shore, came down to welcome us and after a short consultation in low voices he led Pop and Uncle Smith up the hill to a small narrow building on the edge of the cliff. I gathered this was how they were solving the plumbing problem. When Pop came back, much refreshed, he said we ought to visit the place.

"It faces right out to sea," he said. "Most magnificent view I ever saw."

He was quite right. The small building, weathered silver as a piece of driftwood, had no door at all, and from the sun-warmed seat the inmate commanded a panorama of blue sea and sky, with the treeless golden flanks of the opposite islands dividing them.

Pop and Uncle Smith wandered off talking about the difference in wing spread between roseates and common terns, but we three hunted for babies. We discovered a small fresh-water pond, blue as a sapphire, set in the marsh grass above the beach, and here we watched the terns playing over its surface, dipping their bellies in the water like swallows, splashing in the shallows, and even swimming about like ducks. Beyond the pond were a lot more nests. Followed by our cloud of screaming parents we stepped carefully through the grass, around rocks, over salt-silvered driftwood and mops of seaweed. Finally, between two pink granite boulders, I saw the first baby.

He was a newly hatched chick, still in the nest, lying

flat so that his buff and brown markings melted into the buff and brown of his seaweed bed. I picked him up in spite of the screams of his parents, and he immediately opened his carmine-lined mouth for food. After a bit he rolled over on his back, exhibiting a white belly and two rose-petal-pink feet. I stroked his downy stomach with my finger and unfurled the tiny transparent webbed toes. What a miracle of packaging he was, so freshly dried out from his egg, as yet unaware of the danger from above—the cruciform shadow of the herring gull that eats baby terns for breakfast.

These cannibals live out on a point in their own community, and we eventually came out on a grassy knoll where eggs, fishbones, broken shells, and other rubbish were strewn about, liberally whitewashed with droppings. A few downy chicks were flattened in hollows, and they were pretty endearing, being composed entirely of pearl-gray fluff. Very soon in their careers they take to the water; fleets of them were bobbing about offshore like bathtub toys. Young gulls have a revolting habit that one cannot but deplore. If they are alarmed they stagger off toward the sea, pausing for a moment en route to disgorge everything they have eaten, apparently since birth. This is mostly fish, and often quite sizable ones are returned intact. Others not so intact are also returned, and this doesn't add to the charm of the colony. Still, I have to admit that an adult herring gull on the wing is one of the perfect sights in life. When they were all in the air over our heads the effect was of sails, the snow-white curves in the sun, the pointed shapes against blue, the flapping thunder of yards swinging over. A towering cloud of gulls moves you like a square-rigger coming down under full sail.

When we went back to the beach we found Pop and Uncle Smith crouched over a little fire cooking bacon and coffee, while an enraged tern made periodic dives at their heads. Pop said some rather Elizabethan things about the dangers of cooking under so many unhousebroken birds, so we waved them off between forays for more driftwood. Nothing ever smelled so good as that bacon cooking outdoors, its heavenly fragrance mixed with the

smell of smoke and coffee, and the iodine odor of rockweed.
Pop was never allowed in the kitchen at home, but he was
always the cook on cruises or picnics. I can see him now in his
white hat and seaweed wig breaking eggs into a frying pan and
explaining the exact amount of force needed to crack the shell
without rupturing the yolk.

"Just a quick snap of the wrist," he said, tapping an egg on
the edge of the pan, "and then open it up this way." And there
was the egg, looking up at us with its one golden eye.

We ate bowed over our plates to protect them from the terns'
reprisals, while Pop discoursed on the experience of real hunger
and how vital it was for everyone to feel it at some time.

Pop's habit after any picnic was to lie in the sun a while and
rest, but nobody could do this down by the nesting grounds. Also,
after a certain amount of time spent in the middle of that vast din,
you began to think of it as existing wholly apart from the birds.
It was like a great creaking machine of sound, full of individual
squeaks and grindings. You heard a thousand rusty hinges shriek,
armies of squealing wheelbarrows, a million sticks of chalk squeaking on a thousand blackboards, and unoiled pulleys screeching, all
gathered up into one huge engine room.

To escape the birds we climbed the hill back of the beach
and went over to the other side of the island. As we labored up
the lion-colored flank we climbed above the noise into what seemed
like silence. The hot sun baked the fragrance out of bayberry and
sweet fern. Song sparrows bubbled from the tips of wild-rose
bushes, as fresh and cool as little springs after the feverish clamor
below. At the top our heads rose suddenly into the sea breeze
and a wide emptiness of blue water. Penikese is so small that we
could see all around it—south to Nashawena and Cuttyhunk and
Gay Head on the Vineyard, west into the silver glare of the sun
on the open ocean and north across Buzzard's Bay to the violet
haze of the mainland. A white yawl was beating out of Padanaram
and a schooner was running downwind into New Bedford. While
Pop and Uncle Smith dozed in the sun with their hats over their
eyes, we went swimming in a rocky cove below. As a lone female

I had to go and undress in the remains of Agassiz' academy. The water was cold and clear as champagne over the pebbles, blue-green as thick glass over the white sand bottom. I lay on my back and looked up at the soaring gulls and then swam face down, exploring the blurred underworld of water. Afterward I dried myself in the wind and sun and lay in a warm hollow, roasting myself in full view of Buzzard's Bay. When you have cooked and eaten food there, gone swimming from it, and felt against your bare back the soft fur of the island's side you have somehow gotten at the essence of the place. I could, I' thought, feel the earth turn under me, wheeling me up and over through the blue air like a gigantic ferris wheel.

When we went down to the shore we found everybody deep in conversation with a group of Harvard scientists. They were all wearing seaweed wigs under their hats and were gravely discussing the markings of garter snakes. One of them had a burlap bag with a horrible snarl of snakes in the bottom, and he would run one of them through his fingers, exhibiting the beautiful designs of brown and black and cream. The garter snakes of Penikese because of their isolation had, I think, developed their own pattern.

The sail home was wet and rough, and in spite of our oil-skins we were soaked to the skin. It was a real workout clinging to the windward rail, dodging the sheets of salt spray, and riding the boat's bucking motion the way you sit a horse. All this ended abruptly in the heavenly peace of the harbor. In the lee of the Point of Rocks the waves vanished and the wind dropped, and we floated on a level keel without a sound. The scents of grass and flowers came to us off the land; the sun was hot again. I went up on the cabin top and stood there, to dry my bottom and to savor the luxury of a steady deck. In the late-afternoon light the river was a theatrical blue, the grass flats were incandescent. Terns were still flying past, rosy now in the westering sun, and some were fishing in the channel, but their day was about done as ours was. Every sailor knows the special quality of this interlude between the sea and the mooring, when after cold you are warm, after wetness you are dry, and you have a whole blue day under your belt.

Now that we had discovered the sea and the islands our river with its eelgrass and mud flats seemed tame indeed. Compared to the *Spindrift* our pea-green sharpies seemed pitifully small and shabby. Here at last was what we'd read about—the poetry of sail, blue water, and all that business of boats being like birds with white wings. I took to reading Conrad and memorized the names of all the sails on a clipper ship. Dave, on the other hand, pursued a more practical course. He went to work on Pop.

CHAPTER SIXTEEN

Down to the Sea

IN DAVE'S FIRST ATTEMPTS to brainwash Pop into buying a big boat he used the wrong approach. Under the impression that Pop, too, loved the sea and wanted to go to the islands, he explained to him how this could be done. He spoke in poetic language of the joys of cruising, the beauty of the islands, and the excitement of all those terns on Penikese. If we bought a boat—just a tiny little sloop like the *Spindrift*—we could go out there all the time and not have to wait for other people to ask us.

"A man in my position can't afford a big boat," said Pop. "I'm a minister and ministers don't have that kind of money. Big boats are for millionaires."

"Uncle Smith's a minister," Dave said, "and he's got a big boat."

"I have no idea what Smith's financial situation is," said Pop, "but I am familiar with mine."

"You are not," said Mum.

This was true in a way as she controlled the checkbook and paid the bills. Pop was apt to throw away bills unopened, and in the process often threw away checks. He was allowed a few handfuls of change for his own use, but every night when he picked up his pants by the cuffs to fold them all of it fell out on the floor and rolled to the far corners of the room, so he didn't get much. In any case, he despised money most of the time and used to say he felt sorry for rich people, poor jaded creatures ruined by wealth, every want gratified. Now he spoke of a millionaire at the harbor who had a steam yacht.

"Look at them," he said. "There's that great boat lying at anchor and no one ever goes near it."

"Pop," we said, "we don't want a steam yacht, just a seagoing sailboat."

However, nothing came of this. Of course we all knew we couldn't afford a big boat, but ordinarily this would not have prevented Pop from buying one. Finally, Mum extracted from him the fact that not only had he felt green on the *Spindrift* but that on a ghastly voyage with friends in a motor cruiser he had been actively seasick. He didn't like it out at sea. After we discovered that we went to work on him and had almost persuaded him he hadn't been seasick at all when a miracle occurred. A friend of his offered us his Friendship sloop for the summer. This vessel had a mast as big as a telephone pole, several acres of sail, and a boom that could knock a bull cold. Only a gorilla could have managed both sheet and wheel with any kind of ease, and for us to take to sea in such a craft was comparable to a five-year-old child's driving a moving van. The mere thought of doing so made Pop turn green even on land, but he couldn't resist the offer. Friendship sloops were famous and were working boats, not yachts. This seemed to comfort Pop, as he didn't approve of yachting ministers, the nautical equivalent of hunting parsons. What's more a working boat must, he felt, be sound and seaworthy. Actually, the Friendship was held together only with paint, but fortunately he didn't know that. On the whole, I think it was the cabin that finally won Pop over. The Friendship's had the great advantage of headroom; even the tallest of us could stand erect. There was also a forward cabin with a head and two extra bunks. The main cabin followed the classic pattern, with a drop-leaf mahogany table down the middle, a Shipmate stove up against the after bulkhead on the port side, and a little sink on the starboard. There were two excellent bunks and various shelves, racks, bins, and cupboards for stowing supplies, charts, papers, and equipment. The whole thing was painted the thick, shiny white of all proper cabins, and on its walls the sun ripples quivered in a very romantic way. Pop was so entranced with the cabin that he introduced a new kind of picnic—eating on the boat—that became one of the features of the new era. While we were painting and rigging the Friendship we ate on the boat almost every day.

One of the delights of outfitting was the trip to Beckman's, the ship chandler in New Bedford. This marvelous place, built of granite, was on the steep street heading down to the waterfront. It was on several levels, each one with its specialty—rope or hardware or marine paint. It smelled like tar, and around each corner were enchanting objects, furniture of the new world we had entered with the Friendship. Pop was as new to it as we were, and he soon lost all sense of reality, fingering bronze blocks and cleats, running lights polished like gold, and brass lanterns hung in gimbals. He even contemplated seriously a ship's clock but finally dragged himself back to earth and bought what we needed—manila rope and charts. These works of art in pale blue and cream are so dear to the hearts of amateur sailors that few can resist papering walls with them or framing them under glass for trays and coffee tables. Our first collection included "Westport River and Approaches," "Martha's Vineyard to Block Island," "Robinson's Hole to Cuttyhunk Harbor," "Buzzard's Bay," and one or two others.

The Professor heard about our love affair with the Friendship and came over to invite us out on his yawl for a practice run. He would, he said, take us out for a day on Nashawena, his favorite of the Elizabeth chain. Then he really let himself go on the subject of islands—the eternal symbols of escape and freedom, tiny continents just the right size for one man, a little world unspoiled by so-called civilization. He sang the praises of cruising—stopping at a different harbor every night, exploring new islands, swimming off strange beaches, but always taking along with you the cozy refuge of your vessel's cabin. To wake in an island harbor and see the sunrise at sea was, he said, one of life's essential experiences. He was like one of those sailors with gold rings in their ears who tell stories of far-off climes to little boys in books. In fact, he so inflamed Pop's imagination that he could hardly wait to go on a cruise himself in his own boat.

The Professor was in great form when we set out the next morning. As we took off the sail covers, coiled ropes, and stowed gear he discoursed on the romance of the sea, the poetry of sail. He remembered, he said, when on a clear day you could count fifty sails between Newport and the Vineyard. Never again, he said, would man be so intimate with the sea as when he was dependent on the winds and moved under a cloud of canvas. He directed a sea chanty for pulling up the anchor, and then taking the wheel sailed us straight across the channel onto a mud-flat.

We spent quite a while there waiting for the tide to float us off and the Professor read aloud to us out of a book called *Blue Water* by Hildebrand. After a while Pop and Dave got into the dinghy, took a line off the stern, and pulled the boat free.

The trip to the islands was a great success, but unfortunately the Professor began reading aloud again from *Blue Water* on the way back and nearly piled us up on the Lumber Rocks. He had gone inside the marker but explained that buoys were an artificial arrangement of man and not part of the eternal plan.

These two incidents had a very bad effect on Pop. If the Professor, who had sailed for years, went aground on mud-flats, what would we do who had never operated in big boats?

"We'll pay attention to what we're doing," said Dave. "Steer the boat, for instance."

Still Pop was not ready. This was abundantly clear when Uncle Smith loaned us the *Spindrift* for an afternoon. The *Spindrift* was only a small sloop and easy to manage, so we got out to sea with no trouble. However, beyond Half-Mile Rock the swells mounted and the wind freshened. Then the whistle of the breeze in the rigging, the crunch of the bow into a green wave, and the tumultuous flapping of sails while coming about caused

Pop to do what we called grim-deathing. He who had taught us to lean on the wind over cliffs, walk ridgepoles, and play tag on the barn roof now gripped the wheel until his knuckles turned white under the strain and spoke in a tense, clipped voice between clenched teeth. He made us take down the mainsail half a mile from the mooring and float down under jib. Even so, we missed the mooring five times, losing the boathook in the process. Dave was furious.

"The whole village probably has the glass on us," he said. "You can't maneuver a boat with the sail down, for Pete's sake."

"That's all right, boy," said Pop, who only called his sons "boy" when he was mad. "The man at the wheel has the last word. When I speak, you jump."

When we finally took the Friendship out, though, the man at the wheel was Dave. From then on he was the skipper, and when he spoke Pop jumped or at least crawled to his post. I don't know whether Dave was a good sailor or not at that point, but he thought he was, so we trusted him.

We will pass over the initial stages of our education in big boats. Suffice it to say that we gave a lot of innocent pleasure to every inhabitant of Westport. Finally, though, we acquired a certain amount of primitive competence, although chimpanzees could probably have done as well.

Dave now decided it was time we went on a short cruise, and after some argument Pop agreed to try it.

No navigator of the ancient world, planning a voyage into the Sea of Darkness, was more apprehensive than Pop when he unrolled the charts of our prospective cruising ground.

The "Approaches" part of the Westport River chart made it all too clear why it was called one of the worst harbors on the Eastern Seaboard. Under the innocent sparkling surface of the summer sea lay all manner of sinister bars, reefs, and ledges, submerged rocks as big as cathedrals and flocks of smaller ones that gave their names to *Hen and Chickens* and *Sow and Pigs* lightships—Dogfish Ledge, Joe Burris Ledge, Browing Ledge, Chickadee Ledge, the Lumber Rocks—a dreadful collection.

"Eye Guy," said Pop, "there's a place here that says 'Wreck' and another that says 'Wreckage.'"

"Leave that chart alone," said Dave sternly.

The day we were to sail dawned hot and steamy—a white day. There was no wind, but Pop was rather pleased at that. The Friendship had an engine and the sea was like glass. We spent all morning loading supplies, set sail at twelve and spent the afternoon slatting around in a flat calm off Half-Mile Rock. Having forgotten lunch we ate sardines out of a can, probably the last thing anyone should attempt while rolling about on oily swells. I haven't eaten them since. The engine refused to start, so we finally towed the boat into the river with the dinghy just as the entire world was swallowed up in fog.

"Well, at least nobody can see us," said Dave. "Let's spend the night right here and maybe we can sneak out early."

We anchored just off the wharf but the fog was so thick we could easily have been out at the islands.

"This is just as good as Cuttyhunk," said Pop happily.

"No, it isn't," said Dave, annoyed, but Pop was clearly delighted to be safe.

The next morning the fog was thicker than ever but we went over the side for a dip. Pop, who had been awake most of the night waiting for the anchor to drag, went below with chattering teeth and hit his head a resounding blow on a beam. When he unfolded the towel he had brought it turned out to be a pale blue one about a foot long with "Baby" embroidered on it.

We sneaked back to the mooring under cover of the fog and arrived home just as the family were eating breakfast.

"That was a pretty short cruise," said Mum.

A spell of fog followed this degrading episode but at last we got a morning when the sea was once more visible. There were clouds, but we decided to load the boat secretly and then pretend we were going for a routine afternoon sail. This time luck was with us. The cloud cover slipped back and left the sky the color of a morning glory. Beneath it the waves rolled, deep purple-blue to the horizon. Dave climbed the mast and lay along the gaff, rocking slowly with the motion of the boat. I lay on the cabin top in the sun, looking up at the sail against the sky, and Pop sat at the wheel in a state of extreme euphoria, captain of his own ship at last.

Running easily before the gentle breeze we passed *Hen and Chickens* lightship at six and saw Cuttyhunk rising out of the sea ahead of us, gold in the sunlight. Terns with shiners in their bills winged by on their way to Penikese and the whole business was like something out of John Masefield.

We dropped anchor in the Chicken Yard, Cuttyhunk's inner harbor, just as the wind vanished completely. While Dave furled the sails Pop and I rowed ashore in the dinghy to get a fish for dinner. Some of the boats were in, and we bought a freshly caught tautog from one of the fishermen. He cleaned it while Pop questioned him about life at sea. It turned out he was a Greek, which somehow made everything even better.

Dave had already lighted the Shipmate stove, and the smell of wood smoke met us as we rowed out.

Pop as the official cook went to work in the galley while Dave and I prepared the Friendship for the night. We hung up the riding light, checked the mooring line, and then went below into a glorious smell of broiled fish and strong coffee. The cabin's white walls gleamed yellow in the light from the kerosene lantern, the stove snapped and crackled, and it was warm. Every porthole was full of the sunset. Pop was in his highest spirits and beamed around the cabin, waving a fork like a conductor's baton.

"Say, how about this?" he asked. "Did you ever see such a cozy little place? And what about that sail out? You'll never forget that. You'll remember it all your life."

The storehouse of joy, our insurance for the future, was bursting with new contributions. There was nothing Pop loved more than to review the latest treasures. He was like a miser counting his gold, but the gold was for us. And what wealth it was.

We sat around the mahogany table after dinner drinking coffee and eating chocolate. Dave and I lighted cigarettes, which tasted wonderful. Pop regarded us with envy.

"Give me one of those," he said.

We did so and he inserted half of it into his mouth.

"Holy smoke, Robert," said Dave, "you're not supposed to eat it. Just put the end in."

Pop removed the cigarette and put the dry end in his mouth. Dave took it away from him and gave him another, adjusting it correctly to his lips. He then lighted it. A shower of sparks shot over the table.

"Suck in!" we yelled. "Inhale!"

After Pop had recovered from his fit of coughing he sat up with streaming eyes.

"Gosh almighty," he whispered, "I don't see how you do it. It looks so comfortable."

"You aren't supposed to smoke the whole cigarette in one long drag," said Dave, removing the wreckage from Pop's nerveless fingers. "Forget the whole thing."

After this episode Pop said he thought he needed some fresh air, so we rowed ashore and climbed to the top of the island under a sky full of stars.

That night I lay in my bunk and heard the water gurgling against the side; the peak halyard tapped against the mast. Sometime in the early morning the tide turned and we woke up feeling the boat swing around on her mooring. Pop got up to check the anchor, and I stood in the companion way looking at the constellations, which had all changed position while we slept. Over the dark curve of the islands they seemed brighter and larger than they did at home. It was so still that the harbor was full of their reflections, and we floated in space surrounded by stars.

When I woke the next morning the sun ripples were already running across the cabin ceiling. Every porthole was full of blue. I heard the harsh cries of terns outside and the music of water against the wood by my head. The day was well on its way, but when I scrambled up on deck I saw that the sky was still rosy with dawn. The lighthouse on shore, the boats, the white houses of the village, and the breasts of the terns were all flushed pink. A film of pink lay over the blue of the harbor and the sea, a

color so tender and soft that it made me think of apple blossoms. During the night a yawl had anchored near us, the *Sea
Dream* from Oyster Bay, elegant as a swan. No one aboard her
was awake. No one anywhere seemed awake but me and the
terns. Standing there in my pajamas with my bare feet cold in
the dew I greeted the new day. After our mud flats and eelgrass
it seemed unbelievably pure and unused, the water clear as a
jewel, the dew-washed air sweet with wild roses and salt and
the magic islands asleep in the sunrise.

I woke to many other mornings at sea but this was the first.
When I look back on it I am glad to remember that I knew just
how miraculous it was to be alive at all, and on top of that young
on a summer morning.

Pop joined me in the cockpit and looked about him as though
he owned the world.

"This is the day the Lord hath made," he cried. "Make a
joyful noise unto the Lord!"

Until about two-thirty in the afternoon the level of euphoria
continued to rise. After the exalted moment at dawn we went
swimming in the harbor, then ate bacon and eggs on deck in the
lovely sunlight. Then we made sail and ran down Buzzard's
Bay to Quicks's Hole, the passage between Nashawena and
Pasque islands, where a crescent of white sand curved around a
little bay as blue as the eye of a peacock feather. We anchored in
the lee of the island and rowed ashore in the dinghy. It was as
hot and still as a beach in the tropics, but when we stood on the
sand we could hear the bleating of sheep on the moors and the
song sparrows singing.

"You'll never forget this," said Pop rapturously. "You
cannot not have had it."

After a swim we ate on the boat—Pop's classic meal of broiled
swordfish and canned corn. The sun was hot, we were ravenously
hungry, and our spirits were so high that we spoke boastfully of
our prowess as navigators and of the excellence of our ship.

Pop admitted freely that we had been right about the need
for a seagoing vessel of our own. He said he thought the Friend-

ship was, without any question, the best craft he had ever sailed on.

"Sound as a dollar. A great old boat," he quavered, for already the Friendship was one of the family, part of the home.

Then we put up the sails and headed across Vineyard Sound toward Menemsha—the harbor at the western end of the Vineyard. Almost at once everything fell apart. The wind rose to a screaming gale, the Friendship heeled over with a loud cracking of timbers and bellowing of sails. Every seam opened up, and in no time at all the cabin was awash. Once, when I was feeling slightly seasick, I lay in my bunk and watched the toilet paper sailing back and forth in the bilge that covered the floorboards. After a while a lot of this bilge, liberally mixed with gasoline, surged up the side and onto the mattress, so I stuck my head out the hatch.

"I think we're sinking," I said.

"Never mind that," said Pop in a harsh voice. "Hold on to this wheel when I put her up into the wind. We'll have to reef."

"We can't," said Dave. "The waves are too high." Then the boom came across and jammed my head down against the cabin top until my eyebrows were almost touching my chin. Pop and Dave burst into hysterical laughter.

"Your face is about an inch high," yelled Dave above the wind. Pop could only point at me and wheeze. After this episode I was so mad that I hoped we would go straight to the bottom. That would teach them.

"Go ahead, sink," I said when I could move my jaw. "I'm leaving. I don't feel well."

It was a little hard to leave just then, but I abandoned ship in Menemsha, bummed my way to a hotel, and borrowed money to go back on the steamer. After I had cooled down I began to worry about the others, who had decided to sail back across the Sound to Quicks's. What if they really did sink?

Late that night when we were about to go to bed the telephone rang and it was Pop. They were at the shipyard. Somehow they had sailed across the bay in the dark. Nobody, including themselves, had any idea how they had done it.

"It was awful," said Pop, when he finally tottered into the house, green in the face, soaked as to clothing and trembling in every limb. "When we anchored in Quicks's it was so dad-gasted lonely we couldn't stand it. The wind moaning in the rigging—" He broke off as a fit of shivering made his teeth rattle in his head.

The end of the Friendship was very sad. The shipyard men pulled out some of her planking and reaching in scraped out a handful of something like coffee grounds.

"There's your beams," said one of them. "She's just held together with paint, that's all. Just paint."

The Friendship was beached in the shallows near the shipyard and the tide rose and fell in her wonderful cabin. Dave and I gave Pop no time to brood about things and went straight over to the yacht agency to look for another boat. We came back with a flimsy typewritten sheet that had on it a photograph of a boat.

"*Calmar*, Yawl," it read. "Thirty feet over all, etc., etc., $1000 fully found."

She lay in Quisset harbor up the Cape, and the next day we all piled into the car and drove down there. When we went out on the dock we asked where the *Calmar* was.

"There," said the man, pointing. "There she is, out there next to the sloop."

There she was—a snub-nosed black yawl, broad beamed, sturdy—the *Calmar*, that was to be ours for twenty years. It makes me weep just to think about her. Pop bought her with his first royalty check, for he had published a book and was now an author as well as a dean.

CHAPTER SEVENTEEN

Watch Hill

AS DEAN OF THE Princeton Chapel Pop became more and more sought after as a speaker. His engagement book was filled up to two years ahead; he was away every summer Sunday. But for years he refused to charge a fee for speaking and even paid his own travel expenses. If there was one thing Pop despised it was working to *make money*. A man's job, he said, was his contribution to humanity and should not be mixed up with anything as crass as cash.

"Cash may be crass, but I haven't found any way of buying food without it," Mum said. She felt very strongly about this business of preaching for nothing, and spending his own money on travel was the last straw.

"With five children you can't afford to be so revoltingly Christian," she said. "Yale and Harvard are not going to go hungry if you ask a fee for your services. And those people at Watch Hill have more money than you've ever seen in your whole life. You just like to make a noble gesture."

"I do not," cried Pop, rising to the bait.

"Yes, you do. You love to go down there and be treated like the Lord of Creation. That trip cost you over fifty dollars," she said, "and we can't afford it. You like to make grand gestures and have everybody fawning on you. 'Oh, dear Dean Wicks, you're so wonderful,'" she said in the voice she used to imitate Pop's female admirers.

"That's right. Make me out an ass," said Pop. "Your mother always attributes to me the lowest motives."

"Well, then, start charging a good fat fee," said Mum. "That old Ghost gets paid for working in summer. You don't catch him making gestures so a lot of rich women will worship him."

"Your mother is jealous," said Pop to us, but after a while he gave in and began charging a small fee. Of course he often lost the check they gave him or threw it away unopened but gradually he began to depend on speaking engagements to supplement his income. The next thing we knew he was making long strings of baccalaureate addresses in June and signing away his summer Sundays years in advance. Even so he hardly made any money on these transactions because he lost so many of his clothes on the trips.

Every trip he took alone was fraught with peril, as he was the most absent-minded living man. He used to drive our car up to the Chapel to his study, then call a taxi to take him home. While he waited he rested against the fender of a car parked outside—his own. However, at home we could look after him.

The most incredible things happened to Pop the minute he left home, and we never knew whether we'd ever see him again. On his winter trips his secretary always provided him with a typed list of directions, including train times, tickets, detailed descriptions of the places he was going, and his own home address and telephone number, ending with the line: "Your name is Robert Russell Wicks."

Even these precautions were insufficient and Pop would charge into the railroad station, grab a redcap, cry, "Take me to the three-o'clock train," and end up on his way to Baltimore instead of New Haven. Fantastic things happened to his clothing—things that never happened to anybody else's. In a way he seemed to be the victim of his apparel. Once a man threw up on his back in a bus and Pop abandoned his brand-new overcoat without a qualm. He was always leaving his hat somewhere or picking up somebody else's, which was the size either of a washtub or of an egg cup. Once he sat on his hat all the time he was on the train, so when he arrived at the place he was staying he sneaked into his hostess's kitchen and tried to iron it. He had a dim idea that people put a damp cloth over woolen materials when they ironed them so he used a dishrag he found under the sink. The result was a kind of waffle pattern of grease all around the brim.

The boys used to spend hours trying to train him how to buy and wear clothes.

"Why is it," Dave once said, "that no matter what kind of a hat you buy it turns into a violet balloon with a crown a foot high? What in God's name do you do to them?"

"Nothing at all," said Pop. "If you don't like my hats, pick out one for me."

Dave did this and in two days it was a violet balloon.

Then there were his pants all of which were known in the family as Abraham and Isaac.

"When you buy pants," Dave told him, "you don't need to get them so big you can pull them right up over your head and look out the fly. You could get a grown man in each leg. Don't you ever try anything on? What do you do, shut your eyes and grab the first thing you touch?"

"Go ahead, laugh at the old man," said Pop. "I'm just a poor old geezer off the farm. I'm not a Princeton smoothie like you." (Princeton smoothies were the dandies of the thirties. The species is now extinct.)

"Stop saying you're off the farm," said Mum as usual.

"I'm just a hick, just a simple fella, doin' his best," said Pop, becoming a gnarled son of the soil.

Even if his clothes escaped destruction Pop himself was liable to all kinds of damage. If somebody met him at the station they drove the car through the back of the garage or smoked cigars with the window shut until Pop was carsick.

These disasters occurred everywhere he went, but the place where the worst things happened to him was Watch Hill.

Pop went to Watch Hill every summer, and it used to take

him about two days to catalogue the misfortunes that occurred during his stay in that infernal region. The week before he left Mum spent training him, checking his clothes, and going over every item in his suitcase. It was as though he were off to the wars.

"Next Sunday is *Watch Hill!*" she told us, rolling her eyes.

"Oh, boy!" we'd say. To me Watch Hill was a vast sinister stronghold, lashed by perpetual rain, existing in everlasting night, and peopled by a group of characters like those in a Charles Addams cartoon: sinister butlers, burglarous valets, ladies and gentlemen of enormous size dressed in evening clothes, and armies of chambermaids working night and day to hide all Pop's possessions—these passed before our fascinated eyes as Pop told his tale.

I have never seen Watch Hill and I would be scared to go there, but Pop loved it. He used to stay with some very wealthy persons and be entertained like a king in their huge house, but I'm convinced that house was fatal. In fact, we all began to be afraid he'd be killed in it or disappear forever.

On one occasion he decided that rather than risk his life in a public conveyance he would drive his own car from the Point. We tried to dissuade him but to no avail.

"Why don't you just stay here and cut your throat?" Dave asked him. "It would be quicker and easier."

Pop said we were being silly, but all the time he was gone we waited for a telephone call from the police or a hospital.

"He must have made it," Mum said wonderingly, but when he came home he had a heavy cold and was very low in his mind. Apparently he had actually gotten to the town of Watch Hill, but just as he was congratulating himself he had a flat tire, and a thunderstorm broke at the same time. He changed the tire in the rain, wearing his only suit. Hours later, soaked to the skin, he staggered into the house in the middle of a musical soirée with everyone in evening dress. His suit was a mass of wrinkles as well as wet and he developed a severe chill. His hostess insisted that he turn the pages for the pianist, which he did with his teeth chattering like castanets.

"Ibe a sig bad," he said gloomily to us.

On the very next trip one of the legendary characters who seemed to haunt Watch Hill took him swimming after church. Then when Pop was treading water out beyond the breakers his host brought up a steady stream of people to be introduced. Every time Pop shook hands he went under; he nearly drowned before he could get to shore. Then he contracted an even worse chill than he had the previous year, and they had to revive him with hot soup.

The next time he got stuck in a gigantic bathtub and barely made dinner.

"How can anybody get stuck in a bathtub?" I asked him.

"It's easy," said Pop, "when the sides are about six feet tall."

"You'd better keep away from water in that place," said Dave.

When he came back after another round in the house of fear, he had a Band-aid on his chin and carried his head at a queer angle.

"*Now* what have you done?" asked Mum.

"Well," said Pop, "I was just going down to dinner and I tripped on the top step and dove the whole length of the stairs. I landed with my chin on a chair, and I think I've dislocated my jaw or neck or something. I can hardly chew."

"Did anybody see you?" asked Mum.

"All of them," he said. "I think they thought I was drunk."

Once he really did get drunk. He had driven down during a heat wave, and when he arrived he was parched with thirst. When he came downstairs he was offered what he believed to be orange juice. He tossed off several glasses of this refreshing beverage and only later realized it was an Orange Blossom. Not that Pop knew what an Orange Blossom was, but when his head began to spin he knew he had been drinking cocktails.

"Holy cats, Pop," I said, "can't you tell the difference between orange juice and booze? Anyway, who would serve orange juice before dinner?"

"Well, that's great," said Mum. "Just great. First you dive the length of the stairs on your chin and then you get drunk."

Sometimes he came back from Watch Hill with almost nothing left in his suitcase.

"They hid everything," he cried. "Couldn't find my pajamas. No socks. No underwear. I looked all over the whole dadgasted room."

"Listen," I said, "it's perfectly possible for a person to go to Watch Hill without losing all his clothes."

"That's what you think," said Pop. "Why, they get my suitcase away from me and then hide everything I own."

The affair of the tuxedo occurred after we moved to Princeton. Until this period Pop hadn't owned a tuxedo because he believed that ministers should live simply. Now, though, he had to go to so many black-tie functions that he decided to do violence to his ideals and get one. As usual we had hardly any money so Mum unearthed an old tuxedo that had belonged to Uncle Scott, a great uncle who had been a "dandy."

"Uncle Scott," as the tuxedo was called, was made of beautiful material, and the tailor altered it to fit Pop. At this time my brothers were fairly grownup and Uncle Scott was used by all three of them as well as Pop. However, they all wore different pants as Pop's—Abraham and Isaac—were too big.

The minute Pop arrived in Watch Hill somebody ran over his suitcase with his car and broke a medicine bottle. When Pop went up to dress for dinner he found that both legs of the tuxedo pants were slashed across the knees. Still, this to him was of no particular consequence as he felt lucky to have any extra pants at all in Watch Hill. Unfortunately, when he put them on he found they were not Abraham and Isaac, but the pants of his youngest son. The fly wouldn't do up and I think he finally wore the pants of a tweed suit.

"Well, they were on the hanger with Uncle Scott," he cried in self-defense. "How was I to know they were Bob's? Eye Guy!"

The next summer Uncle Scott had a trial run and all was in correct order.

"Now don't let those maids unpack you," Mum said. "Lock your suitcase. Hang up Uncle Scott yourself."

"Your mother thinks I'm an idiot," said Pop. "She doesn't give me credit for any intelligence."

We all waited apprehensively for his return, and finally he drove in with the car door hanging open on a length of clothes line.

"The heater's on. Won't turn off," he said, climbing stiffly out of the car. "Hot as Tophet in there."

"What did you turn it on for?" we asked. "Don't tell us you got another chill."

"I did not turn it on," said Pop with dignity. "It turned itself on."

"Well, never mind that," said Mum. "How did things go? Was Uncle Scott all right?"

"Not exactly," said Pop. "Now don't all jump on me. I hung Uncle Scott up myself. It's not my fault."

"What isn't?" asked Mum. "What's the matter with Uncle Scott now?"

"Nothing at all," cried Pop. "It's just that he's gone."

"Gone?" we said in chorus.

"That butler must have stolen him," said Pop. "A shady character if you ask me. He had shifty eyes."

All summer long Pop had nightmares about Watch Hill and all kinds of other places, some imaginary, where he appeared in the pulpit naked or in his underwear or in a wet bathing suit. I could hear him on the other side of my wall telling them to Mum to the accompaniment of her shrieks of laughter. Actually, his nightmares weren't very different from his real experiences, and the affair of the *Reader's Digest* was even more improbable than most.

One Sunday night as Mum was waiting for Pop to come back from a trip he walked in the door holding a copy of the *Reader's Digest* in what we will call fig-leaf position.

"What's that supposed to be?" asked Mum suspiciously.

"That," said Pop, "is a copy of the *Reader's Digest* as worn by R. W. during the past two days."

Apparently while he was on the train Pop had noticed that his zipper was open, a routine business as far as he was concerned. This time, however, when he zipped himself up the little gadget you zip with came right off the top of his pants. He had a copy of the *Reader's Digest* with him at the time so he used it as a fig leaf until he arrived at his destination, where he explained his predicament to his host. This individual attacked the zipper with a pair of pliers and managed to destroy it completely. Pop said it didn't really matter as his gown would cover it in the pulpit, and this proved to be the case. Afterward he had to go to a luncheon, so the *Reader's Digest* was once more put to work. He kept it in place all through the cocktail hour and luncheon and eventually caught his train and traveled home without once losing his grip on that invaluable magazine.

"But how did you explain to the people at the luncheon?" cried Mum in horror.

"Why should I explain?" asked Pop. "It's a free country, and if a man wants to hold a *Reader's Digest* over his fly it's nobody's business but his own."

We often begged him to write a testimonial to the *Reader's Digest* and invented a great many ourselves, all unprintable, but somehow he never got around to it. Like the testimonial we were going to write to the *New York Times* praising its usefulness in housebreaking puppies, we never did compose one that would pass even a liberal censor.

CHAPTER EIGHTEEN

Pop and the Demon Rum

AFTER POP GOT DRUNK ON Orange Blossoms at Watch Hill we saw that the time had come to train him to drink like a gentleman. It was difficult to know where to start as none of us knew how to drink either. The only liquor bottles we ever saw the whole time we were growing up were advertisements in the London *News*. Prohibition reigned darkly over the land, and Pop was a law-abiding minister who had spent many years salvaging drunks in the slum districts of the city.

It was sometimes hard to understand why drinking was so evil; people did it incessantly in books by Dickens, Thackeray, Dumas, and practically every author Pop read aloud to us. Mr. Pickwick drank to excess as did all his friends; Mr. Micawber in *David Copperfield* was always whipping up hot toddies out of rum, lemons, and other ingredients. Bob Cratchit in *The Christmas Carol* made a bowl of hot gin and lemons and Tiny Tim, that golden-haired Christian child, raised his tiny glass and cried, "God Bless us All!" At least that seemed to be what he said. Pop croaked and sobbed so himself when he read it that the whole Tiny Tim sequence was pretty confused. We had to skip the part where he died as Pop couldn't read any of it.

Even Robin Hood drank like a fish. If it wasn't nut-brown ale, it was "malmsey" or "sack." As for the Three Musketeers, they were hardly ever separated from bottles of wine. They seemed to have a wonderful time sitting in cellars or on tops of towers getting drunk together, and I envied them.

"What's so wicked about drinking wine?" I asked Pop. "Look at D'Artagnan. You love him and he drinks gallons of wine all the time."

Pop said the French were a loose, immoral lot. His year in France during the war had given him a very low opinion of the French, although we never understood why.

"What's wrong with the French?" I asked now. "You're supposed to be a Christian minister and love all mankind."

Mum said Pop had had some interesting experiences in Paris after dark. Then she shrieked with laughter.

"Stop that!" cried Pop.

"He got chased by prostitutes," said Mum. "He was scared blue."

"But, Pop," Dave said, "we have prostitutes over here. All over the place."

"Now drop the subject!" cried Pop. "How did we ever get on it?"

"You said the French were no good," I said.

"Well, they aren't," said Pop. "A rotten bunch, Latins."

"All right, look at the English," said Aldie. "Boy, at Christmastime all they do is drink. Wassail, wassail all over the town, and all those dirty old men in *Pickwick Papers* pinching housemaids behind the door at Old Wardle's. And look at this," he said, holding out a copy of the London *News*. "Gin. Whiskey. Port. Sherry—" He pointed to the advertisements.

"I don't give a damn what the English or the Scots or the blasted Frogs do," said Pop. "I'm not serving liquor in this house!"

With three of his children practically grownup Pop was finding parenthood a little more rugged than he'd expected.

Prohibition was still going on when we moved to Princeton, but as far as we could see this had no effect on the drinking habits of the natives. When we first arrived I was too innocent to believe that anybody but depraved criminal types ever touched a drop, but after a few months in Miss Fine's School the facts of life in a university town filtered down to me.

People drank all over the place. Members of the faculty drank, the students drank, the fox-hunting gang drank, even people's *parents* drank.

Some of the students went out to a "joint" in Hopewell where a farmer ran a still and manufactured a liquid called applejack. Others, more corrupt, went in to New York to places called "speakeasies" where hordes of drunks were drinking moonshine out of teacups. Some persons made bathtub gin and after drinking it went blind and then insane. All this was nothing to the amazing discovery that perfectly respectable people had their own private *bootleggers*. Bootleggers! I had always pictured these individuals as fiends in human form, rough villainous men, red-faced and un-shaven. Now it appeared that they were just like everybody else, and in some cases a lot better looking.

When Repeal hit, an English graduate student who had been brought up on liquor (cf. the London *News*) took me somewhere and fed me a glass of 3.2 beer. It was at this point that I recognized Mum's nursing medicine. When Targ was born Mum had taken a really great medicine called Pabst's Extract to help the milk supply, and we often sampled it. It came in squatty brown bottles with "Pabst's" on the label and tasted nutty and good, prickling the tongue.

"Hey, I've had this before," I said, draining my glass.

"You have?" he said. "Where?"

"Oh, my mother gave it to me," I said. When I got home I told the family about this extraordinary discovery.

"You say drink is so bad," I said to Pop. "Well, Mum drank cases of it. So did we. So did you."

"I have never had a drop of liquor in the home," cried Pop. "What are you talking about?"

"Pabst's Extract," I said. "It was beer."

What the alcoholic content, if any, of Pabst's Extract was I have no idea, but it was indistinguishable from 3.2 beer and served as a good weapon in our arguments with Pop.

"How are we ever going to learn about liquor if you don't let us try it?" we asked. "All the students drink beer."

"Well, I'm going to give them some place to get away from it," said Pop in his loudest voice.

"But, Pop," we said, "they don't want to get away from it."

"They're going to here," he said. "No one can say that a nice chap took his first drink in my home."

As far as Pop was concerned it was the first step that was fatal. In no time at all the demon rum took hold and you ended up in the gutter and shortly afterward died raving and were buried in a drunkard's grave. The gutter was a place that figured heavily in these dramas of vice and seemed to be the final destination of those who did things behind the barn. You could also learn a lot in the gutter but you weren't supposed to. We used this argument, too.

"If you don't want us to learn about liquor and sex in the gutter," I said, "why not teach us yourself?"

Pop didn't think this at all funny. It shocked him deeply to hear a nice girl like me use that word.

"What word?" I said, trying to make him say it, but he simply shook his head sadly.

"This isn't you," he said.

"Yes, it is!" I cried.

It was not easy, believe me.

Down at the Point all hell had broken loose. There was a bar at the foot of the street, a real bar with a sign in red neon letters. Baba and Aunt K. were full of the scandal, and Baba refused even to speak the word. When she was forced to refer to this den of iniquity she spelled it out.

"We heard that So-and-So was seen going into the B-A-R," she would report and all summer she kept track of those who entered its doors. So did Tink, who became an authority on the subject.

Tink had acquired a large new vocabulary as a result of the radio at Synton—a radical purchase which brought jazz, prize fights, opera, and other aspects of modern life right into Baba's drawing room. Aunt K. once revealed in an unguarded moment that Baba liked to listen to the fights, but Baba herself never mentioned this secret vice. She refused to listen to opera, and only church services were allowed on Sundays or so I remember. Tink, of course, adored the radio and was a walking catalogue of commercials. That summer he had a new one which at first we couldn't translate.

"Mother Ann's Codfish," Tink would intone. "Absolukally bumlass."

It turned out that the last phrase was "absolutely boneless," but it finally entered into Tink language and everyone used his version.

When a new name was added to his list of B-A-R victims Tink would report it to us with great relish.

"Call that pretty?" he would say. "I call absolukally bumlass!"

As a result of the B-A-R, we were told, one of the local residents had fallen off the wharf into the river, and some other person was discovered lying in the gutter in broad daylight. Tink took much pleasure in these anecdotes, but Baba wouldn't let him talk about the B-A-R in our presence, so we had to pump him in private.

Right in the middle of all these alcoholic excesses Pop went to Watch Hill and got drunk on Orange Blossoms. We moved in on him.

"Now see what you've done," we said. "You won't learn how to drink like a gentleman so you get drunk in public and disgrace yourself. A man in your position is supposed to be an example to the young. How can you be an example to the young if you swill Orange Blossoms by the dozen and go plunging downstairs on your chin? Do you want people to think you're a hick who doesn't know the difference between orange juice and booze?"

Above Pop's shouts of protest we went on to say that all really sophisticated men drank.

"Winston Churchill," we said. "King George. It's possible,

you know, to drink without getting drunk. Probably Abraham Lincoln drank."

"Holy Caesarea Philippi," cried Pop. "I've had enough of this talk! I am not serving liquor in this house and that's that!"

"Well, if you're not going to teach us to drink in the home, we'll just have to go out behind the barn," said Aldie.

When we went back to Princeton I took that first fatal step—a pink cocktail in a bar called The Peacock Alley, where ladies were allowed. This cocktail—the most repellent stuff I'd ever sipped from a glass—was called a Pink Lady, and when my graduate student left me at the door of the home, pinwheels were going around in my head and I was walking about a foot and a half off the ground. The whole world looked bright, clear, and beautiful.

"Hi, group," I said, tacking into the dining room, where they were all assembled.

"Where have you been?" they asked.

"Oh, uptown," I said, falling over the rug.

Nobody seemed to notice anything, but when Aldie took his fatal step—actually went to a cocktail party—he returned in a far less euphoric condition. He was, not to mince words, a ghastly pale green in color and his gait was unsteady. Pop went over and put his arm around him and then recoiled as from a serpent.

"You are drunk, boy," he said, and for an hour thereafter people kept opening doors and saying things and then going back in and slamming the doors hard. The place was like one of those clocks you see in Germany.

The cocktail party had been given by some missionary friends of the family, and more respectable human beings I would not care to know. Poor Aldie had tried one drink, his first, and his sufferings had been extreme. Pop, though, acted as if his son had returned from nameless orgies in a red-light district. We were very indignant and Mum was, too. It was true that Pop was deeply upset but this was simply because he knew nothing about liquor. We couldn't do much with him at that moment as it was Commencement time and he had a long string of baccalaureate addresses ahead of him. We waited until he had rested up a bit at the Point, then gave him the treatment. Our tactics were frankly diabolical.

Pop's Achilles heel was his inability to sleep. From his morning reports he hardly closed an eye all night. If he got two hours' sleep he felt lucky, he said, although we could hear him snoring lustily every time we woke ourselves during the night. In any case, we played upon this weakness in our campaign.

"If you can't sleep, why not take a shot of whiskey in hot milk at bedtime?" I said casually one morning. "Doctors prescribe it."

"Nonsense," said Pop, but he looked interested. Anything to do with doctors, sleep, or medicine intrigued him.

"No, really, they do. Whiskey is a medicine. A hot whiskey toddy with lemon is great for a cold or a chill."

"I don't believe it," said Pop.

"Oh, Pop," Dave said. "Everybody knows that. Doctors prescribe a drink of whiskey every day for high blood pressure."

"I read somewhere that anybody over forty should drink whiskey regularly to keep his arteries from hardening," I said.

"Whiskey isn't like an Orange Blossom," Aldie said. "It will just make you feel drowsy and you'll sleep like a log. Try it."

Pop would have drunk poison if he had thought it would make him sleep, and we saw he was weakening.

"Well, I haven't any whiskey," he said, "and a man in my position can't be seen in liquor stores."

"Mum can buy it," I said.

"Not on your life!" cried Pop. "I won't have your mother cross the threshold of one of those places."

"They're just stores," Aldie said. "People don't drink in there," but Pop was adamant.

After this interchange Mum came to us in gales of laughter and said Pop had sent Bruce to the liquor store to buy a bottle of whiskey. He was going to try it that night but we weren't to be allowed to see him drink it.

The next morning when Pop emerged from his room he looked haggard and wore the sweet, saintly expression he always assumed after a bad night. Behind his back Mum rolled her eyes and shrugged her shoulders and her lips formed the words "Sweetly chee," the family phrase for describing this mood of Pop's.

"How did it go?" we asked, but without hope. "Did you sleep?"

"No, I didn't sleep," said Pop in a martyr's voice. "That blasted stuff doesn't do any good at all."

"How much did you take?" we asked.

"He took one teaspoonful in a glass of milk," said Mum. "I told him it wasn't enough."

"For Pete's sake, Rob," said Aldie. "A newborn baby could drink a teaspoon of whiskey and never know the difference. You need a good slug."

"I am not going to turn into an alcoholic to please you," said Pop. "Thanks just the same."

We waited a few days for him to recover from this experience and then approached him again.

"Now," we said, "we'll have a nice cozy evening by the fire and you can read Wodehouse and we'll make you a whiskey toddy so you'll sleep. Whiskey is supposed to be sipped slowly so it goes into the system a little at a time. Then it won't hit you like a bomb and you'll feel great and sleep. Drinking is supposed to be fun. It's a social thing. People sit around talking and having a good time while they sip their drinks. You don't want to take it in milk like an old lady. Drink like a man and enjoy it. This way it goes into the bloodstream gradually."

Pop loved any little technical details about the system and the bloodstream and he also liked the delightful picture of himself, the Dean of the Chapel, sitting by the fire in the privacy of the home, his loved ones around him, his dogs at his feet, a glass of good whiskey at his elbow. He agreed to cooperate.

Dave built him a huge fire after dinner and we pulled up his footstool, gave him his slippers, and settled him in his favorite chair. It was a nice crisp evening, the fire snapped and crackled in the fireplace, and the living room looked snug and inviting. Mum sat in her corner of the sofa mending. The dogs were stretched out on the oriental rug in front of the fire.

"Say, I like this," said Pop, beaming around the room. "It's nice to have the whole family looking after the old man—" Here his voice broke.

"Watch it, Father," said Dave. "You haven't even started drinking. Don't go on a crying jag now."

Pop gave a croaking laugh.

"Where's the bottle?" we asked.

"It's up in my closet," he said. "Behind my shoes."

When we unearthed it we found it was Old Grandad.

We got Bruce to help us mix up a toddy. As I remember, it had lemon and sugar in it and a lot of hot water. It tasted horrible.

"Now don't you give the doctor any more than that," said Bruce sternly. "He's not a drinking man."

"He's going to be," we said.

Bruce shook his head doubtfully.

We placed the glass at Pop's elbow and it steamed pleasantly, just like the bowl of hot toddy that Bob Cratchit made. We all settled ourselves around the room, Pop opened *Brinkley Manor,* one of our favorite Wodehouse classics, and started reading. By an odd coincidence it was the chapter about a man called Gussie Fink-Nottle, who never drank anything but orange juice and as a result couldn't face life. His friends were plotting to spike his orange juice for his own good.

"Just sip a little as you go," we said as Pop lifted his glass. "Enjoy the taste."

Pop sipped delicately, and then a pleased smile spread over his face.

"This is good," he said, and took another sip.

"Take it easy," said Aldie. "That's got to last you all evening."

As the tale of Gussie Fink-Nottle's downfall unfolded, Pop's spirits rose. He became absolutely incandescent, and after a while he got laughing so much he could hardly read more than a few words at a time. Presently he laid the book down in his lap and doubled up with his famous wheeze. Then he put his head back and whooped until the rafters rang. We all exchanged glances, and I saw Bruce open the kitchen door a crack and peer out.

"Oh, Gad," whispered Pop with streaming eyes, "haven't had so much fun in a month of Sundays." He finally stumbled up to bed still laughing. The thing looked like a sensation.

The following day Pop came bounding in to breakfast and said he felt like a million dollars.

"Slept like a log," he said. "Why, that stuff's terrific."

"See, we told you," we said.

We tried to make him have another drink that night but he said no, he didn't want to get the habit. He would take it when he needed it.

Everything seemed to be fine, and then one day Pop came down to breakfast with his hand over his eyes. Then he sat down and worked his head back and forth as though to loosen it.

"What's the matter?" I asked.

"I'll tell you what's the matter," he said gloomily. "I tried your dad-gasted whiskey last night and now I've got a splitting headache. That's the last time I listen to you."

"Did you sleep?" asked Dave.

"How could I sleep with my head spinning like a top? I told you liquor made my head spin."

"How much did you take?" I asked.

"Oh, not very much. An orange juice glass full."

"Good God, Father," said Aldie. "That's a lot of whiskey."

"That's what I told him," said Mum, "but he wouldn't listen. He just sat on the edge of the bed and drank it down."

Pop had a special way of drinking medicine which he called "opening his throat." When you didn't want to taste something—castor oil, for instance—you just "opened your throat" and poured the liquid down. This was said to be the way Germans got down so much beer.

"Did you open your throat and drink it all at once?" I asked.

"Of course I did," said Pop, irritated. "The stuff tastes awful by itself."

"Oh, boy," said Aldie. "It's a wonder you didn't pass out cold. Why didn't you sip it the way we told you? People drink for pleasure. They don't just crouch on the edge of their beds and gulp it down. You see what happens when you don't learn how to drink like a gentleman."

"What do you know about drinking like a gentleman?" asked Pop peevishly. He was not in a good mood.

We never did train him to drink like a gentleman. He finally began keeping a bottle of cheap port under his bed; whenever he couldn't sleep he reached down and took a swig. We tasted it once and it was ghastly—like heavy syrup.

"Really, Pop," Dave said, shuddering, "this kind of thing is disgraceful. The Dean of the Chapel keeping a bottle of this junk under his bed and swilling it all night long. A fine way to act in the home. What would God say?"

"Now, you leave God out of this," said Pop. "You and your mother have no respect for anything. The old man is just a clown, just a laughingstock. Anyway, port is only a liqueur, not alcohol."

He really believed it, too.

I don't want to give the impression that we wasted much time trying to make Pop over. We really didn't want him to change, as he was just right the way he was. Anyway, when we were down at the Point there was no cocktail-party circuit that we knew about. The most heady social event of the week was Saturday-night folk dancing. The rest of the time people just swam together at the beach or went out sailing. Now that we had the *Calmar* and had learned to sail her we ourselves went out every afternoon, weather permitting, and if Dave and I felt restless after dinner on moonlight nights we took the *Calmar* out to sea and played Narrow Escape around the Spindle, coming about so our wash swirled up on the silver rocks and the rudder almost touched them.

As the summer went downhill toward September we clung to

the old traditions of the hill. With the trials of another Princeton year coming up I fortified myself by going on bird walks with Pop or beelines with the boys. The Hideons were still too young for us, but I felt kindly toward them and took Targ with me to hunt for shells, while Bobs, who was rapidly becoming the ace beachcomber of the family, scoured the sand for loot. I found it sweet to have a little sister, so gentle and easy compared to the boys. She slept in my room now, and although she nearly drove me mad whispering things to herself at dawn it was nice having her there. The fascinating but exhausting business of survival in a man's college town was ahead of me, but in the last weeks of summer I rested in the peace of the old life on the hill. There were certain rituals to be performed, and one of them was graping.

CHAPTER NINETEEN

Graping Time

THERE ALWAYS CAME A DAY around the first week in September when something—a darker blue on the water or a sudden scatter of diamonds across the bay—spelled fall. We had been seeing golden-rod for weeks and watching the cut hayfields fill up with Queen Anne's lace and the swallows gather on all the telephone wires, but we still felt summery. Then this moment arrived and anyone going out on the upstairs porch recognized the special clarity of the air, the burnished look of the oak leaves. The birds had stopped singing in the woods but showers of little warblers went tumbling from tree to tree, flickering a yellow feather here, a greenish wing there. "Confusing fall warblers" these were, on their way south. The whole day throbbed with cricket song, golden and drowsy, and up from the woods came the scent of ripe grapes and dry leaves. The wind was in the north. Graping time was with us.

Graping on our hill was a form of self-torture rather than a genuine search for grapes. There were other places by roadsides or along stone walls where you could sit in comfort and pick a bushel in no time. As all grapers know, there is hardly any under-brush under the canopy of big leaves so you step inside as into a green-and-gold cave and there are the grapes, hanging in dark, heavy bunches right over your head. No thorns, no poison ivy, no grubs. We had all three in our graping place at the Point and, to be baldly frank, very few grapes. This was all beside the point.

The great thing about our grapes was that they grew in the

very tops of the red cedars beside the path to the river, and, to make it even more exhilarating, so did poison ivy, greenbrier, honeysuckle, roses, and bittersweet. In the tree I called mine there was one of those gorilla poison-ivy vines, hairy and horrible, and an old honeysuckle as big around as a boa constrictor.

The poison ivy writhed up to the very tip of the tree, sending out side branches that spread into awnings of dangerous shiny leaves. Fierce bundles of greenbrier stretched from the ground into and throughout the tree, so what you had in effect was a poisonous barbed-wire entanglement. Honeysuckle and bittersweet were harmless and fun to be with, but they often tied things so tightly together that you couldn't get through. This, of course, was a condition devoutly to be wished as the whole point of graping was hardship, not grapes.

It took a while to get organized for the ordeal. Somebody had to take the long ladder down into the woods, and each participant had to be provided with a rake to rip out some of the worst poison ivy. After this you put on your graping costume. The last time I went up my tree I wore a pair of Pop's old white ducks tied on with a rope and closed around the ankles with string. On top of this I had a giant sweatshirt I found in the sea chest. I stuffed all my hair into a beret, and to protect hands and wrists I used a mismated pair of paint gloves which at some point had been soaked in kerosene. This was a bad choice, as they were both left-hand gloves and easily big enough to fit King Kong.

Everybody else dressed much the same way, with those little personal touches that make all the difference. It was considered bad form to look nice or wear too many of your own clothes.

We all tied pails around our waists and went down into the Tunnel, the official graping territory. No one was allowed to cut vines in this area for fear of spoiling the jungle effect and reducing the high quality of torture so essential to graping.

We took turns using the ladder for the first stretch, leaning it up against the curtain of vines and clawing our way into the tree from its top rung. That year was a good one for grapes, and I could see them overhead in thick, dusky clusters. The air was heavy with their fragrance, the true breath of fall. Getting in to the trunk of the tree was always a grim business, especially with a pail slung around your middle. I removed mine and stuck it in a crotch while I did a little poison-ivy raking. The good thing about all those other vines was that while using the rake you could lean out into space supported by a hammock of assorted vegetation. Some of it was, of course, bristling with thorns, but if you had dressed properly they only penetrated to the flesh in a few places. For this reason oilskins were a popular item of clothing if you could stand the heat. After loosening up some of the worst poison ivy I hooked the rake in a branch and started climbing. On the whole I found it easier to go up close to the trunk because the various vines branched mostly toward the outside of the tree. I shut my eyes and hauled myself upward a branch at a time, forcing a passage through the tangle with my head. I could hear the others screaming with pain from their trees and I screeched in reply. Inside my tree the smell of grapes was mixed with the powerful odor of red cedar—pungent as turpentine. I liked to sit back against the net of vines at intervals and feel the tree sway slightly in the breeze. The higher I climbed, the wider it swung. Up near the top, where the branches were no bigger than my finger, you could really get quite a sweep, thus adding the spice of danger to the whole affair. I climbed until my head emerged into the sun at the very tip of the spire thirty feet in the air. From there I could see the river's blue through the oaks and feel the cool air off the water. Then, winding my legs around the trunk, I rocked in space and listened. The surf sound of the oaks was stilled and the trees seemed transfixed in yellow sunlight, as thick and clear as amber. The cricket throb went on, the pulse of the earth, and somewhere there were chickadees, dee-deeing through the trees.

After this respite I retreated into the depths of the tree and began picking. I was eventually able to fill two pails, which meant that I had to lower the first on a rope to Mum, who replaced it with an empty one. This is tricky stuff, believe me, and entailed hanging out at an alarming angle in a kind of vine sling. Picking grapes which are out of reach from any secure foothold is a stimulating experience. My own system was to throw myself out backward in a loop of vine with my toes hooked under something, preferably a branch. On this occasion I had to use a vine, thus setting the stage for one of the most invigorating episodes of my graping career. Hanging with my feet in a wreath of greenbrier, I suddenly felt something give. I was at the time picking some superior grapes under a poison-ivy canopy at the top of the tree and hated to stop before I had them all. As a result I reached once too often, and with a loud rending and tearing sound I dived head first toward the earth. Targ was in the next tree and promptly went into fits of laughter, this kind of thing being well received by fellow grapers. My head was about ten feet above a rock when I stopped moving and hung like a pendulum, with my face in a hazel bush. I thought Mum would die, and as for myself I'm surprised I didn't have some sort of seizure. I don't know whether you've ever tried to laugh hanging by the feet but it's as close to apoplexy as I care to go.

"Hey, you guys," I cried in a gargling upside-down voice, "for Pete's sake, help!"

Nobody did anything and I heard them wheezing and squeaking nearby.

"I think I'm going to die," I yelled. "Help! Help!"

Then laughter almost strangled me and I got some leaves in my mouth gasping for air. Things were going black before my eyes when Pop came down the path.

"What in Sam Hill do you think you're doing?" he asked, peering down into my inverted face.

"I'm reading a book," I screamed. "Can't you see?"

I think it was Pop who finally got me down, but the whole thing is vague. I have the feeling I hung there for several hours while the others shrieked and howled below. I sometimes wonder what I would have done if I had been alone, but then nobody goes graping alone.

In the evening after a graping expedition the ladies picked over the grapes for jelly, discarding green ones and those containing grubs. Pop used to read P. G. Wodehouse aloud to us on these occasions, and we had a huge fire roaring and snapping in the fireplace.

The next morning Mum and the maids made grape jelly and jam.

The business of jelly making was a proper part of fall at the Point, and I think Mum would have done it if only to smell the rich grape perfume that filled the house and poured out into the September sunlight. Every child should know that smell, along with the sharp vinegary scent of pickles, hot raspberries cooking down, and, of course, fresh bread just out of the oven. Less amateur head shrinking and more jelly- and bread-making are what mothers should give their young in the brief happy time the house is full. Mum always made a lot of jams, jellies, pickles, and preserves, and the kitchen door of our house was something to pass. Hardly anybody could resist going in to see if there was some scum or a spoon to lick. Mum would be in there in her blue-checked overall, attended by the cook, peeling and chopping and stirring in a splendid cloud of incense.

Mum used a jelly bag made of cheesecloth—triangular in shape, so that it tapered to a sharp piont. This she hung by a strong cord to a broomstick laid across two chair backs with a kettle underneath to catch the drip. The jelly bag was always called "the pig" and the sight of it slowly twirling and dripping at one end of the dining room was a faintly revolting but familiar sight in September. This method produced a jelly as clear as rubies as long as you didn't commit the sin of squeezing the pig. When nobody was looking I always sneaked in and squeezed the pig. It felt slippery and squishy and the resulting stream of juice was most satisfying.

Baba, who ordinarily never entered the kitchen, did so in the grape season, when she put on a violet-flowered apron and stood over the stove stirring the royal purple sludge with a wooden spoon. She would tell me how in the days before paraffin they used to cover jelly jars with circles of brown paper dipped in brandy. It was easy to see that Baba was at that moment being the lady of the manor in her stillroom, not just somebody making grape jelly in a kitchen.

Unmarried girls and children did not participate in the delicate business of jelly making, but after I had a young gentleman come to visit Baba decided I must have a lesson.

"Now, dear Jan," she said, "just come over here and watch."

I went and stood beside her, peering into the bubbling caldron.

"Always measure cup for cup," she said. "One cup of juice to one cup of sugar. *Never* use commercial pectin!"

Having never heard of the stuff I found this easy to promise.

Baba took a clean silver spoon and dipped out a bit of the crimson juice. Then she tilted it and let it slide off. It clung to the edge of the spoon in a sticky sheet.

"There," she said with satisfaction. "It's ready when it aprons."

I helped her line up the red-hot jars, then watched while she ladled out the syrup. The full jars looked like rows of carbuncles on the kitchen shelf and gave me a mysterious pleasure. Somewhere deep inside I felt an atavistic urge to make jelly.

Unlike graping, beach plumming was an aesthetic experience, in which torture played only a minor role. The purpose of the expedition was to acquire as many beach plums as possible before the Labor Day crowds got them first. We left the actual picking to the ladies, although we sometimes deigned to pick the biggest blue plums off the most accessible bushes. There were better things to do on a beach-plum expedition than pick beach plums.

There were two places to go for beach plums—one a hollow back of the dunes at Horseneck's tip; the other the Sand Hill Property, where they grew on the highest ridges.

When we were little Baba used to lead the expedition to the Sand Hill Property. We'd file through the huckleberry bushes and bayberry, under the pitch pines, to a long slope of loose sand that flowed like sugar from the crest of the dune wall. It was a little hard for Baba in her long skirts to get up, but she did so without loss of dignity. We scrambled up on all fours and suddenly we were on the roof of the forest, our bare toes in the top twigs of buried trees. From this perch the panorama of marsh, village, and sea was enough to take your breath away. The "halleluiah blue," as the

Professor used to call it, wrapped the sand-dune country on three sides, and the river spread out inland like a peacock's tail.

The ladies would hurry along the ridge to the beach-plum thickets while we took off into the dunes, slipping and sliding or jumping far out over the ivory valleys.

The expedition to the Horseneck beach-plum area was by water and was usually combined with a picnic. In the beach-plum season there were enchanted mornings when the river lay dreaming in the rich fall sunlight, the channels pale blue between the fox-red stretches of marsh. It was so still you could hear the cricket song from the fields of goldenrod and smell the sticky, polleny sweetness of those yellow jungles above the shores. These were thistledown days, days when a gull feather rested so lightly on the water that it stayed perfectly dry. The wind would be just enough to fill the curve of the feather and send it sailing. When we let go the mooring the boat moved off without a ripple, the sails hanging straight. Even though the day might be blue and warm as July you could feel the fall in it. I never knew how, but perhaps it was the cricket song or the quality of the sunlight, which seemed thick and fragrant like honey poured over the land. If we were lucky, we had a full tide brimming up to the edges of the grass flats and just on the turn so that we rode out on it as on a great sliding floor of glass.

When we emerged from the rustling golden tunnel of grass everybody would crane his neck to see if there were people in the beach-plum thickets. Once a small army of women were in the process of entering the sacred place and we were all outraged. Usually, though, we got there first.

Across the boat channel we floated over the mussel beds and edged up onto the sand on our bow wave. Back in the dunes the beach-plum thickets were always half buried in sand, and on some of the nearly drowned bushes the fruit was as big and blue as Concord grapes. I remember while we picked the monarch butterflies drifted by like scraps of flame, heading out to sea on their mysterious annual migration.

Pop sometimes picked for a brief period, but Mum soon threw

him out because she never liked to see him engaged in any feminine operation. If he ever tried to help with the dishes on maid's night out she said it drove her crazy to see him with a dish towel in his hand. She also couldn't stand watching him puttering around in the beach-plum bushes swearing at mosquitoes and getting scratched on thorns.

"Go away," she'd cry. "Go look at birds!"

"Nobody wants the old man around," he'd say pitifully, but he went and I usually went with him, for we had a lot of work to do checking in the shore patrol.

Like the warbler waves in spring the arrival of the shore birds in the fall was a peak in our bird-watching year. Streaming down the coast from their arctic breeding grounds they dropped down to feed and rest wherever land and water met. In those constantly shifting margins of saturated ground we would find them —sand-colored, pebble-colored, grass-colored, neat and sleek as carved and painted decoys. Their coming was one of the signals that summer was almost over.

When I went out on my porch in the starlight or in the blue-white brilliance of a full moon I could hear the voices of the migrating hosts going across the Milky Way overhead. Sometimes I saw them cross the moon's face, high and lonely, reassuring each other on their journey with sweet whistling calls.

One day the mud flats in the river would be alive with small scampering forms. In the creeks and pools among the salt marshes yellowlegs stalked about on lemon-colored stilts, mysterious long-billed silhouettes moved against the golden sunset in freshwater ponds, and when we walked on Horseneck we put up flock after flock that flashed out over the breakers in silvery squadrons, then wheeled and alighted farther up the beach. On the mirror of wet sand they chased the backwash, speeding along on twinkling feet like clockwork toys. They were endlessly fascinating to watch and maddeningly difficult to identify in their fall plumage. Like the confusing fall warblers, they never seemed to have the correct field marks. We would check out bills, eye streaks, rumps, wings, and everything would be fine, and then their legs would be the wrong color. In those pre-Peterson days life was tough for bird-watchers as we had a choice only between the Reed pocket guides, in which the bird portraits were all on separate pages, and the three-volume set of Forbush's *Birds of Massachusetts,* each one of which weighed a ton. You can't go out on beaches or into swamps lugging a great book in your arms, so we always took a final despairing look at the colored plates before we set out. The group that caused us the most trouble was the small streaked sandpipers known as "peeps." There were five species and even hardened bird watchers threw up their hands when it came to identifying them in the fall season. However, Pop was determined to conquer them.

"There's no reason," he said one day, "why two intelligent people should allow themselves to be defeated by a bunch of sandpipers. I refuse to knuckle under to anything that calls itself a 'peep.' "

"They don't call themselves that," I said. "We do."

"Why is it," he said, staring at one of the Forbush plates, "that all the sandpipers on the beach look alike and none of them look like this?"

"It's all that stuff about juveniles and fall plumage," I said.

If there was one thing we resented it was the vacillating manner in which shore birds assumed seasonal coloring.

"May retain breeding plumage into late fall," Pop would read in an angry voice. "May be confused with spring sanderling—Eye Guy, it's enough to drive a man mad."

"We don't have to go, you know," I said.

"Of course we do," he said. "They can't go through without us."

Actually we wouldn't have missed the shore patrol for the world. Our annual struggle with the peeps was part of the pattern of family summers, just as beach plumming was.

"I've got an idea," said Pop. "First we'll go to the beach and study them at our leisure and in comfort. Then we'll go out to the mud flats and creep up on them through the water."

"How are you going to carry binoculars and guides under water?" I asked.

"We won't need them. We'll be so close we can see every feather. We'll just keep our eyes and nose above water."

"You'll get a chill," I said, for Pop was always imagining he had chills when it was too cold to have a touch of the sun.

"We'll pick a hot day," he said.

On Horseneck the feeding flocks raced at the foam's edge as far as we could see, and on the upper beach among the mops of dried seaweed and shells were companies of small sandpipers and plovers asleep with heads tucked into their back feathers. They looked like a lot of ping-pong balls scattered through the tide wrack.

"One thing about these guys is that they don't go sneaking around in the underbrush or hiding in the tops of trees," said Pop. "They just sit there in plain sight and let you look at every blasted feather. Not that it does any good,'" he added gloomily.

"A lot of those are ring-necked plovers," I said. I was much attached to these charming little birds, so distinctive with their black collars and orange bills and feet.

"Yes, but what about that gang coming toward us? Peeps, every one of them."

I looked and in the circle of my binoculars I saw the familiar forms of the Horseneck patrol—all practically the same size, all soft brown above, with white breasts faintly streaked.

"Dad-gast it," said Pop. "All exactly alike as usual. How am I supposed to measure their bills from here? Does anybody's bill droop at the tip?"

"I think one has a white rump," I said.

After some minutes Pop dropped his binoculars and wiped his eyes.

"I can't afford to go blind looking at the rumps of birds," he said. "Let's go on up the beach."

We did this and were rewarded by some spectacular black-bellied plovers and two golden plovers, their spangled backs clearly visible to the naked eye.

"Now there's a bird I like," said Pop, "a decent size with nice obvious markings. Good of them not to be in winter plumage."

After that we saw a flock of turnstones, gay harlequins in russet, black, and white with turned-up bills. No other shore birds look anything like them. We watched them rooting among the piles of iodine-brown kelps and red seaweed whose coloring they matched so well, and Pop said it was a pleasure to see them. It did a man good.

"Thank God for turnstones," he said. "It's birds like that that restore one's faith in bird watching."

On the next hot, still day we rowed out to the grass flats and tested Pop's new bird-watching system. We picked a place where a deep channel ran along the edge of a large mud flat on which the shore birds swarmed like ants. Entering the water at a good distance we submerged to the nose and let the outgoing tide carry us downstream. The flocks paid no attention to us, and we were able to come within a few inches of those feeding near the edge.

"Pleeps," said Pop in a bubbling whisper.

Clinging to the rim of the flat I was practically nose to bill with one of the little feeders, and Pop's chin was all but resting on the mud in front of a group of others. Mine was a masterpiece of coloring, each soft mushroom-brown feather edged with black and with a flush of brown on his chest. If he had had greenish legs, he might have been a least sandpiper—if he'd been smaller and had a streaked breast.

Suddenly Pop disappeared beneath the surface but he emerged at once blowing like a grampus. The whole flat went up in a flurry of wings.

"Lost my footing," he explained. "Forgot where I was." Then he frowned.

"I was so close I could have spit in that bird's eye," he said. "It's no good. They don't read the blasted guides. There's no such bird as that one. It doesn't exist."

In spite of our struggles with the peeps the hours we spent hunting the shore patrol were enchanting additions to the storehouse of joy Pop was building for me. The sense of wonder and excitement that he gave to all our expeditions made these simple events into adventures, treasures of living, clear and vivid in every detail.

I remember the time we saw our first phalaropes. We had rowed up our bay and landed on the shore of the point below the Howland farm whose pastures and fields were then kept open by cows and provided good walking. It was a late afternoon in September and a spectacular purple-and-orange thunderhead was piling up over Adamsville. The sunlight that escaped from this cloud castle was a strange red-gold and it gave the whole scene the theatrical brilliance of a stage set.

Underfoot the turf was soft and springy and our steps made no sound. We knew of a pool in the swamp, much favored by migrating birds, and soon we saw it lying like a rose-pink mirror in the hollow ahead. Three greater yellowlegs were already there, two up to their bellies in the water, the third stalking in the shallows, balanced high on its stilts. We hid behind a stone wall and rested our binoculars on top of it.

"Deluxe bird watching," said Pop, "and not a peep in the place, thank the Lord."

Presently three small grayish birds swam out from behind a tussock. They looked suspiciously like peeps, but they swam in a peculiar way, spinning in circles and all the while dabbing at the water with their bills.

"Phalaropes," hissed Pop, "the swimming sandpiper."

But, as they say in bad novels, more was yet to come. A large bird which had passed for one of the yellowlegs now waded out into the sunlight and, like the leading man in a play, took the center of the stage. Instead of the freckled pearl gray of the yellowlegs he was dark reddish brown with a striped crown and very long bill. Placing his bill in the water he kept it there and went through a series of fast pumping motions as he moved forward. This was the famous Wilson's snipe, Pop told me, much excited.

"This is more like it," he said. "We can rest on our laurels for a while and forget those damned peeps."

We stayed behind the wall so long that the thunderhead was

upon us before we knew it. The red glow disappeared, and silver trumpets of light fanned out over the fields. Just before we rose to leave three more birds came out of the sky to our pool, folding their pretty wings with a satisfied chirruping sound. Pop recognized them at once by their brown-striped bibs and russet backs and said they were pectoral sandpipers.

Another precious vignette remains with me from our shorebird expeditions—the nuptial song flight of the woodcock over the mill-pond in Adamsville. It was after sunset on a July evening and the bird climbed with a whistling of wings into the pink twilight, bursting into a sweet canarylike warbling as he reached the peak of his flight and sank earthward. I saw the short round body, the short rounded wings, and the absurdly long bill. The "whinnying" sound was clear and the whole performance was very moving, like the performance of a great actor or singer.

On our trips we crawled on our bellies over marshes, hitched on our bottoms across damp sand bars, or plunged through beds of gigantic reeds that clattered in the breeze like a thousand newspapers. While we watched the birds, feeding busily in the shallows or sleeping in neat formation on sword-shaped flats, Pop told me that some of these same species patrolled the shores of newborn continents fifty million years before Homo sapiens appeared at all. It is possible, he said, that their fantastic migration patterns were originally determined by the great ice sheets. I liked to think when I saw the flocks silhouetted against the flamingo clouds of the sunset in our salt creeks and river channels that nothing much had changed since the ice receded. The waves broke on Horseneck or beaches like it, Pop said, in exactly the same way fifty million years ago. On these sand bars, in salt creeks and marshes, in dreaming estuaries full of the sky the ancient time still lived as the shorebird flocks came down to feed. When we sat near them and watched their charming ways we would pretend we were back in the remote past before people were around to hear the sweet, sad calls of plovers flying over or see the yellowlegs wading in the sunset at the end of a September day.

One of the last rituals before the boats were pulled out was to sail to Adamsville for marsh rosemary and a hunk of the famous Adamsville cheese. The summer was running through our fingers in a stream of blue days and we clung to it like drowning men to a rope. At no time was the Point so beautiful, never were the colors so intense.

Sailing inland on a September day was all peace. The whole scene looked like a landscape by Constable. Ahead of us the little islands blurred together in the pale blue haze, and beyond them lay the white houses of Adamsville asleep in their cloud of trees. Cows came down to cool themselves in the shallow water, yellow butter-flies fluttered in pairs over the mast, and instead of the fresh breeze off the sea we sailed through heat and the smell of corn-fields and goldenrod. The drowsy purr of insects came to us from the shores.

We used to tie up at an old dock in the salt marshes, where the water was coffee brown and a sunken rowboat lay on the mud. A kingfisher lived there, and his electric blue rattle interrupted the drugged peace of the little backwater.

The men would walk up the village street to the country store and buy cheese, and the women picked marsh rosemary. It grew in the marsh among pink marsh asters and other tiny precious flowers. When dried it lasted all winter, and like the grape and beach-plum jellies and the shells I gathered, was a tangible piece of summer, a talisman to see us through until next year.

CHAPTER TWENTY

Labor Day and Approaches

AS WE SLID DOWNHILL toward summer's end, the final rock of Labor Day, we all dug in our heels. Nobody wanted to admit summer was over, so the last rites of closing up, pulling boats, dismantling the dock, and so forth were put off as long as possible. However, we always noticed that the grownups at this season tended to gather together on the front lawn or assemble in the living room and try to come to some decision about affairs on the hill. Pop usually started these discussions.

"While we're all here," he would say, "why don't we see what we can do about the road this winter?"

The road was a constant problem, as it had a valley in the middle of it, and all the sand or gravel anyone put on it washed down there in the heavy rains. There was no set policy, no real organization to deal with this problem, and it nearly drove Pop crazy. Every year he built up thank-you-ma'ams and dug neat drains to divert the water into the ditches, but during the fall Baba might take a dislike to the thank-you-ma'ams and either hack them out herself or hire a man to remove them.

One year, I remember, Pop made a herculean effort to get things under control. It was a blue morning just before Labor Day and the grownups were standing around on the front lawn visiting.

"Now that we're all here," I heard Pop say, "let's see if we can't decide about the road. Last spring it was just like the bed of a mountain stream."

Nobody said anything.

"Last year," said Pop in the high voice he used when the family were involved, "they ordered a load of cobblestones instead of gravel. Now they might just as well have dumped them directly into the ditch." ("They" were Baba and Aunt K.)

Somebody cleared his throat and Pop waited but nothing happened.

"Then there was the time they put sand on," said Pop, "and they might just as well have put it right in the valley to start with. I suggest that we elect someone to be responsible for the road, find out what to put on it, and then we'll divide the cost."

Everybody said that was a good idea and that it was time to go get the mail.

"Dad-gast it," said Pop, after they'd left, "how in Sam Hill is anything to be decided around here? Nobody will ever discuss anything."

"Well, don't worry about it," said Mum comfortingly. "Come on down for a swim. It's high tide."

The next morning down at the river they were all ready to go in swimming, and Pop said now that everyone was present they might talk about the pump. In his opinion it was running all day long, and he thought there must be a leak in the pipe. Either that or people were careless about leaving the toilets running. A pump that ran twenty-four hours a day wouldn't last long, would overheat and burn out.

Nobody said anything, and finally Mum said she didn't know what anybody was going to do but she for one was going in swimming.

Some time later we saw Pop and Uncle Basil pacing off the area between our guest room and the wall and we knew they were talking about the boundaries and Riverside Drive, which ran through the house. Some weeks before the neighbors had, with great difficulty, driven a car through the woods to keep one of the invisible rights of way open, and this always started Riverside Drive up again. Compared to our Riverside Drive the one in New York City was nothing—a mere cowpath. Ours had a classic quality—it was invisible, it didn't actually exist but it was immortal.

Another thing that disturbed Pop was that Baba had caused all the electric and telephone wires to be laid underground. Nobody knew where they were any more and the electric-company men said they didn't know either.

"If anything goes wrong," one of them told Pop, "you'll just have to start all over again. We can't dig up the whole property."

The same was true of the telephone cables wandering somewhere through deep woods from the last pole below Synton. It gave Pop an uneasy feeling to think that any time he shoved a spade into the ground he might cut the telephone cable or be electrocuted.

"If only everybody could get together and make a plan we'd know where we were," he used to say. He liked things out in the open. He would tell anybody anything and liked to share his ideas, but Baba, like Queen Elizabeth, never revealed her plans in advance. She did what she had decided and you were faced with a *fait accompli*. Of course, this system was eminently successful and Pop's wasn't. The only way we ever learned about some of Baba's plans was through Tink, who was a valuable secret agent.

At summer's end Tink virtually lived with us. Before we left he and Pop always had a wrestling match, from which Pop barely escaped with his life. Its pattern never changed. At some point when Pop was not looking Tink would creep up on him from behind and steal the handkerchief out of his back pocket. Then he'd run off cackling with glee. Pop would wheel around, slap his pocket, and give chase. When he caught up with Tink they grappled for a moment, and then Tink hurled him to the ground and started tickling him. Pop's howls could be heard for miles, and he grew so weak from screaming and laughing that Tink easily overpowered him.

"Call quits, Tink," he would gasp, but Tink refused to let him up until he put on a stern voice: "No more, see? I'm tired."

Then Tink would rise instantly, haul Pop to his feet, and tenderly brush grass and leaves from his person.

Summer at the Point was officially over on Labor Day and was marked by the Labor Day Picnic, a folk festival whose origins lay far back in the past. Uncle Smith's family, I believe, had had the first one, but they had gradually expanded it to include the families of two or three close friends from the Boston area. After a while the thing snowballed, and by the time we were included most of the summer people we knew went to it. Not, however, *all*. It was impossible for Johnny-come-latelys like ourselves to trace the mystic relationships that made some people eligible for the Labor Day Picnic, some not. One thing was clear: only summer people were involved. No native of Westport ever appeared, but I have no idea whether or not they were invited. It seems to me now that the year-round inhabitants of the village would have taken a dim view of the whole operation, which not only wasted a whole day but entailed much physical labor and quite a lot of pain and discomfort.

It was also clear that nobody who lived up the East River was asked, but then nobody knew anybody who lived up the East River. We didn't even realize they were there.

Nobody from the harbor ever came either, but this, too, was easy to understand. People at the harbor lived high—playing golf and tennis at the country club, dancing every Saturday at the Casino, and, according to legend, going to cocktail parties every day. After Aldie crashed the harbor society we realized that everybody over there was just like everybody at the Point, only a little more conventional. However, before that we considered the harbor on a par with the Left Bank of the Seine—a haunt of hard-drinking Bohemians.

The Labor Day Picnic took place in the East River on a small rock island—a dome of granite covered with broken clamshells and gull droppings and sporting lush thickets of poison ivy and wild-rose bushes. We sat on the clamshells and anyone wanting to swim changed back in the poison ivy. All old-timers felt it their duty to sail up there, and when there was an outgoing tide and a headwind some people didn't make it until the first arrivals were leaving. Fish chowder was the only food served, this famous concoction being cooked in two gigantic iron kettles, real witches' caldrons, impregnated with the salt-pork grease of untold summers. The position of chowder maker was handed down from father to son, although in our youth one lady, the great Jessie Luther, shared the job with Pop and Uncle Smith.

Pop was elected to the post when a vacancy appeared, but, as we often pointed out to him, he would never have been eligible for the honor unless we had forced him to rent a bathhouse. Before that momentous occasion we hadn't been asked to the Labor Day Picnic. We had seen the hordes struggling up the river like a run of herring in spring, we had observed them crawling on the rock, and later we had watched them fighting their way home under the bridge against the tide. To be perfectly frank we pitied them and had no desire to join the fray. After the bathhouse era dawned, however, we were taken into the charmed circle and Pop became a chowder maker as authentic as any of the old guard.

The chowder makers left for the rock at dawn, bearing kettles; firewood; a battery of giant spoons, ladles, and forks; fish stock; salt pork; and other equipment. They then built the fire and, as far as anyone knew, put the salt pork in to try out.

In the meantime a hard core of ladies and girls gathered at one house, sliced onions with streaming eyes, and pared and cut potatoes in the traditional wedge shape, thick at one end, paper-thin at the other. The thin end was supposed to cook off and thicken the chowder. One of the leaders of the female contingent had already procured quantities of haddock, which had been cooked in advance and had to be boned.

During the slicing, boning, and cutting party every bit of Point gossip was brought out and discussed with scholarly thoroughness. As an unmarried girl I never got to the table but worked on the porch steps listening in.

When the fish, potatoes, and onions were ready they were sent up the river in the care of various little boys who owned outboard motors.

That part of the summer population whose boats were kept in the East River started sailing people over to the rock about midmorning, and if it was low tide the most elderly ladies were dragged over the mud flats in rowboats by the stronger young males.

Those of us who kept boats in the West River had to sail around to the foot of the street, take down our masts, row under the bridge, put them up again, and continue under sail until we reached the island. We often sailed in one place for hours, but it was considered beneath contempt to accept a tow.

Toward noon all the docks and landings on the East River side of the bridge showed clusters of persons waiting to be ferried to the rock. These were either boatless individuals, grandparents, or people too weak or too lazy to go through the ordeal of de-masting boats and rowing them under the bridge against the tide rip. Some of them were guests or remote relatives of the founders of the feast, who had traveled miles for a bowl of chowder. By twelve o'clock things were getting pretty tense, as once the chowder was broken out it vanished instantly. The troops who had reached the rock had worked so hard for so long that they were weak from hunger and would wolf two bowlfuls without pausing for breath.

We used to arrive at the bridge in *Hawick* and *Dehra Doon,* the latter so full of gear and human freight that she was barely afloat. Dave, Aldie, and I wrestled the masts loose and lowered the hideous tangle of sails, rigging, and spars on top of Mum, Bobs, Targ, and the picnic baskets. Then one of us inserted himself into the middle of the wreckage and tried to row. Other boatloads labored nearby, and every now and then a rower would collapse over his oars and his craft would spin around in the eddies and shoot backward. Low moans of anguish, yells of rage, and oaths echoed hollowly under the bridge.

Once on the other side we tied up at a little dock and put the masts back up, usually getting the halyards twisted or the lazy jacks looped over the gaff. When everything was sorted out we let go the painters and started backward toward the bridge. There were various schools of thought on the subject of how to get away from the bridge. Some sailors sneaked up the far side of the channel;

others went boldly up the middle; we edged across the flats as long as there was any water on them. If you could muster enough labor you could drag a sharpie right across the mud, but this was not looked on favorably by true sailors and Dave refused to descend so low. He preferred to starve.

While we hung in the tide, squinting at trees on the shore to determine whether we were going forward or backward, we saw the rock in the middle distance swarming like a kicked anthill, with a lovely row of sails fluttering below the cliffs. As we approached we could smell the heavenly fragrance of fried onions and salt pork—the chowder seething in its caldron—and observe the cooks standing around tasting it out of gigantic spoons like the witches in *Macbeth*. Pop always wore his Labor Day uniform— an L. L. Bean red-checked shirt, a lobsterman's duck-billed cap and his classic pants, Abraham and Isaac. He always burned his tongue on the chowder, and we could hear him yelping with pain at intervals.

With so many aboard it was difficult to uphold the honor of sail for very long. People started whining for food and Mum wanted to get up to her place on the rock before some usurper grabbed it. Mum's place was near the top of the rock, in an alcove framed by poison ivy and rose bushes, and there she would spread out her gear and deal out bowls, spoons, and supplementary food. Sitting out in the channel with the smell of chowder on the breeze was more than she could stand, and the skipper of *Debra* usually accepted a tow or took to the oars.

We landed the boats around the back of the rock and climbed up through the crushed clamshells and poison ivy to where the starving crowds stood in line, a bowl in each hand. The chowder makers were down on a stone platform by the water, and the edge of the cliff above this shrine was lined with hungry observers. You could look down into the kettles and see the brown bits of salt pork and onion floating on the creamy surface, where eyes of beautiful grease shone in the sun.

Miss Luther always put in the cream and the Worcestershire sauce at the end while Uncle Smith stirred. There were dashes of salt, sprinklings of pepper and more tasting. Then, at last, it was said to be done, and everybody up above raced to the line.

I don't know what gave the Labor Day chowder its special flavor. Maybe it was the kettles or the pieces of seaweed that sometimes blew into it, or the wood smoke that swirled in clouds over it, dropping bits of ash into the brew. It could be that we were all so famished from the struggle of getting there that we would have eaten the fish raw. In any case, those bowls of chowder were so heavenly that greed made us choke down the first one at top speed in order to get a second. We never had enough time to savor Labor Day chowder in a leisurely fashion. We simply guzzled it and then sat back on the rock and looked around, swollen like boa constrictors.

When I was young, it seems to me, all Labor Days were hot and dark-blue, throbbing with crickets and smelling of goldenrod. From the rock the village showed up crisp and clean, the white houses standing on emerald lawns, the small boats lying at their little docks at the bottom of each garden, and the blue water wrapping it all around. Gulls played on the rising air currents, wheeling and side-slipping against the sky, with the sun illuminating their wing tips. Thistledown and milkweed silk glistened in the blue air, and the sails of racing sharpies made white triangles all over the river. Down by the bridge those sailors too proud to accept a tow or use oars hung in the tide rip, quietly starving.

There wasn't much time to loll around enjoying the view, once the chowder was gone. The job of getting everybody off the rock and back to civilization still lay ahead. The older members were already making their way down to the edge of the water, where the most-powerful boys waited to assist them into the boats. Outboards were summoned to resume ferry duty, the racing sailboats waved in. If it was dead low tide some of the elder ladies could be dragged or pushed across a mud flat in a rowboat and deposited on a dock nearby. However, most of the multitude piled into whatever craft had been assigned to them and headed for the bridge. Boatless persons tried to bum rides, and there was a certain amount of panic about being the last people on the island. Without the crowds and the chowder it reverted to its original state—a rock covered with broken clamshells, gull droppings, and poison ivy. Nobody wanted to be there alone. The picnickers were like swallows who have flocked before migrating south and were now ready to take off. Last-minute jobs had to be done—boats had to be pulled out, bags packed, water turned off, houses closed up for winter. Pop's one idea was to get back to the house for a nap, as he often said he felt as though he'd been on the rock since he was a small child. We helped him get under the bridge, and then we went for the last sail. As long as we were sailing summer was still going on, but the final sail was like the breakfast a condemned man eats before being executed. The Point never looked so beautiful as on Labor Day afternoon. Never was the water so blue, the red-gold of the marshes so intense, or the odor of rockweed and salt water so sweet as in those hours just before we dismantled the boats.

The big boats lay at anchor off the shipyard and among them was the *Calmar* stripped of her sails, her spars as bare as bones. There was something sad about the sight of the gaff and boom touching with no furled canvas between them. We could barely look at her.

The air had a nip in it when we ran home through the marshes, and we sailed straight in to the dock. While we took off the sail and unstepped the mast, we reviled school.

"Do you realize," Dave said with disgust, "that day after tomorrow we'll be in New Jersey? Boy, what a state!"

We dragged the spars and sail up to the boathouse and heaved them across the rafters. Then we went back for the rudder, the oars, and the bailer. The boats without their sails were birds without wings, and we ourselves were grounded too. Trudging drearily up the path through the woods I smelled the autumn in the air—a mixture of dry leaves and crushed ferns, mushrooms and overripe grapes—and then deep inside me anticipation stirred. The joys of the new season rose up—trees in gold and scarlet, the smoke of leaf fires at dusk, football games, new textbooks and class bells and all those Princeton men in their tweed jackets and gray flannels. It seemed there was never an ending without a new beginning and growing up was not bad at all.

Epilogue

WE WENT DOWN TO THE POINT this year in four cars. I drove my two cats and Foxy, the dog, in the station wagon. Tim, my youngest son, took the television set and his guitars in his Volkswagen, and later Peggy, my youngest daughter, drove her two cats down in hers. I also had in the back of the station wagon a bed, two orange trees, some maidenhair ferns, and the cat box. Mum came down separately in her car with Tabby, her cat, a lot of African violets, and another maidenhair fern.

With the new superhighways it takes only two hours to get to Westport from Exeter in New Hampshire, and it was midmorning when I topped the rise by the Santos farm and saw the sea. As I slowed down to turn into our lane I smelled the wild roses and honeysuckle on the verge and the old happy feeling came back, the feeling of summer and the Point.

The lane no longer has a green grass strip down the middle where Gyp trotted, and all the Scotch pines along the sides went down in the '38 hurricane, but the baby rabbits with powder-puff tails still bounced down the ruts ahead of my station wagon just the way they did ahead of the buckboard and the Artful Dodger.

On top of the hill Synton still stands. All her great trees, including the twin spruces, went down in the hurricane, and they had to tear off the veranda because the supports had rotted out. When her spruces fell and the gardens were buried in the wreckage of her other beloved trees, Baba never showed a quiver of emotion, but her light seemed to have blown out. When we wished her many happy returns on her August birthday she said with a smile that she wanted no more birthdays. After she had presided at the funeral of Aunt Sis, her only surviving sister, she quietly went upstairs to bed. In two weeks she was gone. I have no doubt at all but what she simply decided to die. It was the way she did things, giving as little trouble as possible and behaving to the end with grace and dignity. At the last she had forgotten us all and was a little girl again, merry and gay. So she went away and the old Synton went with her as far as I was concerned.

Aunt K. stayed on and did the best she could, but Tink, without his manager, lost his old zest and died too. He lived long enough, though, to play with my children.

Aunt K. made some changes in Synton, the most interesting of which was to raise the bathroom floor up to the rim of the bathtub. This necessitated raising the toilet and washbasin on stalks to get them above grade, so to speak. I forget why she did this. The other innovation was to cut an opening from the dog pen off the kitchen into the flour bin under the counter in the butler's pantry. This bin, which had once contained a large flour barrel, had a hinged lid, and now when you opened it a gang of small dogs erupted right in your face.

The family, who were worried about Aunt K., somehow tracked down The Fiddle and persuaded her to live at Synton, as the Scotch accent seemed just what Aunt K. needed. However, this didn't work; The Fiddle, besides being beyond communication, was, if possible, more eccentric than ever, wore the skating cap all the time, and refused to do any work. After a long series of experiments Aunt K. decided to move out, and Dave, on leave from the Navy, designed and built for her a tiny Cape Cod cottage on the lane. Here she lived happily for many years, completely surrounded by birds, plants, and animals. When she had had enough, she died just like Baba, but not before she had indoctrinated our grandchildren in the ways of hens and goats.

When I drove by Synton my cousin Anne was sitting outside in the sun, and I stopped for a visit. My Scotch bluebells have spread along the crack of the granite steps and out into the lawn. They were in bud. Anne, who now owns Synton, was cleaning it for the renters, she said. The hill has reached that stage in the life history of a family summer place, when the original house has to be rented to pay the taxes and all the outbuildings contain members of the third and fourth generations. There are no boats in the boathouses, no horses in the stable, no carriages in the carriage house, no wood in the woodsheds, no cars in the garages, just people. Anne and her husband live out in the barn, sleeping in Gyp's box stall, while their children sleep in the hayloft. There is a john in the grain closet, and the carriage house is a living room, and I believe there is a double bed in Rajah, the peacock's, apartment. The barn swallow still nests up on the beam by the harness closet, but last summer the cat got the babies.

Anne said they had some Harvard professor this year and that she had been up half the night washing floors.

Down at Snowdon I parked at the top of the lawn and got out. Everything was exactly the same, and it could have been any other summer. Over the treetops I saw the river's blue and the checkerboard pattern of fields on the opposite shore. It was low tide and the air smelled of salt flats, bayberry, and juniper. The front door of the house was open and the phoebe that nests over it was fluttering nervously nearby.

Snowdon is no longer cocoa brown but weathered gray with white trim. Pop finally said he was sick of that dad-gasted brown and just stopped painting the shingles. This happened after he had dropped a gallon of cocoa brown onto the roof of the guest room from the top of a ladder. The paint had shot up like a geyser and come down on his head, and he said that was the last straw. After that he kept putting white on the trim until the brown didn't show, and pretty soon the paint wore off the shingles and he was delighted. As usual the trim needs painting again. Tim painted part of it last summer, and my oldest son, Chip, who was home on combat leave before going to Vietnam, painted the whole back porch in one hour in preparation for a cocktail party we gave in his honor. This was the first cocktail party ever given under Snowdon's roof, and we could almost hear Pop saying, "Not in the home, boy, not in the home." However, in his last years he had become so corrupted by his children that he allowed Mum to serve sherry and even tolerated the introduction of more powerful liquors by us when we were visiting.

The front porch was covered with droppings from the baby phoebes who looked fatly down on me over the edge of their nest. When I went inside I saw the deck chairs stacked in a corner, last summer's bunch of marsh rosemary on the mantelpiece, and the usual piles of the London *News* and the *Geographic*. Somebody was in the cellar. It was Dave, down for the weekend from the school where he is headmaster. He met me at the top of the cellar stairs and said the pipes had burst.

"Oh, great," I said. Mum and I now share the responsibility for Snowdon's maintenance, and last year she gave me a new toilet for my birthday. This was after the one upstairs burst during the winter because somebody had forgotten to bail it out and put kerosene down it. Last September I bailed it out myself with a cup and even reached down the hole with a sponge. Sometimes I think plumbing is more trouble than it's worth. Now I was back in the old familiar world where water, toilets, and the well are major topics of conversation.

"You guys ought to overhaul your whole plumbing system," said Dave. "It's a mess."

We went down in the cellar, where it was just like the fountains of Rome: jets of water spouting in all directions and splashing into pools on the dirt floor. The place was a sea of mud and smelled like fungus.

We turned off the water, and as we went back upstairs Dave said how about paying our dues for the Eldridge Heights Improvement Society, as the tractor needed a new tire and we had to put some more loads of gravel on the road. Those characters who rented Synton, he said, came up the hill about ninety miles an hour and the curve by the laurel was just like a washboard.

Dave, by some mystic process, has become road commissioner on the hill, and on almost any foggy day when the sailing is no good he can be found down there with the tractor scraping the crown or trimming the verges with the cutter bar. Pop would be pleased with the businesslike way the road is now managed, although as far as I can see it looks just the same as it always did except that the central grass strip and the horse manure are missing.

Snowdon is full of so-called modern improvements, but it's much harder to open up than it used to be. The age of kerosene has given way to the age of propane gas, and there's a little thing outside the kitchen window that turns red when the cylinder is nearly empty. We have a gas stove, a gas refrigerator, a gas hot-water heater, and a gas floor furnace, and I'm always afraid they're going to blow up.

Opening up now involves a great deal of lying on the floor under appliances and lighting matches. The hot-water heater has a sheet of directions in Pop's handwriting tacked up on the wall beside it, with some further warnings in Mum's writing and a large typed list of instructions by my son Chip. First somebody has to crawl up a mud bank under the floor of the kitchen to do something to a petcock or all the water runs into the cellar and you burn up the boiler. Then there's the business about lying on your back holding a lighted match, keeping your finger on some button and peering through a little window near the floor all at the same time. You might manage it if you were a midget or had three hands and a match a foot long, but as it is, I either burn my fingers or the match goes out and I let go the button.

You have to light something under the refrigerator too, and the instructions for this in my handwriting are up on the wall nearby, but I never can understand what they mean in June so Dave has to do it.

When everything was going I went up to Targ's house with a couple of gallon jugs and filled them at her sink. Targ and her family live in the garage, and her kitchen is in the woodshed. Her refrigerator stands on the exact site of the old two-hole privy where Tim's crib was when we lived there. Pop gave us the garage and the woodshed after we outgrew the boathouse, but we outgrew the place before we finished fixing it up so we gave it to Targ.

The boathouse was the first of Snowdon's outbuildings to go. Pop fixed it up as a honeymoon cottage for newly married members of his brood. He spent many sleepless nights planning how to handle the sudden increase in population.

The emotional strain of officiating at the weddings of his three older children had been severe. They had occurred in fairly rapid succession, and in my case he had played a double role—taking me up the aisle, turning around to become the minister, and then giving me away. Before my wedding, which was the first, the whole family was very apprehensive.

"Pop will never be able to speak a word," I said. "How are we going to get married? We'll have to live in sin."

"It'll be just one long croak," said Mum. "I don't think he can do it."

Pop claimed he could.

"Eye Guy," he said, "you and your mother think I'm just a sentimental old fool."

"Well, how are you going to give me away?" I asked. "Are you going to say, 'Who gives this woman?' and then switch around and say, 'I do'?"

"No, I am not," he said. "I'll simply say, 'I give this woman.'" His voice broke.

"See?" said Mum. "You can't even do it here in the dining room. How are you going to do it in the Princeton Chapel?"

He did, though, in a firm, clear voice, although when we started down the long aisle he couldn't speak at all. He explained later that he pretended he had never heard of any of us.

He married Aldie and Dave in naval uniform, and they went

off on their ships, so for a short time the housing situation was under control. Pop had it all worked out.

"Each of you will start in the boathouse," he said, "and we'll give you a piece of land and then you can build your own place."

"Using what for a medium of exchange?" I asked, but Pop said one thing at a time.

The boathouse was an enchanting little house full of reflections from the water and moving shadows of leaves from the big oak outside. There were a main room with a Franklin stove, a tiny kitchen, and a cell made out of two of the bathhouses, where Hilly, our first baby, slept in Aldie's old walnut crib. I used to get up early, light a little fire in the Franklin stove, and go for a swim. While I dried myself on the dock I could smell the cedar smoke from the stove. The osprey fished over the shallows and the kingfisher rattled from his branch. We were very happy there. Ernie liked the privacy, but he got a little tired of carrying ice and groceries and Hilly up and down the hill. Marrying into our family was, he said, a strenuous experience.

The summer before Chippy was born Ernie had to push me up the hill from the river, and I felt just like a spawning salmon going up a waterfall. After Chippy was born there wasn't any room for him at the boathouse, and then Ernie went into the Navy and I moved back to Snowdon. When the war was over there were so many additions to the tribe that the moves became like a chess game. Aldie, who, true to Baba's prediction, really became a painter, had married a girl from the Left Bank—the other side of the river—so he moved over there. We moved into the garage-woodshed with our two smallest children, but the other two had to sleep down the hill at Snowdon, so we moved out and into Synton, as Aunt K. had moved out of there by then. This was about the same time that Dave moved out of the boathouse and Bobs and his wife moved in. The family tried to persuade us to take on Synton permanently, but Ernie said if there was one thing we didn't need at that point it was a gigantic Victorian house in need of repair, so we moved out.

After Dave moved out of the boathouse he built with his

own hands a house for himself on the other side of the fabled Riverside Drive. By some legal hocus-pocus he caused Riverside Drive to be erased forever, and Pop was able to sit in his own living room without imagining some law-crazed stranger bull-dozing his way through the wall.

Last summer Dave was just putting the finishing touches to a new shed when his daughter got married and moved into it. This is the quickest turnover of a building on record, although Aunt K.'s garage comes in a close second. For as long as two years it actually contained a car, but she soon turned it into a barn and put goats and chickens in it. Members of the fifth generation helped her get the eggs and feed crackers to the goats just the way we and our children did.

The only outbuildings that still serve their original purpose are the shop and the new boat shed.

The shop is a real antique carpenter's shop that used to stand, buried in pink roses, back of a house on the village street. Pop had coveted it for years. One day I was driving by and saw two men with wrecking tools starting to take it apart, so I bought it for Pop for twenty-five dollars. He was so happy he couldn't speak to me for three days. Will Brightman, the local carpenter, cut the shop in half, moved it up on trucks and put it together again. Pop lovingly arranged his precious tool collection, in-stalled an air-tight stove, and scattered curled blond shavings around the floor to give atmosphere and produce the right shop bouquet of pine and cedar. He made a bin of junk lumber for his grandchildren to use and built a set of little drawers for nails, screws, and other items. Finally he took up his rocking chair and lap board so he could write sermons in there.

"Coziest damned place on the hill," he said to me once when we were cooking hamburgers over the stove. In his latter years he used real swear words quite freely.

The shop is a communal operation at present, where those who are adding wings to their houses, building boats, or scraping down furniture can work. Anyone who tried to turn it into a house would be shot on sight.

The seven family houses are all connected by intercom telephones that somebody got at an army surplus place. There are also three outside lines, shared with one or two unknown parties. All telephones ring incessantly, and I often wish we were back in the old megaphone-foghorn days when children of kindergarten age couldn't ring up on intercoms to argue about coming home or to report that a fellow sibling has bitten them. Still, to summon the youngest member of the tribe would now take twenty-three toots on the foghorn, so you can see how matters have progressed. On the whole, though, nothing has changed much.

One slight change is that I am now a grandmother, but compared to Baba and Mum, who is now a great-grandmother, I am an impostor. Mum is the kind of grandmother who knits socks, makes brownies and mends the clothes of all her descendants. She looks at television with her grandchildren and goes snowshoeing.

I always promised myself that when I became a grandmother I would do it up brown, dress like one, act like one, and sit peacefully in rocking chairs knitting tiny garments for the latest babies. Unfortunately, I find that it's much harder than I thought to buckle down and wear violet print dresses, gun-metal stockings, and black health shoes the way Baba did. I'm sorry to report that I wear shorts, old shirts cast off by my sons, and frequently no stockings or shoes at all. I never knit garments, tiny or otherwise, but I can cook and make bread, which is something. Anyway, Deborah and Pieter think grandmothers wear shorts and go barefoot and do the cooking. When Hilly, their mother, was here we practically lived in the kitchen. There was always a large crowd in there eating, cooking, or running the washing machine. This glorious article is the source of much contention in local circles because it uses *water*. One day during Hilly's visit Dave came down while we were feeding diapers through the wringer and said it was time we thought seriously about the well. With five families on it (Synton and Catamaran had their own) the pump ran day and night, and any minute now the well could go dry.

"It's that washing machine," he said. "Why can't you and Targ take your laundry up to the laundromat the way we do?"

He went on to say that ever since Hilly came there seemed to be someone taking a bath or flushing the john every hour of the day.

"Why do you have to take baths all the time?" he asked. "I don't."

"I heard the pump go on at 11:30 last night," I said, "and it ran a long time, so somebody at your house must have taken a bath. It went on again at 3 A.M."

"That wasn't our house," he said.

Targ said it wasn't her house either, so it must have been somebody going to the john down at the boathouse.

Baba, of course, would never have descended to such coarse interchanges on the subject of plumbing, but I am not capable of her queenly reticence. Still, there are treasures even a grandmother in cut-off dungarees can give to her grandchildren. The earth, after all, is as rich in miracles as it was when I was little on the hill; life, in spite of sorrows, is as glorious and full of joy, summer as magic. It arrives every year in the same way, with fields full of daisies and buttercups, strawberries, new peas, and roses. The purple milkwort that I used to pick for Baba blooms in its old place, and I took Deborah up there to pick some. I did not have an amethyst pin to wear it in but I taught her the name.

On the hill, though, it is hard to remember that I'm a grandmother at all and not just a fellow child arriving at the Point in June. When we throw open the windows the rooms fill with the old sounds of leaves, birds, and wind and the sounds and smells of the sea. The air comes through the rusty screens flavored with salt, the iodine reek of rockweed and mud flats. A west wind still brings the odor of cow barns and hay fields from the farms on the other shore, and when there's no wind at all you can hear the bobwhites calling across the water.

There are eight sailboats now moored in the cove and not a single one of them is pea green. All but one are painted white, and those with names are called after sea birds. Our catboat is named *Whistler* after the golden-eye duck. The *Whistler* is white with a blue deck, a dacron sail, dacron lines, a tapered center-board, and toe straps for racing.

Boat painting in this era of purists is not the relaxed, care-free business it was in the old pea-green days. The boys use an electric sander and work on her until her topsides are like glass. They put on two coats of paint and sand between them and then they sand down the spars until they are the color of honey. Everybody else does the same, and the fleet is a pretty sight when it sets out for the Sunday race or for the routine afternoon sail.

Nobody is supposed to mess around in the *Whistler,* but when I get her to myself I go aground a lot, and it's much quicker to climb overboard onto the mud flat and pull her across. I also take her quahogging, for I still love the middle of the river on a hot blue day. The sandpiper flocks go up in front of me and flash out over the water. The white herons stand like Japanese prints against the golden marsh grass. Once I saw what could have been a western sandpiper but it could just as easily have been a semi-palmated. I read in Peterson, "This one is a sticker, hard to iden-tify; when with Semipalmated Sandpipers it appears a little larger and more coarsely marked."

"Hear that?" I said to Pop, for I often talk to him now the way I used to. " 'More coarsely marked'! How coarsely would you say he was marked?"

This year I went to the Labor Day Picnic in an outboard motorboat, and you wouldn't believe how easy it was. One minute we were down at the town landing on the west side of the bridge, ten minutes later we were in the East River approaching the rock. On its point we saw the chowder makers standing around the caldron sipping and stirring. One of them was Uncle Smith's son, Lewis; the other was Dave. Both wore red pants, a daring innova-tion, but Dave had on a duck-billed cap just like Pop's. The smell of wood smoke and chowder was exactly the same and the clamshells crunched underfoot in the old way. Mum was sitting up in her place, surrounded by grandchildren, and the usual frieze of starving chowder watchers stood looking down at the kettle.

When we had climbed to the top of the rock we could see the sailboats hanging in the tide.

There are so many generations on the rock these days that it's almost standing room only. The place looked like a mob scene in a Cecil B. De Mille super-movie. The chowder was gone in a flash, and the first arrivals began lining up at the water's edge almost before the late comers had reached the kettle with their bowls. There were the customary exchanges of time tables, packing reports, and house-closing bulletins. We, however, envied by all, felt none of the annual Labor Day pressures and regrets. We were not leaving because we have decided to live at the Point the year round. The only thing more miraculous and joyful is that, after two years of widowhood, I am a bride. In July when I was beachcombing on Horseneck another beachcomber collected me, and now it is summer all the time.

THE AUTHOR

JANET GILLESPIE spent her childhood years in Holyoke, Massachusetts, where her father, Robert Russell Wicks, was minister of a large church. When he became Dean of Princeton University Chapel, she moved to Princeton and attended Miss Fine's School. After four years at Mt. Holyoke College (class of '36) she became an apprentice teacher at Shady Hill School in Cambridge, Massachusetts. She then went back to Princeton, where she taught English and History at Miss Fine's and became engaged to William Ernest Gillespie, Princeton '33, whom she married in '38. When Mr. Gillespie accepted a teaching job at his old school, Phillips Exeter Academy, they moved to Exeter, New Hampshire, and built the house and garden she described in her two garden books, *The Joy of a Small Garden* and *Peacock Manure and Marigolds*. In 1956 they took their four children to Europe—a trip Mrs. Gillespie made into her first book, *Bedlam in the Back Seat*. Mr. Gillespie was Dean of the Faculty and Vice-Principal of Exeter when he died in '67. At this time Mrs. Gillespie wrote the present book about the happy summers of her youth and the family summer place in Westport Point, in Massachusetts. In '69 she married Robert F. Grindley, formerly of Detroit. They now live the year round at Westport Point, where they are doing over an old house and making a new garden.